Collins
World Atlas

Collins

Title	Scale	Page
Map Symbols and Time Zones		2
National Statistics		3–5

D0510708

World		
World Countries		6–7
World Landscapes		8–9

Europe		
Scandinavia and the Baltic States	1:5 000 000	10–11
Inset: Iceland	1:6 000 000	
Inset: Faroe Islands	1:5 000 000	
Northwest Europe	1:5 000 000	12–13
England and Wales	1:2 000 000	14–15
Scotland	1:2 000 000	16
Inset: Shetland Islands	1:2 000 000	
Ireland	1:2 000 000	17
France	1:5 000 000	18
Spain and Portugal	1:5 000 000	19
Italy and the Balkans	1:5 000 000	20–21
Western Russian Federation	1:7 500 000	22–23

Asia		
Northern Asia	1:20 000 000	24–25
Central and Southern Asia	1:20 000 000	26–27
Eastern and Southeast Asia	1:20 000 000	28–29
Japan, North Korea and South Korea	1:7 000 000	30–31

Africa		
Northern Africa	1:16 000 000	32–33
Inset: Cape Verde	1:16 000 000	
Central and Southern Africa	1:16 000 000	34–35
Republic of South Africa	1:5 000 000	36–37

Oceania		
Australia, New Zealand and Southwest Pacific	1:20 000 000	38–39
Australia	1:13 000 000	40–41
Southeast Australia	1:5 000 000	42
New Zealand	1:5 250 000	43

North America		
Canada	1:16 000 000	44–45
United States of America	1:12 000 000	46–47
Inset: Hawaiian Islands	1:12 000 000	
Northeast United States	1:3 500 000	48
Southwest United States	1:3 500 000	49
Central America and the Caribbean	1:14 000 000	50–51

South America		
Northern South America	1:14 000 000	52–53
Inset: Galapagos Islands	1:14 000 000	
Southern South America	1:14 000 000	54
Southeast Brazil	1:7 000 000	55

Polar Regions		
Arctic Ocean and Antarctica	1:35 000 000	56

Index		57–65

Settlements

Population	National capital	Administrative capital	Other city or town
over 10 million	**BEIJING** ✪	**Karachi** ◉	**New York** ◉
5 million to 10 million	**JAKARTA** ✪	**Tianjin** ◉	**Nova Iguaçu** ◉
1 million to 5 million	**KĀBUL** ✪	**Sydney** ◉	**Kaohsiung** ◉
500 000 to 1 million	**BANGUI** ✪	Trujillo ◉	Jeddah ◎
100 000 to 500 000	WELLINGTON ✪	Mansa ◌	Apucarana ◎
50 000 to 100 000	PORT OF SPAIN ✿	Potenza ◌	Arecibo ◌
10 000 to 50 000	MALABO ✿	Chinhoyi ◌	Ceres ◌
under 10 000	VALLETTA ✿	Ati ◦	Venta ◌

🔲 Built-up area

Boundaries

— International boundary

–·–·– Disputed international boundary or alignment unconfirmed

— Administrative boundary

········ Ceasefire line

Miscellaneous

---------- National park

············ Reserve or Regional park

✱ Site of specific interest

🔗🔗🔗 Wall

Land and sea features

⋯ Desert

⌄ Oasis

⋰ Lava field

1234 △ Volcano height in metres

⋯ Marsh

◨ Ice cap or Glacier

⌐⌐⌐ Escarpment

○○○○ Coral reef

⌐ *1234* Pass height in metres

Lakes and rivers

Lake

Impermanent lake

Salt lake or lagoon

Impermanent salt lake

Dry salt lake or salt pan

123 Lake height surface height above sea level, in metres

— River

— Impermanent river or watercourse

‖ Waterfall

| Dam

| Barrage

Relief

Contour intervals and layer colours

Height

metres		feet
5000		16404
3000		9843
2000		6562
1000		3281
500		1640
200		656
0		0
below sea level		
0		0
200		656
2000		6562
4000		13124
6000		19686

Depth

1234 ▲ Summit height in metres

-123 · Spot height height in metres

123 · Ocean deep depth in metres

Transport

→ ⤍ ····· Motorway (tunnel; under construction)

→ ⤍ ----- Main road (tunnel; under construction)

→ ⤍ ----- Secondary road (tunnel; under construction)

·········· Track

━━━ ⤍ ----- Main railway (tunnel; under construction)

━━━ ⤍ ----- Secondary railway (tunnel; under construction)

━━━ ⤍ ----- Other railway (tunnel; under construction)

——— Canal

✈ Main airport

✈ Regional airport

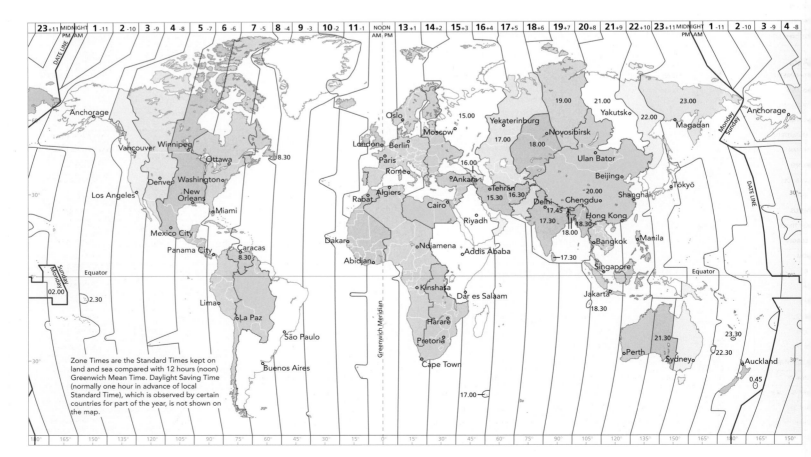

Zone Times are the Standard Times kept on land and sea compared with 12 hours (noon) Greenwich Mean Time. Daylight Saving Time (normally one hour in advance of local Standard Time), which is observed by certain countries for part of the year, is not shown on the map.

Map Symbols and Time Zones

Europe

Europe		Area sq km	Area sq miles	Population	Capital	Languages	Religions	Currency	Internet Link
ALBANIA		28 748	11 100	3 155 000	Tirana	Albanian, Greek	Sunni Muslim, Albanian Orthodox, Roman Catholic	Lek	www.km.gov.al
ANDORRA		465	180	86 000	Andorra la Vella	Spanish, Catalan, French	Roman Catholic	Euro	www.govern.ad
AUSTRIA		83 855	32 377	8 364 000	Vienna	German, Croatian, Turkish	Roman Catholic, Protestant	Euro	www.bundeskanzleramt.at
BELARUS		207 600	80 155	9 634 000	Minsk	Belorussian, Russian	Belorussian Orthodox, Roman Catholic	Belarus rouble	www.belarus.by
BELGIUM		30 520	11 784	10 647 000	Brussels	Dutch (Flemish), French (Walloon), German	Roman Catholic, Protestant	Euro	www.belgium.be
BOSNIA-HERZEGOVINA		51 130	19 741	3 767 000	Sarajevo	Bosnian, Serbian, Croatian	Sunni Muslim, Serbian Orthodox, Roman Catholic, Protestant	Marka	www.fbihvlada.gov.ba
BULGARIA		110 994	42 855	7 545 000	Sofia	Bulgarian, Turkish, Romany, Macedonian	Bulgarian Orthodox, Sunni Muslim	Lev	www.government.bg
CROATIA		56 538	21 829	4 416 000	Zagreb	Croatian, Serbian	Roman Catholic, Serbian Orthodox, Sunni Muslim	Kuna	www.vlada.hr
CZECH REPUBLIC		78 864	30 450	10 369 000	Prague	Czech, Moravian, Slovak	Roman Catholic, Protestant	Koruna	www.czech.cz
DENMARK		43 075	16 631	5 470 000	Copenhagen	Danish	Protestant	Danish krone	www.denmark.dk
ESTONIA		45 200	17 452	1 340 000	Tallinn	Estonian, Russian	Protestant, Estonian and Russian Orthodox	Euro	www.valitsus.ee
FINLAND		338 145	130 559	5 326 000	Helsinki	Finnish, Swedish	Protestant, Greek Orthodox	Euro	www.valtioneuvosto.fi
FRANCE		543 965	210 026	62 343 000	Paris	French, Arabic	Roman Catholic, Protestant, Sunni Muslim	Euro	www.premier-ministre.gouv.fr
GERMANY		357 022	137 849	82 167 000	Berlin	German, Turkish	Protestant, Roman Catholic	Euro	www.deutschland.de
GREECE		131 957	50 949	11 161 000	Athens	Greek	Greek Orthodox, Sunni Muslim	Euro	www.primeminister.gr
HUNGARY		93 030	35 919	9 993 000	Budapest	Hungarian	Roman Catholic, Protestant	Forint	www.magyarorszag.hu
ICELAND		102 820	39 699	323 000	Reykjavík	Icelandic	Protestant	Icelandic króna	www.iceland.is
IRELAND		70 282	27 136	4 515 000	Dublin	English, Irish	Roman Catholic, Protestant	Euro	www.gov.ie
ITALY		301 245	116 311	59 870 000	Rome	Italian	Roman Catholic	Euro	www.governo.it
KOSOVO		10 908	4 212	2 153 139	Prishtinë	Albanian, Serbian	Sunni Muslim, Serbian Orthodox	Euro	www.rks-gov.net/en-US
LATVIA		64 589	24 938	2 249 000	Rīga	Latvian, Russian	Protestant, Roman Catholic, Russian Orthodox	Lats	www.saeima.lv
LIECHTENSTEIN		160	62	36 000	Vaduz	German	Roman Catholic, Protestant	Swiss franc	www.liechtenstein.li
LITHUANIA		65 200	25 174	3 287 000	Vilnius	Lithuanian, Russian, Polish	Roman Catholic, Protestant, Russian Orthodox	Litas	www.lrv.lt
LUXEMBOURG		2 586	998	486 000	Luxembourg	Letzeburgish, German, French	Roman Catholic	Euro	www.gouvernement.lu
MACEDONIA (F.Y.R.O.M.)		25 713	9 928	2 042 000	Skopje	Macedonian, Albanian, Turkish	Macedonian Orthodox, Sunni Muslim	Macedonian denar	www.vlada.mk
MALTA		316	122	409 000	Valletta	Maltese, English	Roman Catholic	Euro	www.gov.mt
MOLDOVA		33 700	13 012	3 604 000	Chişinău	Romanian, Ukrainian, Gagauz, Russian	Romanian Orthodox, Russian Orthodox	Moldovan leu	www.moldova.md
MONACO		2	1	33 000	Monaco-Ville	French, Monegasque, Italian	Roman Catholic	Euro	www.monaco.gouv.mc
MONTENEGRO		13 812	5 333	624 000	Podgorica	Serbian (Montenegrin), Albanian	Montenegrin Orthodox, Sunni Muslim	Euro	www.gov.me
NETHERLANDS		41 526	16 033	16 592 000	Amsterdam/The Hague	Dutch, Frisian	Roman Catholic, Protestant, Sunni Muslim	Euro	www.overheid.nl
NORWAY		323 878	125 050	4 812 000	Oslo	Norwegian	Protestant, Roman Catholic	Norwegian krone	www.norway.no
POLAND		312 683	120 728	38 074 000	Warsaw	Polish, German	Roman Catholic, Polish Orthodox	Złoty	www.poland.gov.pl
PORTUGAL		88 940	34 340	10 707 000	Lisbon	Portuguese	Roman Catholic, Protestant	Euro	www.portugal.gov.pt
ROMANIA		237 500	91 699	21 275 000	Bucharest	Romanian, Hungarian	Romanian Orthodox, Protestant, Roman Catholic	Romanian leu	www.guv.ro
RUSSIAN FEDERATION		17 075 400	6 592 849	140 874 000	Moscow	Russian, Tatar, Ukrainian, local languages	Russian Orthodox, Sunni Muslim, Protestant	Russian rouble	www.gov.ru
SAN MARINO		61	24	31 000	San Marino	Italian	Roman Catholic	Euro	www.consigliograndeegenerale.sm
SERBIA		77 453	29 904	7 334 935	Belgrade	Serbian, Hungarian	Serbian Orthodox, Roman Catholic, Sunni Muslim	Serbian dinar,	www.srbija.gov.rs
SLOVAKIA		49 035	18 933	5 406 000	Bratislava	Slovak, Hungarian, Czech	Roman Catholic, Protestant, Orthodox	Euro	www.government.gov.sk
SLOVENIA		20 251	7 819	2 020 000	Ljubljana	Slovene, Croatian, Serbian	Roman Catholic, Protestant	Euro	www.gov.si
SPAIN		504 782	194 897	44 904 000	Madrid	Castilian, Catalan, Galician, Basque	Roman Catholic	Euro	www.la-moncloa.es
SWEDEN		449 964	173 732	9 249 000	Stockholm	Swedish	Protestant, Roman Catholic	Swedish krona	www.sweden.se
SWITZERLAND		41 293	15 943	7 568 000	Bern	German, French, Italian, Romansch	Roman Catholic, Protestant	Swiss franc	www.swissworld.org
UKRAINE		603 700	233 090	45 708 000	Kiev	Ukrainian, Russian	Ukrainian Orthodox, Ukrainian Catholic, Roman Catholic	Hryvnia	www.kmu.gov.ua
UNITED KINGDOM		243 609	94 058	61 565 000	London	English, Welsh, Gaelic	Protestant, Roman Catholic, Muslim	Pound sterling	www.direct.gov.uk
VATICAN CITY		0.5	0.2	557	Vatican City	Italian	Roman Catholic	Euro	www.vaticanstate.va

Asia

Asia		Area sq km	Area sq miles	Population	Capital	Languages	Religions	Currency	Internet Link
AFGHANISTAN		652 225	251 825	28 150 000	Kābul	Dari, Pushtu, Uzbek, Turkmen	Sunni Muslim, Shi'a Muslim	Afghani	www.president.gov.af
ARMENIA		29 800	11 506	3 083 000	Yerevan	Armenian, Azeri	Armenian Orthodox	Dram	www.gov.am
AZERBAIJAN		86 600	33 436	8 832 000	Baku	Azeri, Armenian, Russian, Lezgian	Shi'a Muslim, Sunni Muslim, Russian and Armenian Orthodox	Azerbaijani manat	www.president.az
BAHRAIN		691	267	791 000	Manama	Arabic, English	Shi'a Muslim, Sunni Muslim, Christian	Bahrain dinar	www.bahrain.bh
BANGLADESH		143 998	55 598	162 221 000	Dhaka	Bengali, English	Sunni Muslim, Hindu	Taka	www.bangladesh.gov.bd
BHUTAN		46 620	18 000	697 000	Thimphu	Dzongkha, Nepali, Assamese	Buddhist, Hindu	Ngultrum, Indian rupee	www.bhutan.gov.bt
BRUNEI		5 765	2 226	400 000	Bandar Seri Begawan	Malay, English, Chinese	Sunni Muslim, Buddhist, Christian	Brunei dollar	www.jpm.gov.bn
CAMBODIA		181 035	69 884	14 805 000	Phnom Penh	Khmer, Vietnamese	Buddhist, Roman Catholic, Sunni Muslim	Riel	www.cambodia.gov.kh
CHINA		9 584 492	3 700 593	1 330 265 000	Beijing	Mandarin, Wu, Cantonese, Hsiang, regional languages	Confucian, Taoist, Buddhist, Christian, Sunni Muslim	Yuan, HK dollar*, Macau pataca	www.gov.cn
CYPRUS		9 251	3 572	871 000	Nicosia	Greek, Turkish, English	Greek Orthodox, Sunni Muslim	Euro	www.cyprus.gov.cy
EAST TIMOR		14 874	5 743	1 134 000	Dili	Portuguese, Tetun, English	Roman Catholic	United States dollar	www.timor-leste.gov.tl
GEORGIA		69 700	26 911	4 260 000	T'bilisi	Georgian, Russian, Armenian, Azeri, Ossetian, Abkhaz	Georgian Orthodox, Russian Orthodox, Sunni Muslim	Lari	www.parliament.ge
INDIA		3 064 898	1 183 364	1 198 003 000	New Delhi	Hindi, English, many regional languages	Hindu, Sunni Muslim, Shi'a Muslim, Sikh, Christian	Indian rupee	www.india.gov.in
INDONESIA		1 919 445	741 102	229 965 000	Jakarta	Indonesian, local languages	Sunni Muslim, Protestant, Roman Catholic, Hindu, Buddhist	Rupiah	www.indonesia.go.id
IRAN		1 648 000	636 296	74 196 000	Tehrān	Farsi, Azeri, Kurdish, regional languages	Shi'a Muslim, Sunni Muslim	Iranian rial	www.president.ir
IRAQ		438 317	169 235	30 747 000	Baghdād	Arabic, Kurdish, Turkmen	Shi'a Muslim, Sunni Muslim, Christian	Iraqi dinar	www.cabinet.iq
ISRAEL		20 770	8 019	7 170 000	Jerusalem (Yerushalayim) (El Quds)**	Hebrew, Arabic	Jewish, Sunni Muslim, Christian, Druze	Shekel	www.gov.il
JAPAN		377 727	145 841	127 156 000	Tōkyō	Japanese	Shintoist, Buddhist, Christian	Yen	www.kantei.go.jp
JORDAN		89 206	34 443	6 316 000	'Ammān	Arabic	Sunni Muslim, Christian	Jordanian dinar	www.jordan.gov.jo
KAZAKHSTAN		2 717 300	1 049 155	15 637 000	Astana	Kazakh, Russian, Ukrainian, German, Uzbek, Tatar	Sunni Muslim, Russian Orthodox, Protestant	Tenge	www.government.kz
KUWAIT		17 818	6 880	2 985 000	Kuwait	Arabic	Sunni Muslim, Shi'a Muslim, Christian, Hindu	Kuwaiti dinar	www.e.gov.kw
KYRGYZSTAN		198 500	76 641	5 482 000	Bishkek	Kyrgyz, Russian, Uzbek	Sunni Muslim, Russian Orthodox	Kyrgyz som	www.gov.kg
LAOS		236 800	91 429	6 320 000	Vientiane	Lao, local languages	Buddhist, traditional beliefs	Kip	www.na.gov.la
LEBANON		10 452	4 036	4 224 000	Beirut	Arabic, Armenian, French	Shi'a Muslim, Sunni Muslim, Christian	Lebanese pound	www.presidency.gov.lb
MALAYSIA		332 965	128 559	27 468 000	Kuala Lumpur/Putrajaya	Malay, English, Chinese, Tamil, local languages	Sunni Muslim, Buddhist, Hindu, Christian, traditional beliefs	Ringgit	www.malaysia.gov.my

**De facto capital. Disputed

*Hong Kong dollar

Asia continued

	Area sq km	Area sq miles	Population	Capital	Languages	Religions	Currency	Internet Link
MALDIVES	298	115	309 000	Male	Divehi (Maldivian)	Sunni Muslim	Rufiyaa	www.presidencymaldives.gov.mv
MONGOLIA	1 565 000	604 250	2 671 000	Ulan Bator	Khalka (Mongolian), Kazakh, local languages	Buddhist, Sunni Muslim	Tugrik (tögrög)	www.pmis.gov.mn
MYANMAR (BURMA)	676 577	261 228	50 020 000	Nay Pyi Taw/Rangoon	Burmese, Shan, Karen, local languages	Buddhist, Christian, Sunni Muslim	Kyat	www.mofa.gov.mm
NEPAL	147 181	56 827	29 331 000	Kathmandu	Nepali, Maithili, Bhojpuri, English, local languages	Hindu, Buddhist, Sunni Muslim	Nepalese rupee	www.nepalgov.gov.np
NORTH KOREA	120 538	46 540	23 906 000	P'yŏngyang	Korean	Traditional beliefs, Chondoist, Buddhist	North Korean won	www.korea-dpr.com
OMAN	309 500	119 499	2 845 000	Muscat	Arabic, Baluchi, Indian languages	Ibadhi Muslim, Sunni Muslim	Omani riyal	www.omanet.om
PAKISTAN	803 940	310 403	180 808 000	Islamabad	Urdu, Punjabi, Sindhi, Pushtu, English	Sunni Muslim, Shi'a Muslim, Christian, Hindu	Pakistani rupee	www.pakistan.gov.pk
PALAU	497	192	20 000	Melekeok	Palauan, English	Roman Catholic, Protestant, traditional beliefs	United States dollar	www.palaugov.net
PHILIPPINES	300 000	115 831	91 983 000	Manila	English, Filipino, Tagalog, Cebuano, local languages	Roman Catholic, Protestant, Sunni Muslim, Aglipayan	Philippine peso	www.gov.ph
QATAR	11 437	4 416	1 409 000	Doha	Arabic	Sunni Muslim	Qatari riyal	www.mofa.gov.qa
RUSSIAN FEDERATION	17 075 400	6 592 849	140 874 000	Moscow	Russian, Tatar, Ukrainian, local languages	Russian Orthodox, Sunni Muslim, Protestant	Russian rouble	www.gov.ru
SAUDI ARABIA	2 200 000	849 425	25 721 000	Riyadh	Arabic	Sunni Muslim, Shi'a Muslim	Saudi Arabian riyal	www.saudiportal.net
SINGAPORE	639	247	4 737 000	Singapore	Chinese, English, Malay, Tamil	Buddhist, Taoist, Sunni Muslim, Christian, Hindu	Singapore dollar	www.gov.sg
SOUTH KOREA	99 274	38 330	48 333 000	Seoul	Korean	Buddhist, Protestant, Roman Catholic	South Korean won	www.korea.net
SRI LANKA	65 610	25 332	20 238 000	Sri Jayewardenepura Kotte	Sinhalese, Tamil, English	Buddhist, Hindu, Sunni Muslim, Roman Catholic	Sri Lankan rupee	www.priu.gov.lk
SYRIA	185 180	71 498	21 906 000	Damascus	Arabic, Kurdish, Armenian	Sunni Muslim, Shi'a Muslim, Christian	Syrian pound	www.parliament.gov.sy
TAIWAN	36 179	13 969	23 046 000	T'aipei	Mandarin, Min, Hakka, local languages	Buddhist, Taoist, Confucian, Christian	Taiwan dollar	www.gov.tw
TAJIKISTAN	143 100	55 251	6 952 000	Dushanbe	Tajik, Uzbek, Russian	Sunni Muslim	Somoni	www.prezident.tj
THAILAND	513 115	198 115	67 764 000	Bangkok	Thai, Lao, Chinese, Malay, Mon-Khmer languages	Buddhist, Sunni Muslim	Baht	www.mfa.go.th
TURKEY	779 452	300 948	74 816 000	Ankara	Turkish, Kurdish	Sunni Muslim, Shi'a Muslim	Lira	www.tccb.gov.tr
TURKMENISTAN	488 100	188 456	5 110 000	Aşgabat	Turkmen, Uzbek, Russian	Sunni Muslim, Russian Orthodox	Turkmen manat	www.turkmenistan.gov.tm
UNITED ARAB EMIRATES	77 700	30 000	4 599 000	Abu Dhabi	Arabic, English	Sunni Muslim, Shi'a Muslim	United Arab Emirates dirham	www.uae.gov.ae
UZBEKISTAN	447 400	172 742	27 488 000	Toshkent (Tashkent)	Uzbek, Russian, Tajik, Kazakh	Sunni Muslim, Russian Orthodox	Uzbek som	www.gov.uz
VIETNAM	329 565	127 246	88 069 000	Ha Nôi	Vietnamese, Thai, Khmer, Chinese, local languages	Buddhist, Taoist, Roman Catholic, Cao Dai, Hoa Hao	Dong	www.na.gov.vn
YEMEN	527 968	203 850	23 580 000	Şan'ā'	Arabic	Sunni Muslim, Shi'a Muslim	Yemeni rial	www.yemen-nic.info

Africa

	Area sq km	Area sq miles	Population	Capital	Languages	Religions	Currency	Internet Link
ALGERIA	2 381 741	919 595	34 895 000	Algiers	Arabic, French, Berber	Sunni Muslim	Algerian dinar	www.el-mouradia.dz
ANGOLA	1 246 700	481 354	18 498 000	Luanda	Portuguese, Bantu, local languages	Roman Catholic, Protestant, traditional beliefs	Kwanza	www.governo.gov.ao
BENIN	112 620	43 483	8 935 000	Porto-Novo	French, Fon, Yoruba, Adja, local languages	Traditional beliefs, Roman Catholic, Sunni Muslim	CFA franc*	www.gouv.bj
BOTSWANA	581 370	224 468	1 950 000	Gaborone	English, Setswana, Shona, local languages	Traditional beliefs, Protestant, Roman Catholic	Pula	www.gov.bw
BURKINA FASO	274 200	105 869	15 757 000	Ouagadougou	French, Moore (Mossi), Fulani, local languages	Sunni Muslim, traditional beliefs, Roman Catholic	CFA franc*	www.primature.gov.bf
BURUNDI	27 835	10 747	8 303 000	Bujumbura	Kirundi (Hutu, Tutsi), French	Roman Catholic, traditional beliefs, Protestant	Burundian franc	www.burundi.gov.bi
CAMEROON	475 442	183 569	19 522 000	Yaoundé	French, English, Fang, Bamileke, local languages	Roman Catholic, traditional beliefs, Sunni Muslim, Protestant	CFA franc*	www.spm.gov.cm
CAPE VERDE	4 033	1 557	506 000	Praia	Portuguese, creole	Roman Catholic, Protestant	Cape Verde escudo	www.governo.cv
CENTRAL AFRICAN REPUBLIC	622 436	240 324	4 422 000	Bangui	French, Sango, Banda, Baya, local languages	Protestant, Roman Catholic, traditional beliefs, Sunni Muslim	CFA franc*	www.centrafricaine.info
CHAD	1 284 000	495 755	11 206 000	Ndjamena	Arabic, French, Sara, local languages	Sunni Muslim, Roman Catholic, Protestant, traditional beliefs	CFA franc*	www.primature-tchad.org
COMOROS	1 862	719	676 000	Moroni	Comorian, French, Arabic	Sunni Muslim, Roman Catholic	Comoros franc	www.beit-salam.km
CONGO	342 000	132 047	3 683 000	Brazzaville	French, Kongo, Monokutuba, local languages	Roman Catholic, Protestant, traditional beliefs, Sunni Muslim	CFA franc*	www.congo-site.com
CONGO, DEM. REP. OF THE	2 345 410	905 568	66 020 000	Kinshasa	French, Lingala, Swahili, Kongo, local languages	Christian, Sunni Muslim	Congolese franc	www.un.int/drcongo
CÔTE D'IVOIRE (IVORY COAST)	322 463	124 504	21 075 000	Yamoussoukro	French, creole, Akan, local languages	Sunni Muslim, Roman Catholic, traditional beliefs, Protestant	CFA franc*	www.cotedivoirepr.ci
DJIBOUTI	23 200	8 958	864 000	Djibouti	Somali, Afar, French, Arabic	Sunni Muslim, Christian	Djibouti franc	www.presidence.dj
EGYPT	1 000 250	386 199	82 999 000	Cairo	Arabic	Sunni Muslim, Coptic Christian	Egyptian pound	www.egypt.gov.eg
EQUATORIAL GUINEA	28 051	10 831	676 000	Malabo	Spanish, French, Fang	Roman Catholic, traditional beliefs	CFA franc*	www.ceiba-equatorial-guinea.org
ERITREA	117 400	45 328	5 073 000	Asmara	Tigrinya, Tigre	Sunni Muslim, Coptic Christian	Nakfa	www.shabait.com
ETHIOPIA	1 133 880	437 794	82 825 000	Addis Ababa	Oromo, Amharic, Tigrinya, local languages	Ethiopian Orthodox, Sunni Muslim, traditional beliefs	Birr	www.ethiopar.net
GABON	267 667	103 347	1 475 000	Libreville	French, Fang, local languages	Roman Catholic, Protestant, traditional beliefs	CFA franc*	www.legabon.org
THE GAMBIA	11 295	4 361	1 705 000	Banjul	English, Malinke, Fulani, Wolof	Sunni Muslim, Protestant	Dalasi	www.statehouse.gm
GHANA	238 537	92 100	23 837 000	Accra	English, Hausa, Akan, local languages	Christian, Sunni Muslim, traditional beliefs	Cedi	www.ghana.gov.gh
GUINEA	245 857	94 926	10 069 000	Conakry	French, Fulani, Malinke, local languages	Sunni Muslim, traditional beliefs, Christian	Guinea franc	www.guinee.gov.gn
GUINEA-BISSAU	36 125	13 948	1 611 000	Bissau	Portuguese, crioulo, local languages	Traditional beliefs, Sunni Muslim, Christian	CFA franc*	www.gov.gw
KENYA	582 646	224 961	39 802 000	Nairobi	Swahili, English, local languages	Christian, traditional beliefs	Kenyan shilling	www.kenya.go.ke
LESOTHO	30 355	11 720	2 067 000	Maseru	Sesotho, English, Zulu	Christian, traditional beliefs	Loti, S. African rand	www.lesotho.gov.ls
LIBERIA	111 369	43 000	3 955 000	Monrovia	English, creole, local languages	Traditional beliefs, Christian, Sunni Muslim	Liberian dollar	www.emansion.gov.lr
LIBYA	1 759 540	679 362	6 420 000	Tripoli	Arabic, Berber	Sunni Muslim	Libyan dinar	www.libyanmission-un.org
MADAGASCAR	587 041	226 658	19 625 000	Antananarivo	Malagasy, French	Traditional beliefs, Christian, Sunni Muslim	Malagasy Ariary, Malagasy franc	www.madagascar.gov.mg
MALAWI	118 484	45 747	15 263 000	Lilongwe	Chichewa, English, local languages	Christian, traditional beliefs, Sunni Muslim	Malawian kwacha	www.malawi.gov.mw
MALI	1 240 140	478 821	13 010 000	Bamako	French, Bambara, local languages	Sunni Muslim, traditional beliefs, Christian	CFA franc*	www.primature.gov.ml
MAURITANIA	1 030 700	397 955	3 291 000	Nouakchott	Arabic, French, local languages	Sunni Muslim	Ouguiya	www.mauritania.mr
MAURITIUS	2 040	788	1 288 000	Port Louis	English, creole, Hindi, Bhojpurī, French	Hindu, Roman Catholic, Sunni Muslim	Mauritius rupee	www.gov.mu
MOROCCO	446 550	172 414	31 993 000	Rabat	Arabic, Berber, French	Sunni Muslim	Moroccan dirham	www.maroc.ma
MOZAMBIQUE	799 380	308 642	22 894 000	Maputo	Portuguese, Makua, Tsonga, local languages	Traditional beliefs, Roman Catholic, Sunni Muslim	Metical	www.mozambique.mz
NAMIBIA	824 292	318 261	2 171 000	Windhoek	English, Afrikaans, German, Ovambo, local languages	Protestant, Roman Catholic	Namibian dollar	www.grnnet.gov.na
NIGER	1 267 000	489 191	15 290 000	Niamey	French, Hausa, Fulani, local languages	Sunni Muslim, traditional beliefs	CFA franc*	www.presidence.ne
NIGERIA	923 768	356 669	154 729 000	Abuja	English, Hausa, Yoruba, Ibo, Fulani, local languages	Sunni Muslim, Christian, traditional beliefs	Naira	www.nigeria.gov.ng
RWANDA	26 338	10 169	9 998 000	Kigali	Kinyarwanda, French, English	Roman Catholic, traditional beliefs, Protestant	Rwandan franc	www.gov.rw
SÃO TOMÉ AND PRÍNCIPE	964	372	163 000	São Tomé	Portuguese, creole	Roman Catholic, Protestant	Dobra	www.gov.st
SENEGAL	196 720	75 954	12 534 000	Dakar	French, Wolof, Fulani, local languages	Sunni Muslim, Roman Catholic, traditional beliefs	CFA franc*	www.gouv.sn

*Communauté Financière Africaine franc

Africa continued

		Area sq km	Area sq miles	Population	Capital	Languages	Religions	Currency	Internet Link
SEYCHELLES		455	176	84 000	Victoria	English, French, creole	Roman Catholic, Protestant	Seychelles rupee	www.virtualseychelles.sc
SIERRA LEONE		71 740	27 699	5 696 000	Freetown	English, creole, Mende, Temne, local languages	Sunni Muslim, traditional beliefs	Leone	www.statehouse-sl.org
SOMALIA		637 657	246 201	9 133 000	Mogadishu	Somali, Arabic	Sunni Muslim	Somali shilling	www.tfgsomalia.net
SOUTH AFRICA, REPUBLIC OF		1 219 090	470 693	50 110 000	Pretoria/Cape Town	Afrikaans, English, nine official local languages	Protestant, Roman Catholic, Sunni Muslim, Hindu	Rand	www.gov.za
SOUTH SUDAN		644 329	248 775	8 260 490	Juba	Arabic, Dinka, Nubian, Beja, English, local languages	Christian, Sunni Muslim, traditional beliefs	South Sudanese pound	www.goss.org
SUDAN		1 861 484	718 725	36 371 510	Khartoum	Arabic, Dinka, Nubian, Beja, Nuer, local languages	Sunni Muslim, traditional beliefs, Christian	Sudanese pound (Sudani)	www.sudan.gov.sd
SWAZILAND		17 364	6 704	1 185 000	Mbabane	Swazi, English	Christian, traditional beliefs	Emalangeni, South African rand	www.gov.sz
TANZANIA		945 087	364 900	43 739 000	Dodoma	Swahili, English, Nyamwezi, local languages	Shi'a Muslim, Sunni Muslim, traditional beliefs, Christian	Tanzanian shilling	www.tanzania.go.tz
TOGO		56 785	21 925	6 619 000	Lomé	French, Ewe, Kabre, local languages	Traditional beliefs, Christian, Sunni Muslim	CFA franc*	www.republicoftogo.com
TUNISIA		164 150	63 379	10 272 000	Tunis	Arabic, French	Sunni Muslim	Tunisian dinar	www.ministeres.tn
UGANDA		241 038	93 065	32 710 000	Kampala	English, Swahili, Luganda, local languages	Roman Catholic, Protestant, Sunni Muslim, traditional beliefs	Ugandan shilling	www.statehouse.go.ug
ZAMBIA		752 614	290 586	12 935 000	Lusaka	English, Bemba, Nyanja, Tonga, local languages	Christian, traditional beliefs	Zambian kwacha	www.statehouse.gov.zm
ZIMBABWE		390 759	150 873	12 523 000	Harare	English, Shona, Ndebele	Christian, traditional beliefs	Zimbabwean dollar (suspended)	www.parlzim.gov.zw

*Communauté Financière Africaine franc

Oceania

		Area sq km	Area sq miles	Population	Capital	Languages	Religions	Currency	Internet Link
AUSTRALIA		7 692 024	2 969 907	21 293 000	Canberra	English, Italian, Greek	Protestant, Roman Catholic, Orthodox	Australian dollar	www.australia.gov.au
FIJI		18 330	7 077	849 000	Suva	English, Fijian, Hindi	Christian, Hindu, Sunni Muslim	Fiji dollar	www.fiji.gov.fj
KIRIBATI		717	277	98 000	Bairiki	Gilbertese, English	Roman Catholic, Protestant	Australian dollar	www.parliament.gov.ki
MARSHALL ISLANDS		181	70	62 000	Delap-Uliga-Djarrit	English, Marshallese	Protestant, Roman Catholic	United States dollar	www.rmigovernment.org
MICRONESIA, FEDERATED STATES OF		701	271	111 000	Palikir	English, Chuukese, Pohnpeian, local languages	Roman Catholic, Protestant	United States dollar	www.fsmgov.org
NAURU		21	8	10 000	Yaren	Nauruan, English	Protestant, Roman Catholic	Australian dollar	www.naurugov.nr
NEW ZEALAND		270 534	104 454	4 266 000	Wellington	English, Maori	Protestant, Roman Catholic	New Zealand dollar	http://newzealand.govt.nz
PAPUA NEW GUINEA		462 840	178 704	6 732 000	Port Moresby	English, Tok Pisin (creole), local languages	Protestant, Roman Catholic, traditional beliefs	Kina	www.pm.gov.pg
SAMOA		2 831	1 093	179 000	Apia	Samoan, English	Protestant, Roman Catholic	Tala	www.govt.ws
SOLOMON ISLANDS		28 370	10 954	523 000	Honiara	English, creole, local languages	Protestant, Roman Catholic	Solomon Islands dollar	www.pmc.gov.sb
TONGA		748	289	104 000	Nuku'alofa	Tongan, English	Protestant, Roman Catholic	Pa'anga	www.pmo.gov.to
TUVALU		25	10	10 000	Vaiaku	Tuvaluan, English	Protestant	Australian dollar	
VANUATU		12 190	4 707	240 000	Port Vila	English, Bislama (creole), French	Protestant, Roman Catholic, traditional beliefs	Vatu	www.vanuatugovernment.gov.vu

North America

		Area sq km	Area sq miles	Population	Capital	Languages	Religions	Currency	Internet Link
ANTIGUA AND BARBUDA		442	171	88 000	St John's	English, creole	Protestant, Roman Catholic	East Caribbean dollar	www.ab.gov.ag
THE BAHAMAS		13 939	5 382	342 000	Nassau	English, creole	Protestant, Roman Catholic	Bahamian dollar	www.bahamas.gov.bs
BARBADOS		430	166	256 000	Bridgetown	English, creole	Protestant, Roman Catholic	Barbados dollar	www.barbados.gov.bb
BELIZE		22 965	8 867	307 000	Belmopan	English, Spanish, Mayan, creole	Roman Catholic, Protestant	Belize dollar	www.belize.gov.bz
CANADA		9 984 670	3 855 103	33 573 000	Ottawa	English, French, local languages	Roman Catholic, Protestant, Eastern Orthodox, Jewish	Canadian dollar	www.canada.gc.ca
COSTA RICA		51 100	19 730	4 579 000	San José	Spanish	Roman Catholic, Protestant	Costa Rican colón	www.casapres.go.cr
CUBA		110 860	42 803	11 204 000	Havana	Spanish	Roman Catholic, Protestant	Cuban peso	www.cubagob.gov.cu
DOMINICA		750	290	67 000	Roseau	English, creole	Roman Catholic, Protestant	East Caribbean dollar	www.dominica.gov.dm
DOMINICAN REPUBLIC		48 442	18 704	10 090 000	Santo Domingo	Spanish, creole	Roman Catholic, Protestant	Dominican peso	www.cig.gov.do
EL SALVADOR		21 041	8 124	6 163 000	San Salvador	Spanish	Roman Catholic, Protestant	El Salvador colón, United States dollar	www.presidencia.gob.sv
GRENADA		378	146	104 000	St George's	English, creole	Roman Catholic, Protestant	East Caribbean dollar	www.gov.gd
GUATEMALA		108 890	42 043	14 027 000	Guatemala City	Spanish, Mayan languages	Roman Catholic, Protestant	Quetzal, United States dollar	www.congreso.gob.gt
HAITI		27 750	10 714	10 033 000	Port-au-Prince	French, creole	Roman Catholic, Protestant, Voodoo	Gourde	www.haiti.org
HONDURAS		112 088	43 277	7 466 000	Tegucigalpa	Spanish, Amerindian languages	Roman Catholic, Protestant	Lempira	www.congreso.gob.hn
JAMAICA		10 991	4 244	2 719 000	Kingston	English, creole	Protestant, Roman Catholic	Jamaican dollar	www.jis.gov.jm
MEXICO		1 972 545	761 604	109 610 000	Mexico City	Spanish, Amerindian languages	Roman Catholic, Protestant	Mexican peso	www.gob.mx
NICARAGUA		130 000	50 193	5 743 000	Managua	Spanish, Amerindian languages	Roman Catholic, Protestant	Córdoba	www.asamblea.gob.ni
PANAMA		77 082	29 762	3 454 000	Panama City	Spanish, English, Amerindian languages	Roman Catholic, Protestant, Sunni Muslim	Balboa	www.pa
ST KITTS AND NEVIS		261	101	52 000	Basseterre	English, creole	Protestant, Roman Catholic	East Caribbean dollar	www.gov.kn
ST LUCIA		616	238	172 000	Castries	English, creole	Roman Catholic, Protestant	East Caribbean dollar	www.stlucia.gov.lc
ST VINCENT AND THE GRENADINES		389	150	109 000	Kingstown	English, creole	Protestant, Roman Catholic	East Caribbean dollar	www.gov.vc
TRINIDAD AND TOBAGO		5 130	1 981	1 339 000	Port of Spain	English, creole, Hindi	Roman Catholic, Hindu, Protestant, Sunni Muslim	Trinidad and Tobago dollar	www.gov.tt
UNITED STATES OF AMERICA		9 826 635	3 794 085	314 659 000	Washington D.C.	English, Spanish	Protestant, Roman Catholic, Sunni Muslim, Jewish	United States dollar	www.firstgov.gov

South America

		Area sq km	Area sq miles	Population	Capital	Languages	Religions	Currency	Internet Link
ARGENTINA		2 766 889	1 068 302	40 276 000	Buenos Aires	Spanish, Italian, Amerindian languages	Roman Catholic, Protestant	Argentinian peso	www.argentina.gov.ar
BOLIVIA		1 098 581	424 164	9 863 000	La Paz/Sucre	Spanish, Quechua, Aymara	Roman Catholic, Protestant, Baha'i	Boliviano	www.bolivia.gov.bo
BRAZIL		8 514 879	3 287 613	193 734 000	Brasília	Portuguese	Roman Catholic, Protestant	Real	www.brazil.gov.br
CHILE		756 945	292 258	16 970 000	Santiago	Spanish, Amerindian languages	Roman Catholic, Protestant	Chilean peso	www.gobiernodechile.cl
COLOMBIA		1 141 748	440 831	45 660 000	Bogotá	Spanish, Amerindian languages	Roman Catholic, Protestant	Colombian peso	www.gobiernoenlinea.gov.co
ECUADOR		272 045	105 037	13 625 000	Quito	Spanish, Quechua, other Amerindian languages	Roman Catholic	US dollar	www.presidencia.gov.ec
GUYANA		214 969	83 000	762 000	Georgetown	English, creole, Amerindian languages	Protestant, Hindu, Roman Catholic, Sunni Muslim	Guyana dollar	www.gina.gov.gy
PARAGUAY		406 752	157 048	6 349 000	Asunción	Spanish, Guaraní	Roman Catholic, Protestant	Guaraní	www.presidencia.gov.py
PERU		1 285 216	496 225	29 165 000	Lima	Spanish, Quechua, Aymara	Roman Catholic, Protestant	Nuevo sol	www.peru.gob.pe
SURINAME		163 820	63 251	520 000	Paramaribo	Dutch, Surinamese, English, Hindi	Hindu, Roman Catholic, Protestant, Sunni Muslim	Suriname guilder	www.kabinet.sr.org
URUGUAY		176 215	68 037	3 361 000	Montevideo	Spanish	Roman Catholic, Protestant, Jewish	Uruguayan peso	www.presidencia.gub.uy
VENEZUELA		912 050	352 144	28 583 000	Caracas	Spanish, Amerindian languages	Roman Catholic, Protestant	Bolívar fuerte	www.gobiernoenlinea.ve

The current pattern of the world's countries and territories is a result of a long history of exploration, colonialism, conflict and politics. The fact that there are currently 196 independent countries in the world – the most recent, South Sudan, only being created in July 2011 – illustrates the significant political changes which have occurred since 1950 when there were only eighty-two. There has been a steady progression away from colonial influences over the last fifty years, although many dependent overseas territories remain.

The shapes of countries and the pattern of international boundaries reflect both physical and political processes. Some borders follow natural features – rivers, mountain ranges, etc – others are defined according to political agreement or as a result of war. Some are still subject to dispute between two or more countries, and many remain undefined on the ground.

Facts

- The longest single continuous land border stretches for 6 416 kilometres between Canada and the USA

- Both China and the Russian Federation have land borders with 14 different countries

- Vatican City, the smallest independent country, was created in 1929 as an enclave within Rome, the capital of Italy

- All countries of the world are members of the United Nations except Kosovo, Taiwan and Vatican City

Internet Links

United Nations	www.un.org
Foreign and Commonwealth Office	www.fco.gov.uk
International Boundaries Research Unit	www.dur.ac.uk/ibru
Permanent Committee on Geographical Names	www.pcgn.org.uk
U.S. Board on Geographic Names	geonames.usgs.gov

Abbreviation Key

A.	ANDORRA	HUN.	HUNGARY	R.F.	RUSSIAN FEDERATION
AL.	ALBANIA	ISR.	ISRAEL	ROM.	ROMANIA
ARM.	ARMENIA	JOR.	JORDAN	S.	SERBIA
AUST.	AUSTRIA	K.	KOSOVO	SL.	SLOVENIA
AZER.	AZERBAIJAN	L.	LUXEMBOURG	SLA.	SLOVAKIA
B.	BURUNDI	LAT.	LATVIA	SUR.	SURINAME
BE.	BENIN	LEB.	LEBANON	SW.	SWITZERLAND
BEL.	BELGIUM	LITH.	LITHUANIA	T.	TOGO
B.H.	BOSNIA-HERZEGOVINA	M.	MONTENEGRO	TAJIK.	TAJIKISTAN
BULG.	BULGARIA	MA.	MACEDONIA	TURKM.	TURKMENISTAN
CR.	CROATIA	MOL.	MOLDOVA	U.A.E.	UNITED ARAB EMIRATES
CZ.R.	CZECH REPUBLIC	NETH.	NETHERLANDS	U.K.	UNITED KINGDOM
EST.	ESTONIA	N.Z.	NEW ZEALAND	U.S.A.	UNITED STATES OF AMERICA
GEOR.	GEORGIA	R.	RWANDA	UZBEK.	UZBEKISTAN

High-resolution satellite image of **Vatican City**, the world's smallest country by both population and area.

World extremes

Countries			
Largest country (area)	**Russian Federation**	17 075 400 sq km	6 592 849 sq miles
Smallest country (area)	**Vatican City**	0.5 sq km	0.2 sq miles
Largest country (population)	**China**	1 330 265 000	
Smallest country (population)	**Vatican City**	557	
Most densely populated country	**Monaco**	17 500 per sq km	35 000 per sq mile
Least densely populated country	**Mongolia**	1.7 per sq km	4.4 per sq mile
Capitals			
Largest national capital (population)	**Tōkyō, Japan**	36 094 000	
Smallest national capital (population)	**Melekeok, Palau**	391	
Most northerly national capital	**Reykjavík, Iceland**	64° 08'N	
Most southerly national capital	**Wellington, New Zealand**	41° 18'S	
Highest national capital	**La Paz, Bolivia**	3 636 m	11 910 ft

The earth's physical features, both on land and on the sea bed, closely reflect its geological structure. The current shapes of the continents and oceans have evolved over millions of years. Movements of the tectonic plates which make up the earth's crust have created some of the best-known and most spectacular features. The processes which have shaped the earth continue today with earthquakes, volcanoes, erosion, climatic variations and man's activities all affecting the earth's landscapes.

The total topographic range of the earth's surface is nearly 20 000 metres, from the highest point Mount Everest, to the lowest point in the Mariana Trench. Major mountain ranges include the Himalaya, the Andes and the Rocky Mountains, each of which give rise to some of the world's greatest rivers. In contrast, the deserts of the Sahara, Australia, the Arabian Peninsula and the Gobi cover vast areas and each provide unique landscapes.

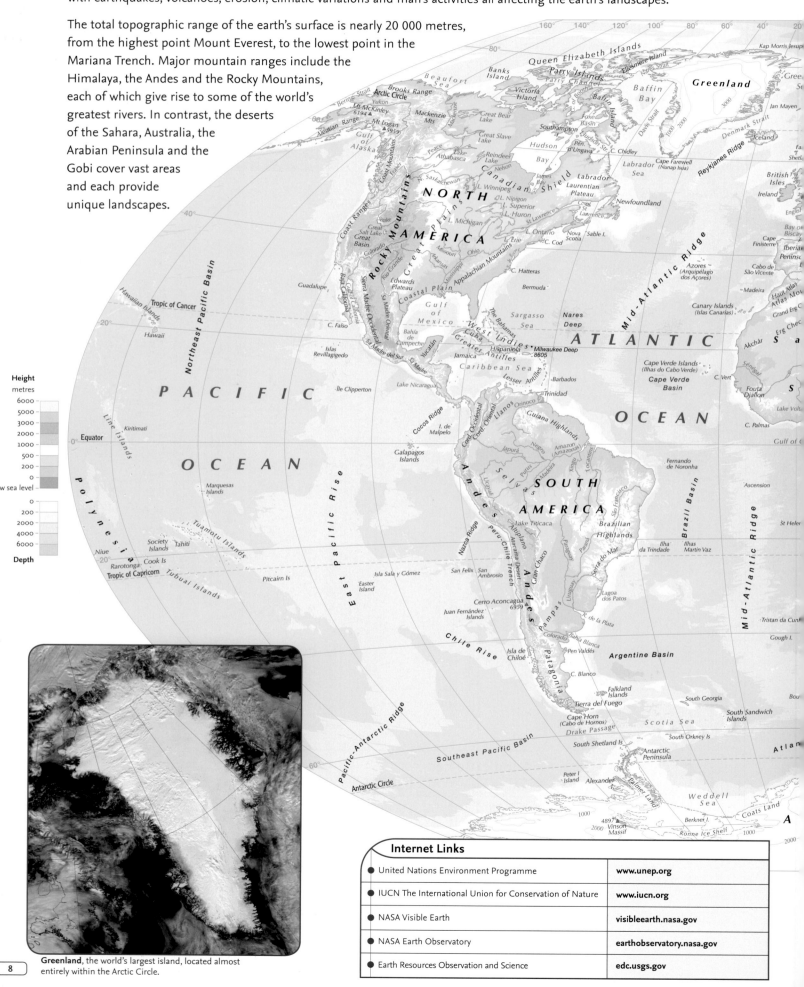

Height

metres
6000
5000
3000
2000
1000
500
200
0
below sea level

Depth

0
200
2000
4000
6000

Greenland, the world's largest island, located almost entirely within the Arctic Circle.

Internet Links	
● United Nations Environment Programme	**www.unep.org**
● IUCN The International Union for Conservation of Nature	**www.iucn.org**
● NASA Visible Earth	**visibleearth.nasa.gov**
● NASA Earth Observatory	**earthobservatory.nasa.gov**
● Earth Resources Observation and Science	**edc.usgs.gov**

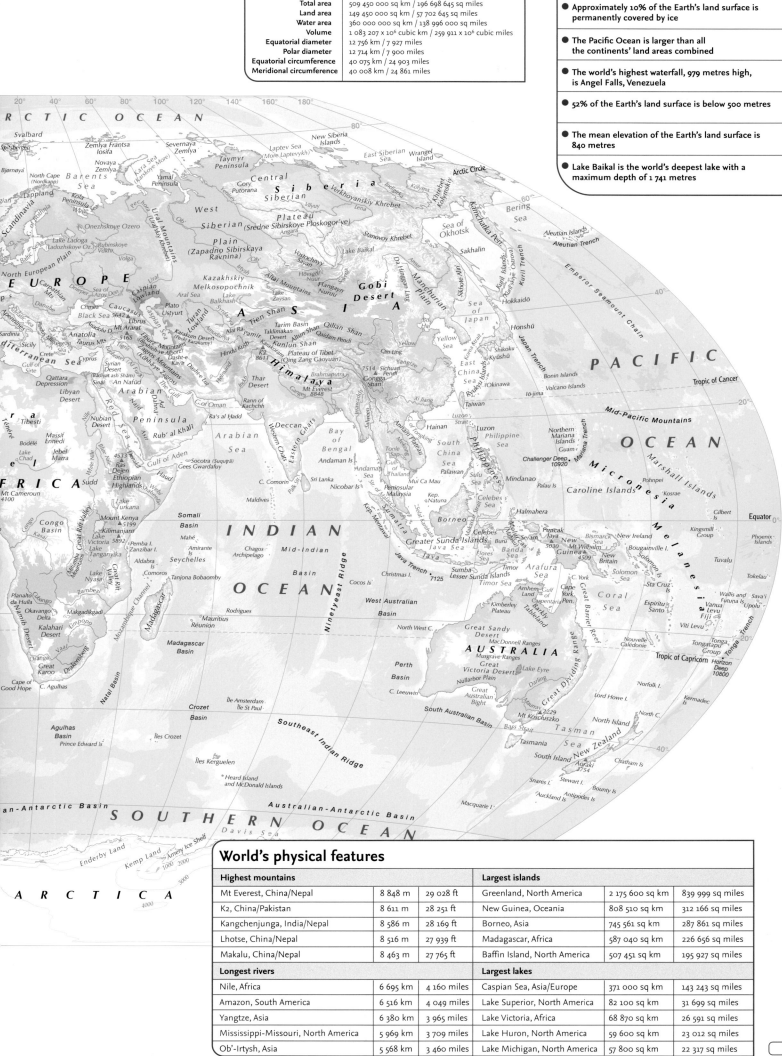

Earth's dimensions

Mass	5.974 x 10²¹ tonnes
Total area	509 450 000 sq km / 196 698 645 sq miles
Land area	149 450 000 sq km / 57 702 645 sq miles
Water area	360 000 000 sq km / 138 996 000 sq miles
Volume	1 083 207 x 10⁶ cubic km / 259 911 x 10⁶ cubic miles
Equatorial diameter	12 756 km / 7 927 miles
Polar diameter	12 714 km / 7 900 miles
Equatorial circumference	40 075 km / 24 903 miles
Meridional circumference	40 008 km / 24 861 miles

(Mass value shown as 5.974×10^{21} tonnes; Volume shown as $1\,083\,207 \times 10^{6}$ cubic km / $259\,911 \times 10^{6}$ cubic miles)

Facts

- Approximately 10% of the Earth's land surface is permanently covered by ice
- The Pacific Ocean is larger than all the continents' land areas combined
- The world's highest waterfall, 979 metres high, is Angel Falls, Venezuela
- 52% of the Earth's land surface is below 500 metres
- The mean elevation of the Earth's land surface is 840 metres
- Lake Baikal is the world's deepest lake with a maximum depth of 1 741 metres

World's physical features

Highest mountains			Largest islands		
Mt Everest, China/Nepal	8 848 m	29 028 ft	Greenland, North America	2 175 600 sq km	839 999 sq miles
K2, China/Pakistan	8 611 m	28 251 ft	New Guinea, Oceania	808 510 sq km	312 166 sq miles
Kangchenjunga, India/Nepal	8 586 m	28 169 ft	Borneo, Asia	745 561 sq km	287 861 sq miles
Lhotse, China/Nepal	8 516 m	27 939 ft	Madagascar, Africa	587 040 sq km	226 656 sq miles
Makalu, China/Nepal	8 463 m	27 765 ft	Baffin Island, North America	507 451 sq km	195 927 sq miles
Longest rivers			**Largest lakes**		
Nile, Africa	6 695 km	4 160 miles	Caspian Sea, Asia/Europe	371 000 sq km	143 243 sq miles
Amazon, South America	6 516 km	4 049 miles	Lake Superior, North America	82 100 sq km	31 699 sq miles
Yangtze, Asia	6 380 km	3 965 miles	Lake Victoria, Africa	68 870 sq km	26 591 sq miles
Mississippi-Missouri, North America	5 969 km	3 709 miles	Lake Huron, North America	59 600 sq km	23 012 sq miles
Ob'-Irtysh, Asia	5 568 km	3 460 miles	Lake Michigan, North America	57 800 sq km	22 317 sq miles

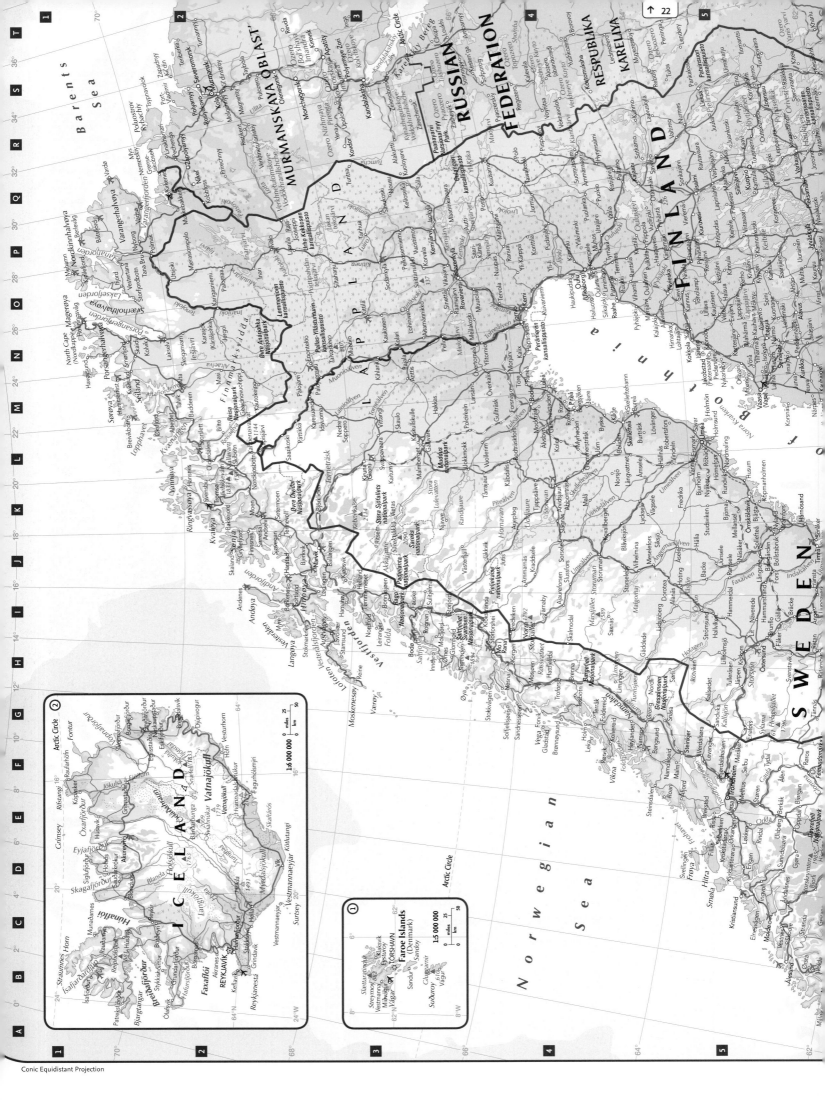

Conic Equidistant Projection

1:5 000 000

| 0 | 50 | 100 | 150 miles |

| 0 | 50 | 100 | 150 | 200 | 250 km |

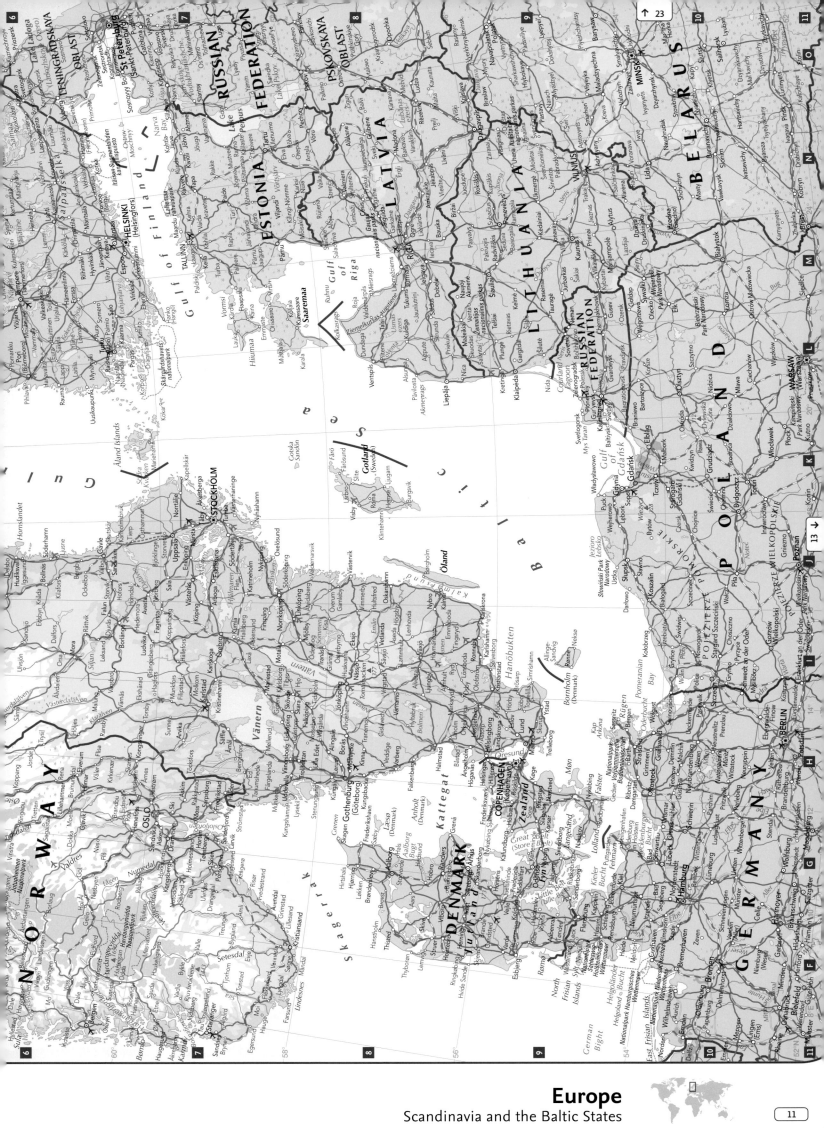

Europe
Scandinavia and the Baltic States

Europe

Northwest Europe

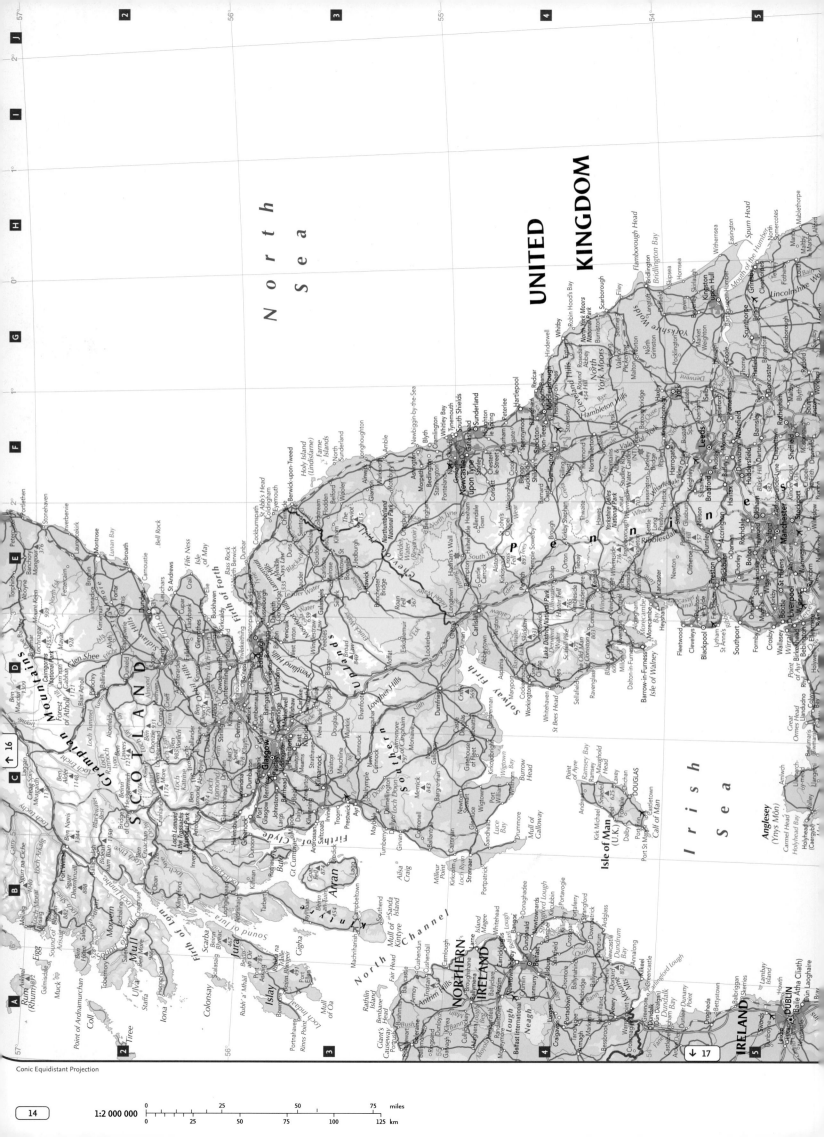

Conic Equidistant Projection

1:2 000 000

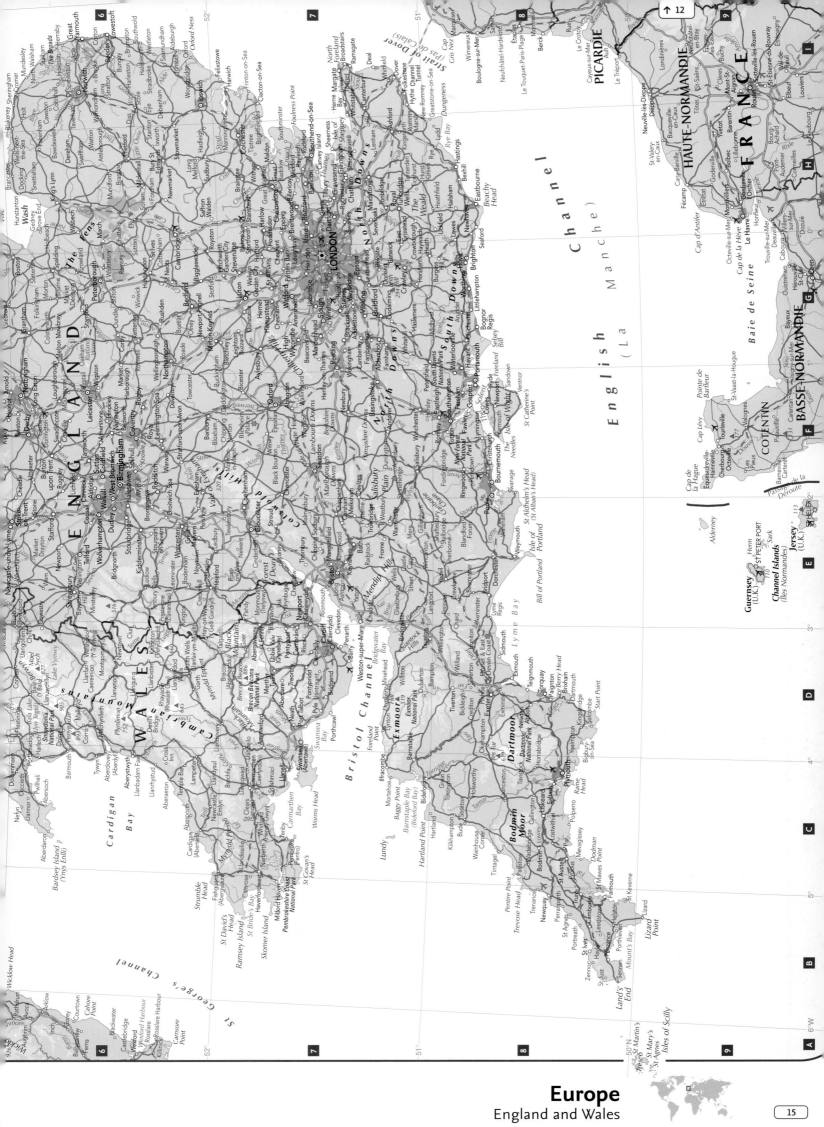

Europe

England and Wales

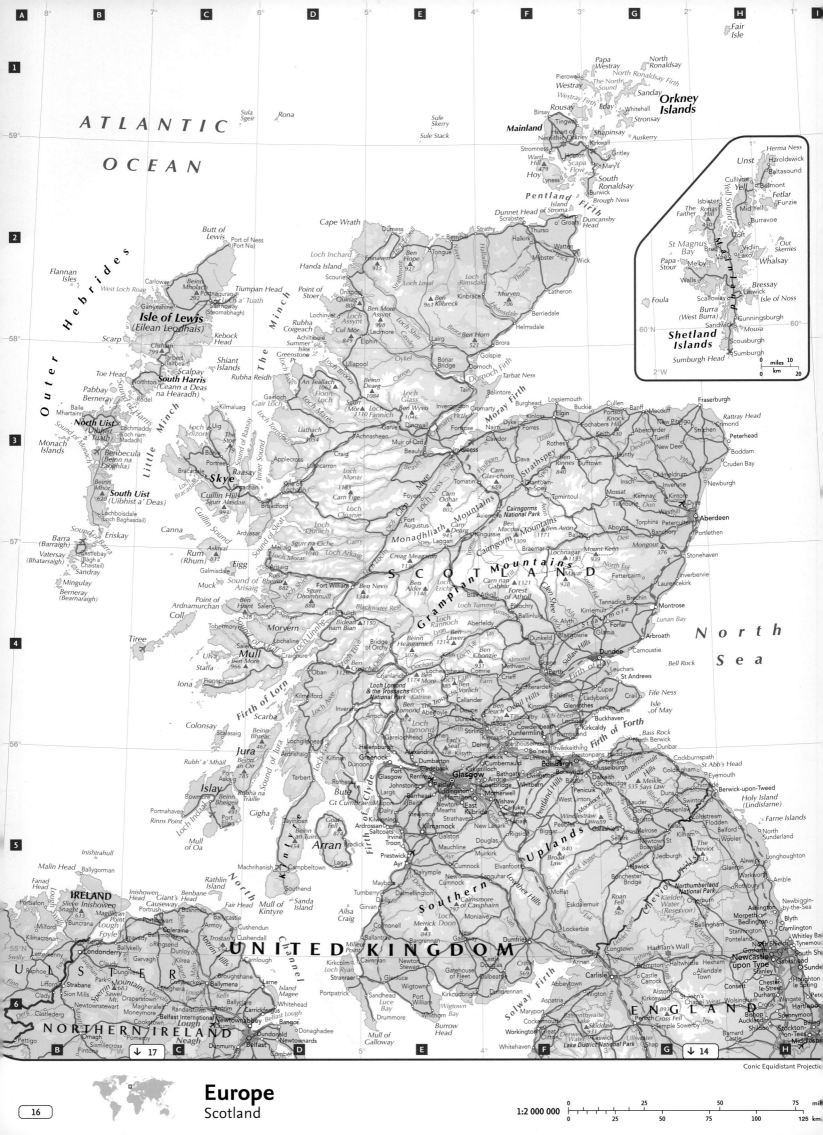

Europe
Scotland

Conic Equidistant Projection

1:2 000 000

Europe
Ireland

Conic Equidistant Projection

Europe
France

1:5 000 000

Europe
Spain and Portugal

Conic Equidistant Projection

1:5 000 000

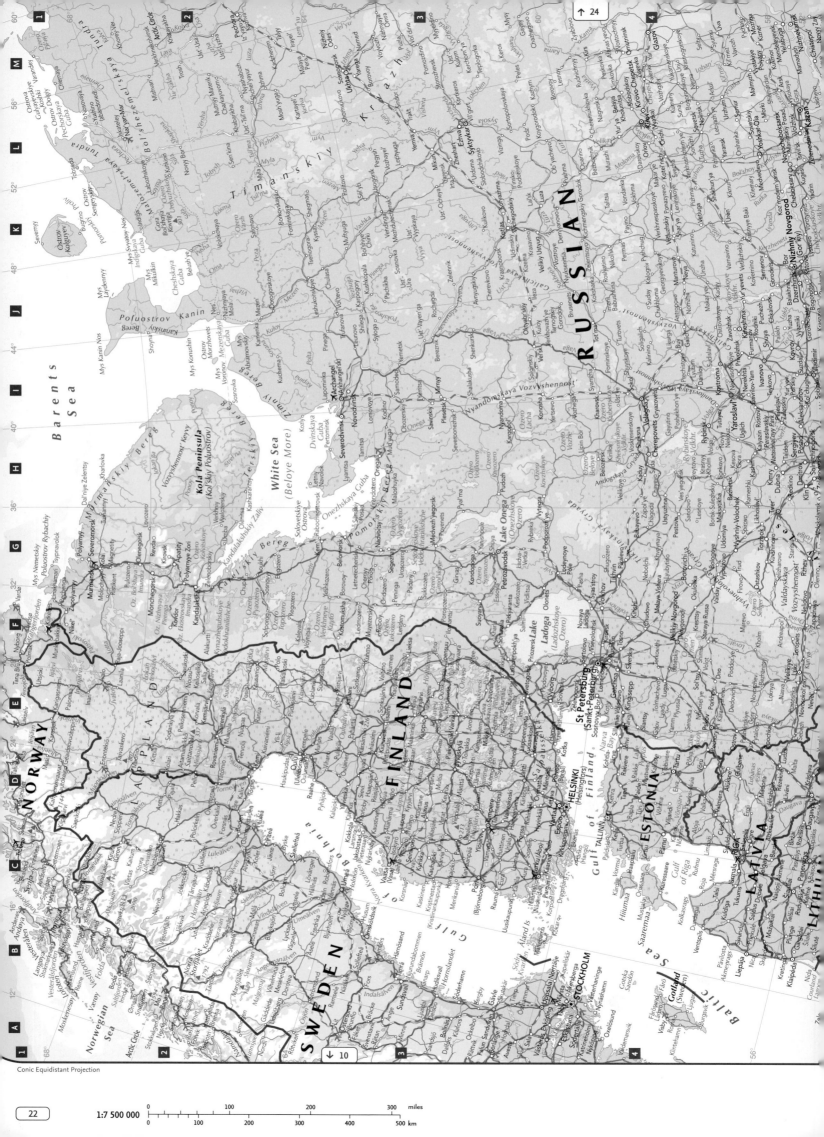

Europe
Western Russian Federation

Asia
Northern Asia

↓ 28

Albers Conic Equal Area Projection

1:20 000 000

| 0 | 200 | 400 | 600 miles |

| 0 | 200 | 400 | 600 | 800 | 1000 km |

Asia

Central and Southern Asia

Albers Conic Equal Area Projection

1:20 000 000

Asia
Eastern and Southeast Asia

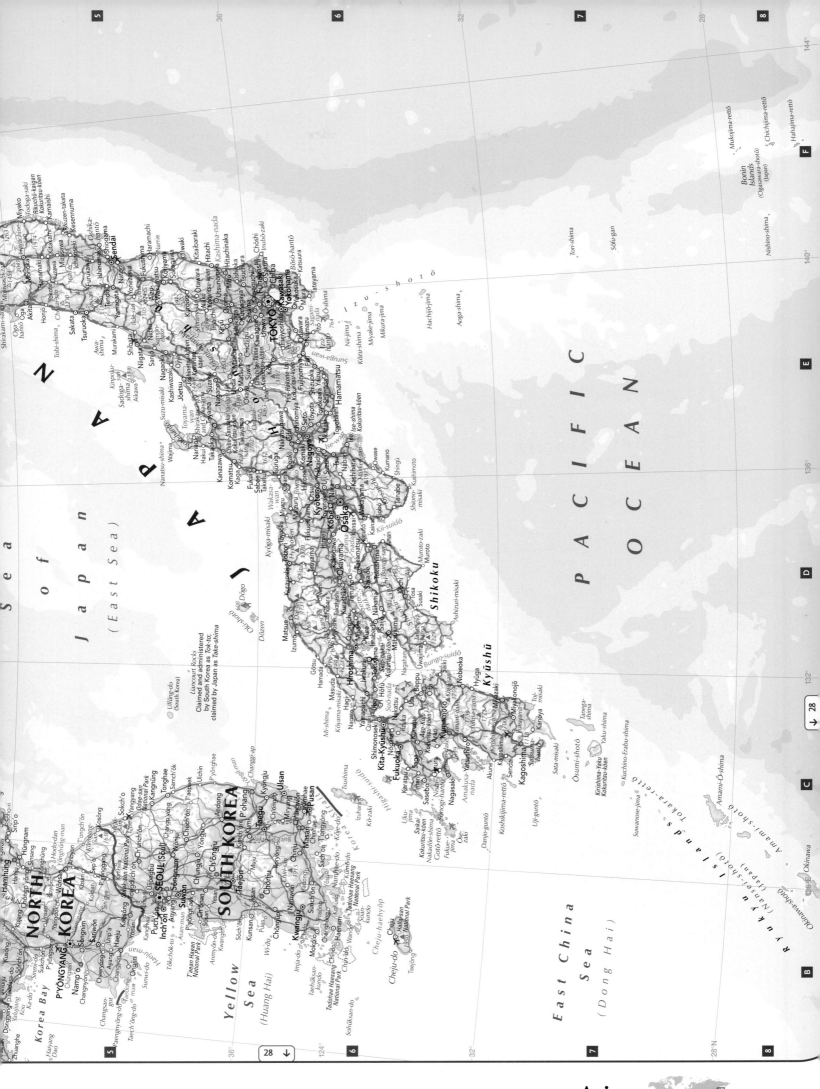

Asia

Japan, North Korea and South Korea

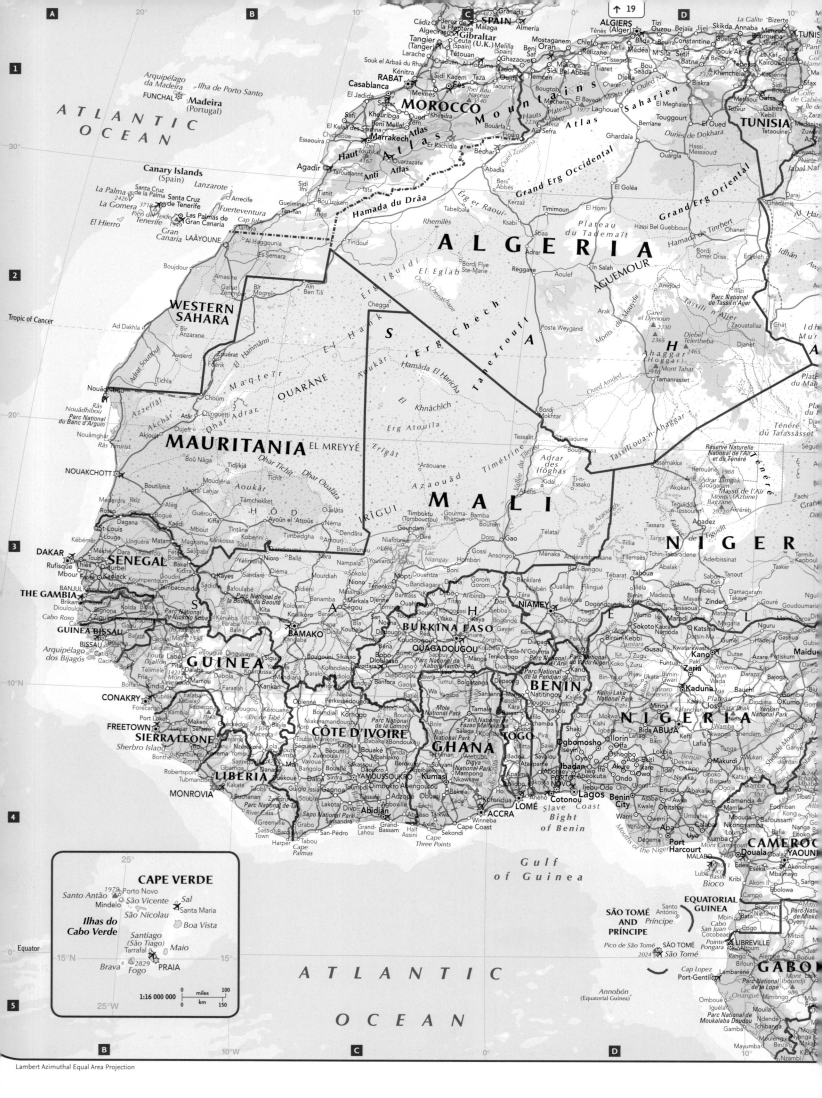

Africa

Northern Africa

Africa

Central and Southern Africa

ATLANTIC

OCEAN

NAMIBIA

BOTSWANA

GHANZI

KGALAGADI

KWENEN

SOUTHE

Kalahari

Desert

REPUBLI

OF

SOUTH AF

NORTHERN

CAPE

WESTERN CAPE

ERONGO

KHOMAS

OMAHEKE

HARDAP

KARAS

GREAT NAMAQUALAND

NAMAQUALAND

Namib Desert

Tropic of Capricorn

Lambert Azimuthal Equal Area Projection

1:5 000 000

0   50   100   150   miles

0   50   100   150   200   250 km

Africa
Republic of South Africa

Lambert Azimuthal Equal Area Projection

1:20 000 000

| 0 | 200 | 400 | 600 miles |

| 0 | 200 | 400 | 600 | 800 | 1000 km |

160° **G** 170° **H** 180° **I** 170° **J**

1

Howland Island (U.S.A.)
Baker Island (U.S.A.)
0°

Aranuka
Nonouti
Nauru YAREN
Banaba
(Ocean Island)
Tabiteuea
Beru
Nikunau
Nonouti
Onotoa Kingsmill Group
Tamana Arorae

NAURU

K I R I B A T I

Phoenix
Islands
Kanton
McKean
Rawaki
Nikumaroro Orona Manra

Takuu
Islands
Nukumanu
Islands

Ontong
Java Atoll
Nanumea
Nanumanga
Niutao

2

Choiseul
Roncador
Reef
Santa
Isabel
Georgia Sound
New
Georgia
Georgia
ands
Buala
Malu'u
Stewart
Islands
Nui
Vaitupu

Malaita
Maramasike
Ulawa Island
Nukufetau

**SOLOMON
ISLANDS**

Florida
Islands
Malaita

HONIARA
Avuavu
Nukulaelae
Tokelau
(New Zealand)
Atafu
Nukunonu
Fakaofo

Guadalcanal
Kirakira
Santa
Ana
San Cristobal
(Makira)

TUVALU Funafuti VAIAKU
Niulakita

Rennell
Indispensable
Reefs

Nupani
Swallow Islands
Ndeni
Santa Cruz Islands
(Solomon Islands)
Swains Island
Pukapuka
(Danger Islands)
Nassau

al Sea

Utupua
Vanikoro
Islands
Mitre
Island
Cherry
Island
Tikopia
Rotuma
(Fiji)

10°

Torres Islands
Uréparapara
Banks
Islands
Vanua Lava
Santa Maria Island
Íles
Wallis
SAMOA
Suwarrow

**Wallis and
Futuna Islands**
(France)
MATĀ'UTU
**American
Samoa**
(U.S.A.)

Espiritu Santo
Mount
Tabwémasana
1879
Aoba
Maéwo
Íles de Hoorn
Savai'i
'Upolu
APIA
Manu'a
Islands
Tutuila FAGATOGO
Rose
Island

VANUATU
Norsup
Pentecost Island
Ambrym
Niuafo'ou
210
Tafahi
Niuatoputapu

Malakula
1270 Epi
Émae
Shepherd
Islands
Yasawa
Group
Great Sea Reef
Bligh
Water
Vanua Levu
Labasa
(Lambasa)
Taveuni
Northern
Lau Group
Vava'u
Group

Récifs
d'Entrecasteaux
PORT VILA Éfaté
Lautoka
Tomanivi
Mt Victoria
Koro
Sea
Koro
Vava'u
Group

Íles Chesterfield
(France)
Grand Passage
Erromango
Viti Levu
Kadavu Passage
SUVA Nasinu
Gau
Lakeba
Southern
Lau Group

Grand Récif
de Cook
Tanna
361
Futuna
FIJI
Moala
Kabara
Tofua 500
Ha'apai
Group

3

Íles Belep
Récif des
Français
Anatom
(Aneityum)
Kadavu
Matuku
Vatoa
Cook Islands
(New Zealand)

Koumac
Grand Récif
de Cook
Nouvelle Calédonie
Ouvéa
Íles Loyauté
(France)
Ceva-i-Ra
(Conway Reef)
Doi
Ono-i-Lau
ALOFI **Niue**
(New Zealand)
Palmerston

New Caledonia
(France)
Bourail
Lifou
Tadin
Maré
Hunter
Island
100
Ata
TONGA
NUKU'ALOFA
Tongatapu
Group

NOUMÉA
Íle des Pins
Yaté
Grand Récif
du Sud
Minerva Reefs

20°

P A C I F I C   O C E A N

Tropic of Capricorn
160°

Norfolk Island
(Australia)
KINGSTON

4

Lord Howe Island
(Australia)
Raoul Island
Kermadec Islands
(New Zealand)
Macauley Island
Curtis Island
Havre Rock
L'Espérance Rock

30°

Three Kings
Islands
North
Cape
Cape
Maria van Diemen
Awanui
Whangarei

**NEW
ZEALAND**

North Island
Great Barrier Island

Takapuna
Auckland
Manukau
Hamilton
Tauranga
East Cape
Te Kuiti
Tokoroa
Taupo
Whakatane
Gisborne

an Sea

New
Plymouth
Mount Taranaki
(Mount Egmont)
Lake
Taupo
Mount
Ruapehu
Wairoa
Mahia Peninsula
Hawera
Wanganui
Napier
Hastings

Cape Farewell
Tasman
Bay
Picton
Levin
Masterton
Palmerston North

Westport
Nelson
Blenheim
Cook
Strait
Lower Hutt
WELLINGTON

5

**South
Island**
Hokitika
Greymouth

Aoraki
(Mount Cook)
3724
Banks Peninsula
Chatham Islands
(New Zealand)

Mount
Aspiring
3030
Christchurch
Ashburton
Timaru
Chatham Islands
(New Zealand)
Waitangi

Mount
Christina
2500
Southern Alps
Queenstown
Oamaru
Pitt Island

Cape Providence
Gore
Dunedin

Foveaux Strait
Invercargill

Stewart Island
South West Cape
Bounty Islands
(New Zealand)

6

Snares
Islands
Antipodes Islands
(New Zealand)

160° **G** 170° **H** 180° **I** 170° **J** 160° **K** 150°W **L**

Auckland Islands
(New Zealand)

40°

Oceania
Australia, New Zealand and Southwest Pacific

39

Oceania
Australia

Oceania
Southeast Australia

1:5 000 000

Lambert Azimuthal Equal Area Projection

Oceania
New Zealand

1:5 250 000

Conic Equidistant Projection

Lambert Conformal Conic Projection

1:16 000 000

| 0 | 200 | 400 | miles |
| 0 | 200 | 400 | 600 | 800 | km |

Lambert Conformal Conic Projection

1:12 000 000

| miles | 100 | 200 | 300 | 400 |

| km | 100 | 200 | 300 | 400 | 500 | 600 | 700 |

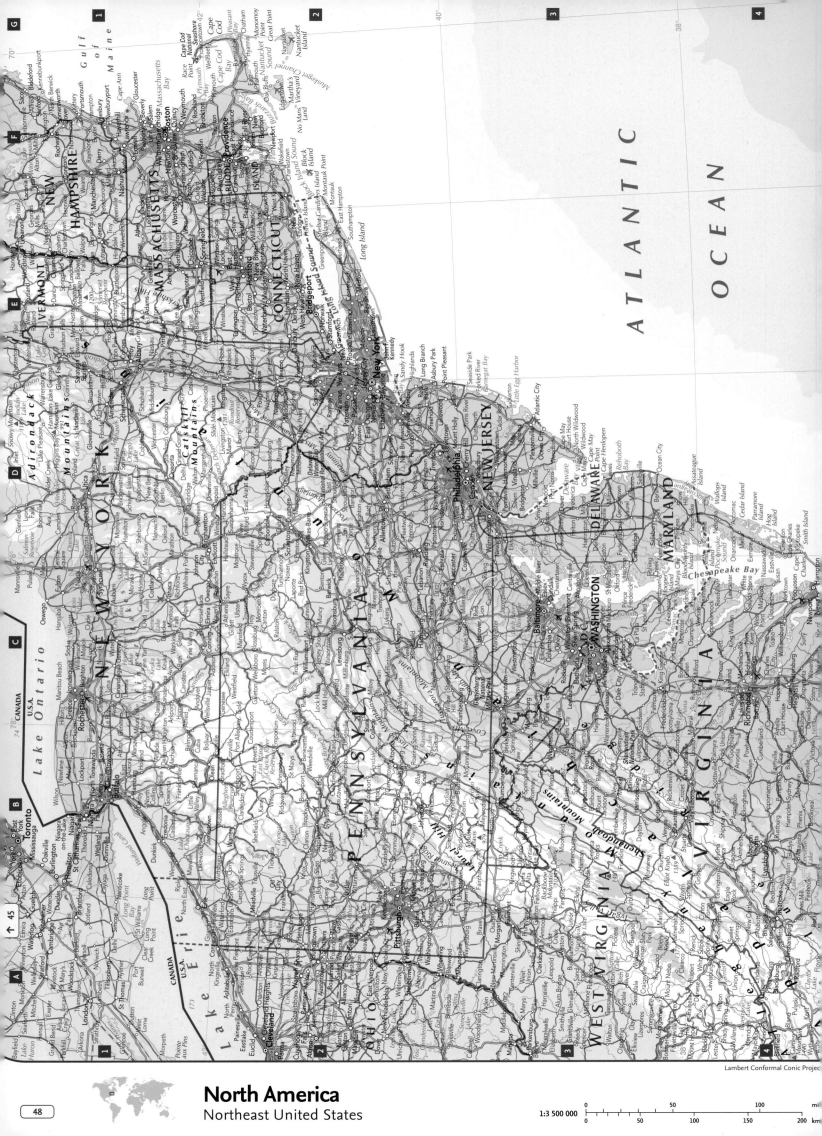

North America

Northeast United States

1:3 500 000

Lambert Conformal Conic Projec

Lambert Conformal Conic Projection

500 000

| 0 | 50 | 100 | miles |

| 0 | 50 | 100 | 150 | 200 km |

North America
Southwest United States

Lambert Conformal Conic Projection

1:14 000 000

| 0 | 200 | 400 | miles |
| 0 | 200 | 400 | 600 | 800 km |

North America
Central America and the Caribbean

PACIFIC

OCEAN

Galapagos Islands

Parque Nacional Galápagos

Equator

Isla Salvador
San Salvador
Isla Fernandina
Isla Santa Cruz
Isla Isabela
Isla San Cristóbal
Santa María
Baquerizo Moreno

Galapagos Islands
(Islas Galápagos)
(Ecuador)

1:14 000 000

NICARAGUA
MANAGUA
COSTA RICA
SAN JOSE
PANAMA
PANAMA CITY

COLOMBIA
BOGOTÁ
Medellín
Cali
QUITO
ECUADOR
Guayaquil
PERU
LIMA
Callao
BOLIVIA
LA PAZ
SUCRE
CHILE
ARGENTINA

VENEZUELA
CARACAS
Maracaibo
GRENADA

1:14 000 000

Lambert Azimuthal Equal Area Projection

0   200   400   miles
0   200   400   600   800 km

South America
Northern South America

South America
Southern South America

1:14 000 000

Lambert Azimuthal Equal Area Projection

0 200 400 mi
0 200 400 600 800 km

South America
Southeast Brazil

Lambert Azimuthal Equal Area Projection

1 : 7 000 000

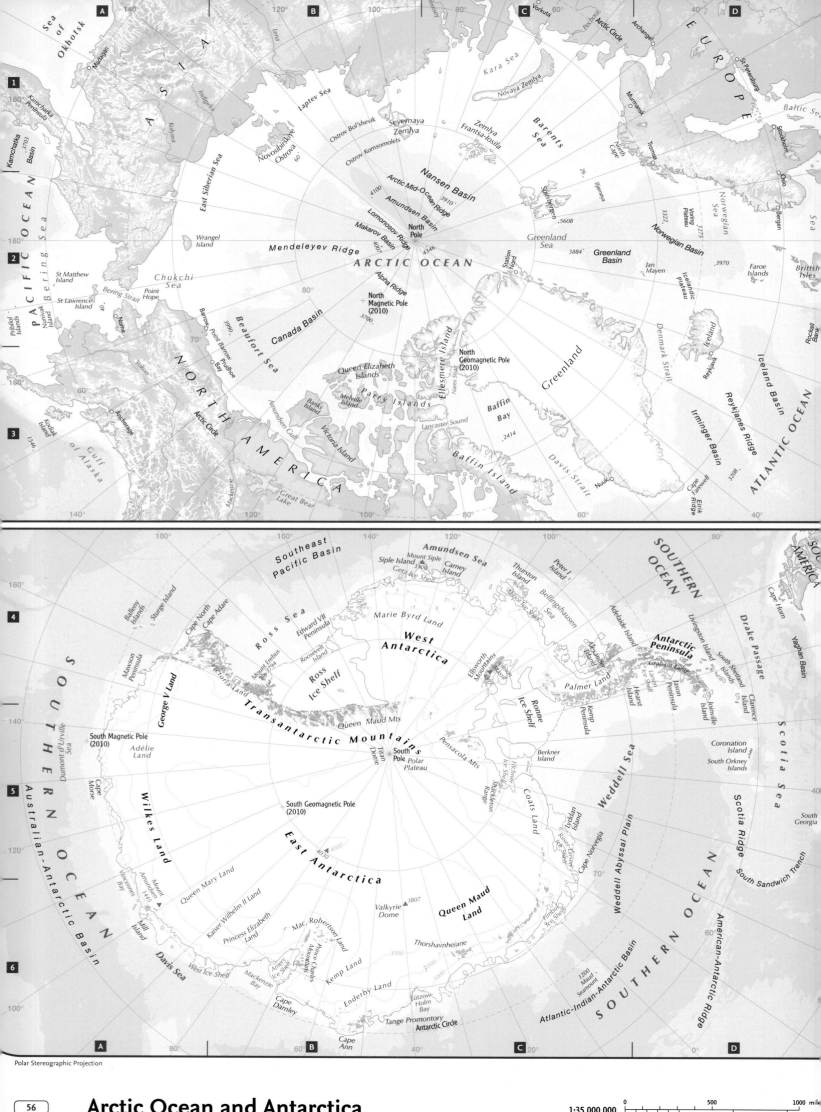

Arctic Ocean and Antarctica

Arctic Ocean (top map)

A — 140° — B — 120° — 100° — 80° — C — 60° — 40° — D

1

Sea of Okhotsk
A S I A
Madagan
Kamchatka Peninsula
.3703
Kamchatka Basin
PACIFIC OCEAN
160°
Bering Sea

Lena
Indigirka
Kolyma
Laptev Sea
Novosibirskiye Ostrova
Ostrov Bol'shevik
Severnaya Zemlya
Ostrov Komsomolets
60°
Arctic Mid-Ocean Ridge
4100
Nansen Basin
3910
Amundsen Basin
North Pole
Lomonosov Ridge
Makarov Basin
4001
4346

Kara Sea
Novaya Zemlya
Zemlya Frantsa-Iosifa
Barents Sea
EUROPE
Vorkuta
Pechora
Arctic Circle
Archangel
St Petersburg
Baltic Sea
Murmansk
Tromsø
North Cape
Stockholm
Oslo
Bergen

2
180°
East Siberian Sea
Wrangel Island
Mendeleyev Ridge
ARCTIC OCEAN
Alpha Ridge
North Magnetic Pole (2010)
3700

Station Nord
Greenland Sea
3884
Greenland Basin
Jan Mayen
Spitsbergen
.5608
Voring Plateau
.1275
Norwegian Basin
Norwegian Sea
Icelandic Plateau
3322
3970
Faroe Islands
British Isles
Sea

Chukchi Sea
St Matthew Island
St Lawrence Island
Bering Strait
Point Hope
Nome
Nunivak Island
Pribilof Islands
PACIFIC OCEAN
40°
Beaufort Sea
Barrow
Point Barrow
Prudhoe Bay
3990.
Canada Basin
70°

Queen Elizabeth Islands
Ellesmere Island
North Geomagnetic Pole (2010)
Parry Islands
Nares Strait
Denmark Strait
Greenland
Iceland
Reykjavik
Reykjanes Ridge
3208
Iceland Basin
Rockall Bank
ATLANTIC OCEAN

3
160°
Kodiak Island
1546.
Anchorage
Gulf of Alaska
Yukon
60°
NORTH AMERICA
Arctic Circle
Amundsen Gulf
Banks Island
Melville Island
Victoria Island
Great Bear Lake
Mackenzie
Parry Islands
Lancaster Sound
Baffin Bay
.2414
Baffin Island
Davis Strait
Nuuk
Cape Farewell
Eirik Ridge

140° — 120° — 100° — 80° — 60° — 40°

Antarctica (bottom map)

180° — 160° — 140° — 120° — 100° — 80°

4
160°
Southeast Pacific Basin
Balleny Islands
Sturge Island
Cape North
Cape Adare
Ross Sea
Edward VII Peninsula
Roosevelt Island
Mount Erebus
3794
Victoria Land
Ross Ice Shelf
Amundsen Sea
Mount Siple
.3100
Siple Island
Getz Ice Shelf
Carney Island
Marie Byrd Land
West Antarctica
Thurston Island
Peter I Island
Bellingshausen Sea
Abbot Ice Shelf
Alexander Island
Ellsworth Mountains
Vinson Massif
SOUTHERN OCEAN
Adelaide Island
Antarctic Peninsula
Graham Land
Livingston Island
South Shetland Islands
Drake Passage
Cape Horn
SOUTH AMERICA
Yaghan Basin

5
SOUTHERN
Mawson Peninsula
George V Land
South Magnetic Pole (2010)
Adélie Land
Dumont d'Urville Sea
OCEAN
Transantarctic Mountains
Queen Maud Mts
Titan Dome
South Pole
Polar Plateau
South Geomagnetic Pole (2010)
Pensacola Mts
Ronne Ice Shelf
Palmer Land
Kemp Peninsula
Jason Peninsula
Larsen Ice Shelf
Hearst Island
Joinville Island
Clarence Island
Coronation Island
South Orkney Islands
Weddell Sea
Berkner Island
Filchner Ice Shelf
Shackleton Range
Coats Land
Scotia Sea
Scotia Ridge
South Georgia
South Sandwich Trench

6
140°
Australian-Antarctic Basin
Cape Morse
Wilkes Land
East Antarctica
4050 ▲ 4000
Queen Mary Land
Mount Amundsen ▲ 1445
Vincennes Bay
Mill Island
Davis Sea
West Ice Shelf
Mackenzie Bay
Kaiser Wilhelm II Land
Princess Elizabeth Land
Amery Ice Shelf
Prince Charles Mountains
Mac. Robertson Land
Kemp Land
Enderby Land
Cape Darnley
Cape Ann
Valkyrie Dome
3807
Queen Maud Land
Thorshavnheiane
3000
2000
1000
Lützow Holm Bay
Tange Promontory
Antarctic Circle
Fimbul Ice Shelf
Cape Norvegia
Riiser Larsen Ice Shelf
Jutul Island
70°
Weddell Abyssal Plain
1200 Maud Seamount
Atlantic-Indian-Antarctic Basin
60°
SOUTHERN OCEAN
American-Antarctic Ridge
0°

A — 80° — 60° — B — 40° — 20° — C — 0° — D

Arctic Ocean and Antarctica

Polar Stereographic Projection

1:35 000 000

0 — 500 — 1000 miles
0 — 500 — 1000 — 1500 km

Index

The index includes the most significant names on the maps in the atlas. The names are generally indexed to the largest scale map on which they appear. For large physical features this will be the largest scale map on which they appear in their entirety or in the majority. Names can be located using the grid reference letters and numbers around the edges of the map. Names located on insets have a symbol □.

Abbreviations used to describe features in the index:

admin. dist.	administrative district	g.	gulf	prov.	province
admin. div.	administrative division	hd.	headland	pt	point
admin. reg.	administrative region	i.	island	r.	river
aut. reg.	autonomous region	imp. lake	impermanent lake	r. mouth	river mouth
aut. rep.	autonomous republic	is.	islands	reg.	region
b.	bay	l.	lake	resr.	reservoir
c.	cape	lag.	lagoon	salt l.	salt lake
depr.	depression	mt.	mountain	sea chan.	sea channel
des.	desert	mts	mountains	terr.	territory
esc.	escarpment	pen.	peninsula	vol.	volcano
est.	estuary	plat.	plateau		
for.	forest	pref.	prefecture		

1

9 de Julio 54D5
25 de Mayo 54D5

A

Aabenraa 11F9
Aachen 13K5
Aalborg 11F8
Aalborg Bugt b. 11G8
Aalen 13M6
Aalst 12J5
Aars 11F8
Aasiaat 45M3
Aba 32D4
Ābādān 33H1
Ābādeh 26E3
Abadla 32C1
Abaeté 55B2
Abaetetuba 53I4
Abakan 24K4
Abakanskiy Khrebet mts 24J4
Abancay 52D6
Abarkū 26E3
Abashiri 30G3
Abbeville 18E1
Abbeville 15E8
Abéché 33F3
Abengourou 32C4
Abeokuta 32D4
Aberdare 32C4
Aberdeen 16G3
Aberdeen 42E1
Aberdeen 46H2
Abergavenny 15D7
Aberystwyth 15C6
Abhā 34E2
Abhar 33H1
Abidjan 32C4
Abilene 46H5
Abingdon 15F7
Abinsk 23H7
Abitibi, Lake 45J5
Aboisso 32C4
Abomey 32D4
Abong Mbang 32E4
Aboyne 16G3
Abqaiq 34E1
Abrantes 19B4
Absaroka Range mts 46E3
Abū ʿArīsh 34E2
Abu Dhabi 26E4
Abu Hamed 33G3
Abuja 32D4
Abū Kamāl 33H1
Abū Ḩadrīyah 34E1
Açailândia 53I5
Acaponeta 50C4
Acapulco 50E5
Acaraú 53I4
Acaraú r. 53I4
Acarigua 52E2
Acatlán 50E5
Accra 32C4
Accrington 14E5
Achaguas 52E2
Acheng 30B3
Achinsk 24K4
Acipayam 21M6
Acireale 20F6
Acklins Island 47M7
Acle 15I6
Aconcagua, Cerro mt. 54B4
Acopiara 53K5
A Coruña 19B2
Acqui Terme 20C2
Acri 20F5
Ada 47H5
Adamantina 55A3
Adams 48E1
Adana 33G1
Adapazarı 21N4
Ad Dafinah 34E1
Ad Daḩnāʾ des. 34E1
Ad Dār al Ḩamrāʾ 34D1
Ad Dakhla 32B2
Ad Darb 34E2
Ad Diwānīyah 33H1
Addis Ababa 34D3
Addlestone 15G7
Adelaide 41I6
Aden 34D2
Aden, Gulf of 34E2
Āḏīgrat 34D2
Adirī 33E2
Adirondack Mountains 48D1
Adjud 21L2
Admiralty Gulf 40F2
Admiralty Islands 38E2
Ado-Ekiti 32D4
Adrano 20F6
Adrar 32C2
Adria 20E2
Adriatic Sea 20E2
Adwa 34D2
Aegean Sea 21K5
A Estrada 19B2
Afanasʾyevo 22L4
Afghanistan country 26F3
Afgooye 34E3
Afogados da Ingazeira 53K5
Afonso Cláudio 55C3
Afuá 53H4
Afyon 21N5
Agadez 32D3
Agadir 32C1
Agadyr' 27G2
Agara 23I7
Agboville 32C4
Agartala 27I4
Ağcabədi 23J8
Agde 18F5
Agen 18E4
Agni 26D3
Agra 27G4
Ağri 26D3

Agrigento 20E6
Agrinio 21I5
Agua Prieta 46F5
Aguadilla 51K5
Aguascalientes 50D4
Águilas 19F5
Agulhas, Cape 36E8
Agulhas plat. 32D2
Ahaggar plat. 32D2
Ahar 26D3
Ahmadabad 27G4
Ahmar mts 34E3
Ahtme 11O7
Ahvāz 33H1
Ahwar 34D2
Aigio 21I5
Aiken 47K5
Aïn Beïda 20B7
Aïn Defla 19F5
Aïn Deheb 19G6
Aïn el Hadjel 19H6
Aïn Oussera 19H6
Aïn Sefra 32C1
Aïn Taya 19H5
Aïn Tédélès 19H5
Aïn Temouchent 19F6
Airdrie 16F5
Aiud 21J1
Aix-en-Provence 18G5
Aix-les-Bains 18G4
Aizawl 27I4
Aizkraukle 11N8
Aizu-Wakamatsu 31E5
Ajaccio 18I6
Ajdābiyā 33F1
Ajmer 27G4
Akçakoca 21N4
Akchâr reg. 32B3
Åkersberga 11K7
Aketi 34C3
Akhali Apʻoni 23I8
Akhdar, Al Jabal al mts 33F1
Akhisar 21L5
Akhtubinsk 23J6
Akhty 23J8
Aki 31D6
Akjoujt 32B3
Akkajaure l. 10J3
Akkol' 27G1
Akkuş 23H8
Akom II 32E4
Akonolinga 32E4
Akordat 33G3
Akranes 10□
Åkrehamn 11D7
Akron 48A2
Aksay 23J6
Akşehir 21N5
Aksu 27H2
Aksubayevo 23K5
Aktau 26E2
Aktsyabrski 23F5
Akure 31C6
Akure 32D4
Akwanga 32D4
Akyazı 21N4
Alabama r. 47J5
Alabama state 47J5
Alaçam 23H8
Alagir 23J8
Alagoinhas 55D1
Al Aḩmadī 26D4
Alajärvi 10M5
Alatyr' 23J5
Alausí 52C4
Alaverdi 23J8
Alavus 10M5
Al ʿAlayyah 34E2
Al ʿAmārah 33H1
Al ʿĀmirīyah 33F1
Al Khaṣab 26E4
Al Khawr 34F1
Al Khums 34F1
Al Khunn 34E1
Alkmaar 12J4
Al Kūt 33H1
Allahabad 27H4
Alakh-Yun' 25O3
Allegheny Mountains 48A4
Allende 46G6
Allentown 48D2
Alliance 46G3
Alloa 16F4
Alma 47M2
Almada 19B4
Al Mahwīt 34E2
Almansa 19F4
Al Manṣūrah 33G1
Al Marj 33F1
Almaty 27G2
Almazny 25M3
Almeirim 19B4
Almeirim 53H4
Almelo 13K4
Almenara 55C2
Almendralejo 19C4
Almería 19E5
Almería, Golfo de b. 19E5
Al Metʿyevsk 24G4
Almhult 11I8
Al Mindak 34E1
Al Minyā 33G2
Al Mubarraz 34E1
Alofi 39J3
Alor Setar 29C7
Alotau 41K2
Alpena 47K2
Alpine 46G5
Alps mts 13M7
Al Qāʿīyah 34E1
Al Qāmishlī 33H1
Al Qaṭn 34E2
Al Quwayʿīyah 34E1
Al Quwayyīyah 34E1

Aldeburgh 15I6
Aldershot 15G7
Aldridge 15F6
Alegre 55B3
Alegrete 54E3
Aleksandrov 22H4
Aleksandrov Gay 23K6
Aleksandrovskoye 23I7
Aleksandrovsk-Sakhalinskiy 30F2
Aleksandry, Zemlya i. 24F1
Alekseyevka 23H6
Alekseyevka 23H6
Alekseyevskoye 22K5
Aleksin 23H5
Aleksinac 21I3
Alençon 18E2
Alenquer 53H4
ʻAlenuihāhā Channel 46□
Aleppo 33G1
Alès 18G4
Aleşd 21J1
Alessandria 20C2
Ålesund 10E5
Aleutian Islands 44A4
Aleutian Range mts 44C4
Alexander Bay 36C5
Alexandria 16E5
Alexandria 21K3
Alexandria 33F1
Alexandria 47I5
Alexandria 48C2
Alexandroupoli 21K4
Aleysk 24J4
Alfeios r. 21I6
Alfenas 55B3
Alford 16G3
Alfred 48C1
Algarve reg. 19B5
Algeciras 19D5
Algemesi 19F4
Algeria country 32C2
Al Ghaydah 34F2
Alghero 20C4
Al Ghurdaqah 33G2
Algiers 19H5
Algoa Bay 37G7
Algona 47I3
Algona 19E2
Al Ḩadīthah 33H1
Alhama de Murcia 19F5
Al Ḩanākīyah 34E1
Al Ḩasakah 33H1
Al Ḩayy 33H1
Al Ḩazm al Jawf 34E2
Al Ḩinnāh 34E1
Aliağa 21L5
Alicante 19F4
Alice 46H6
Alice Springs 40G4
Alihe 30A2
Alindao 34C3
Alingsås 11H8
Aliquippa 48A2
Al Ismāʻīlīyah 33G1
Aliveri 21I5
Al Jahrah 26D4
Al Jawf 33F2
Al Jufrah 33E2
Al Jurmaliyah 34F1
Ajlustrel 19B5
Algoa Bay 37G7
Al Kahfah 34E1
Al Khārijah 33G2
Al Khaṣab 26E4
Al Khawr 34F1

Alto Garças 53H7
Altoona 48B2
Alto Parnaíba 53I5
Altrincham 14E5
Altun Shan mts 27H3
Altus 46H5
Alüksne 11O8
Alva 46H4
Alvesta 11I8
Álvsbyn 10L4
Alyangula 41I2
Alyth 16F4
Amadora 19B4
Amadjuak Lake salt flat 40G4
Amambaí 54F2
Amanzimtoti 37J6
Amarante 53J5
Amareleja 19C4
Amargosa 55D1
Amarillo 46G4
Amasra 23G8
Amazar 30A1
Amazon r. 52F4
Amazon, Mouths of the 53I3
Ambalavao 35E6
Ambam 34B3
Ambato 52C4
Ambato Boeny 35E5
Ambato Finandrahana 35E6
Ambatolampy 35E5
Ambatondrazaka 35E5
Amberg 13M6
Ambergris Cay 50G4
Ambikapur 27H4
Amble 14F3
Ambleside 14E4
Amboasary 35E6
Ambodifotatra 35E5
Ambohimahasoa 35E6
Ambon 29E8
Ambositra 35E6
Ambovombe 35E6
Ambriz 35B4
American Fork 46E3
American Samoa terr. 39J3
Americus 47J5
Amersfoort 12J4
Amersham 15G7
Amesbury 48F1
Amfissa 21J5
Amga 25O3
Amherst 48E1
Amiens 18F2
Amistad Reservoir 46G6
Amlwch 14C5
'Ammān 33G1
Ammanford 15D7
Ämmänsaari 10P4
Amorgos i. 21K6
Amos 45K5
Amoy 30F4
Amparo 55B3
Ampasimanolotra 35E5
Amravati 27G4
Amritsar 27G3
Amstelveen 12J4
Amsterdam 12J4
Amsterdam 48D1
Amstetten 13O6
Am Timan 33F3
Amudar'ya r. 26E2
Amundsen Gulf 44F2
Amundsen Sea 56C4
Amuntai 29D8
Amur r. 30D2
Amursk 30E2
Amurskaya Oblast'
  admin. div. 30C1
Anabar r. 25M2
Anaconda 46E2
Anadolu Dağları mts 26C2
Anadyr' 25S3
Anaga 55C1
Anaheim 49D3
Anajás 53I4
Analalava 35E5
Anamur 33G1
Anan 31D6
Anantapur 27G5
Anan'yiv 23F7
Anapa 23H7
Ánápolis 55A2
Añatuya 54D3
Anbyon 31B5
Anchorage 44D3
Ancona 20E3
Anda 30B3
Andalgalá 54C3
Andalucía aut. comm. 19D5
Andaman Islands 27I5
Andaman Sea 29B6
Andapa 35E5
Andenne 12J5
Anderlecht 12J5
Andernach 13L5
Anderson 47J3
Anderson 47K3
Andes mts 54C4
Andijon 27G2
Andilamena 35E5
Andilanatoby 35E5
Andkhvoy 26F3
Andoas 52C4
Andong 31C5
Andorra country 19G2
Andorra la Vella 19G2
Andover 15F7
Andradina 55A3
Andreapol' 22G4
Andrews 46G5
Andria 20G4
Andros i. 21K6
Andros 47M4
Andújar 19D4
Aneby 11I8
Anegada, Bahía b. 54D6
Anéga 32G4

Ang'angxi 30A3
Angarsk 25L4
Ange 10H5
Ángel Falls 52F2
Ángel Falls 52F2
Angelholm 11H8
Angers 18D3
Anglesey i. 14C5
Angoche 35D5
Angol 54B5
Angola country 35B5
Angoulême 18E4
Angra dos Reis 55B3
Angren 27J2
Anguang 30A3
Anguilla terr. 51L5
Anjalankoski 11O6
Ankara 26C3
Ankazoabo 35E6
Anna 23I6
Annaba 20B6
An Nafūd des. 26D4
Annandale 48C3
Annapolis 48B3
Ann Arbor 47K3
Anna Regina 53G2
Annecy 18G4
An Nirmās 34E2
Annobón i. 32D5
Ansbach 13M6
Anshan 30A4
Anshun 27J4
Antakya 33G1
Antalaha 35E5
Antalya 21N6
Antalya Körfezi g. 21N6
Antananarivo 35E5
Antarctica 56
Antarctic Peninsula 56D4
Antequera 19D5
Anti Atlas mts 32C2
Antibes 18H5
Anticosti, Île d' i. 45L5
Antigua and Barbuda country 51L5
Antikythiro, Steno sea chan. 21J6
Antioch 49B1
Antipodes Islands 39H6
Antofagasta 54B2
Antrim 17F3
Antrim Hills 17F2
Antsalova 35E5
Antsirabe 35E5
Antsirañana 35E5
Antsohihy 35E5
Antwerp 12J5
Anuchino 30D4
Anuradhapura 27H6
Anxious Bay 40G6
Anyang 30A5
Anyang 31B5
Anzhero-Sudzhensk 24J4
Anzio 20E4
Aomori 30F4
Aoraki mt. 43C6
Aosta 20B2
Aoukâr reg. 32C2
Aparecida do Tabuado 55A3
Apatity 10R3
Apatzingán 50D5
Apeldoorn 13J4
Apennines mts 20C2
Apia 39J3
Apiaí 55A4
Aporé 55A2
Appalachian Mountains 47K4
Appennino Abruzzese mts 20E3
Appennino Tosco-Emiliano mts 20E3
Appennino Umbro-Marchigiano mts 20E3
Appleton 47J3
Apple Valley 49D3
Apt 18G5
Apucarana 55A3
Aqaba, Gulf of 33G2
Aquaviva delle Fonti 20G4
Aquidauana 54E2
Arabian Peninsula 26D4
Aracaju 53K6
Aracati 53K4
Araçatuba 55A3
Aracruz 55C2
Araçuaí 55C2
Arad 21I1
Arafura Sea 38D2
Aragarças 53H7
Araguaçu 53I6
Araguaia r. 53H6
Araguari 55A2
Araguatins 53I5
Arak 33H1
Arakan Yoma mts 27I4
Aral Sea salt l. 26F2
Aral'sk 26F2
Aranda de Duero 19E3
Arandelovac 21I2
Aranjuez 19E3
Arapiraca 53K5
Araquari 55B4
Ar'ar 26D3
Araraquara 55A3
Araras 55B3
Ararat 41J7
Araripina 53J5
Arataca 55D1
Arauca 52D2
Arawa 38F2
Araxá 55B2
Arayıt Dağı mt. 21N5
Arbatax 20C5
Arboga 11I7
Arbroath 16G4
Arcachon 18D4

Arcade 48B1
Arcadia 47I6
Arcelia 50D5
Archangel 22I2
Arcos 55B3
Arcos de la Frontera 19D5
Arctic Ocean ocean 56
Ardabīl 26D3
Ardahan 23I8
Ardatov 23I5
Ardatov 23J5
Ardee 17F4
Ardennes plat. 12J6
Arden Town 49B1
Ardestān 26E3
Ardrossan 16E5
Areia Branca 53K4
Arendal 11F7
Arequipa 52D7
Arezzo 20D3
Arganda del Rey 19E3
Argentan 18D2
Argentina country 54C4
Argentino, Lago l. 54B8
Argos 21J6
Argostoli 21I5
Argun 23J8
Argun' r. 28C2
Argungu 32D3
Argyle, Lake 40F3
Århus 11G8
Ariano Irpino 20F4
Aribinda 32C3
Arica 52D7
Arima 51L6
Arinos 53G6
Aripuanã 52F5
Ariquemes 52F5
Arisaig, Sound of sea chan. 16D4
Arizona state 46E5
ʿArjah 34E1
Arkadak 23I6
Arkadelphia 47I5
Arkalyk 26F1
Arkansas r. 47I5
Arkansas state 47I4
Arkansas City 47H4
Arkhara 30C2
Arkhangel'sk 22I2
Arklow 17F5
Arklu 31B5
Arles 18G5
Arlington 48C3
Arlington 48E2
Arlon 13J6
Armagh 17F3
Armant 33G2
Armavir 23I7
Armenia 52C3
Armenia country 26D2
Armeria 50D5
Armidale 42E3
Arnhem 13J5
Arnhem Land reg. 40G2
Arnold 15F5
Arnsberg 13L5
Arran i. 16D5
Ar Raqqah 33G1
Arrábida 55B1
Arras 18F1
Ar Rayyān 34F1
Arrecife 32B2
Arriagá 50F5
Ar Rifaʿī 33H1
Arroyo Grande 49B3
Arsen'yev 30D4
Arsk 22K4
Arta 21I5
Artem 30D4
Artemivs'k 23H6
Artesia 46G5
Artigas 54E4
Art'ik 23I8
Artsyz 21M2
Artvin 23I8
Arua 34D3
Aruba terr. 51K6
Arundel 15G8
Arusha 34D4
Arvayheer 27J2
Arviat 45I3
Arvidsjaur 10K4
Arvika 11H7
Arzamas 23I5
Arzew 19F6
Arzgir 23J7
Asaba 32D4
Asad, Buḩayrat al resr 33G1
Asahikawa 30F4
Asamankese 32C4
Asansol 27H4
Asbury Park 48D2
Ascensión 46F5
Ascension i. 6
Aschaffenburg 13L6
Ascoli Piceno 20E3
Áseda 11I8
Asela 34D3
Asenovgrad 21K3
Aşgabat 26E2
Ashburton 43C6
Asheville 47K4
Ashford 15H7
Ashikaga 31F5
Ashington 14F3
Ashizuri-misaki pt 31D6
Ashkhabad 26E2
Ashland 46C2
Ashland 47I2
Ashmore and Cartier Islands terr. 40E2
Ashmyany 11N9
Ashqelon 33G2
Ashtabula 48A2
Ashton-under-Lyne 14E5
Asilah 19C6
Asino 24J4
Asipovichy 23F5
ʿAsīr reg. 34E1
Askale 23I8
Asker 11G7
Askim 11G7
Asmara 33G3
Åsnen l. 11I8
Aspatria 14D4
Aspen 46F4
Aspiring, Mount 43B7
Assab 34E2
As Salt 33G1

As Samāwah 33H1
Assen 13K4
Assiniboine r. 44I5
Assis 55A3
Assisi 20E3
Astakos 21I5
Astana 27G1
Āstārā 26D3
Asti 20C2
Astorga 19C2
Astoria 46C2
Astrakhan' 23K7
Astypalaia i. 21L6
Asturias aut. comm. 19C2
Asunción 54E3
Aswan 33G2
Asyūţ 33G2
Atacama, Salar de salt flat 54C2
Atacama Desert 54C3
Atakpamé 32D4
Ataléia 55C2
ʿAţaq 34E2
Ataş 27G2
Atascadero 49B3
Atasu 27G2
Atbara 33G3
Atbara r. 33G3
Atbasar 26F1
Atchison 47H4
Athabasca, Lake 44H4
Athens 21J6
Athens 47K4
Athens 47K5
Athens 48C2
Atherstone 15F6
Athlone 17E4
Athol 48E1
Athy 17F5
Ati 33E3
Atico 52D7
Atka 25O3
Atkarsk 23J6
Atlanta 47K5
Atlantic 47I3
Atlantic City 48D3
Atlantis 36D7
Atlas Mountains 32C1
Atlas Saharien mts 32D1
Atlas Tellien mts 19H6
Aţ Ţāʾif 34E1
Attu Island 25S4
Åtvidaberg 11I7
Atwater 49B2
Atyashevo 23J5
Atyrau 26E2
Atyrauskaya Oblast'
  admin. div. 23K7
Aubagne 18G5
Aube r. 18F2
Auburn 48C1
Auburn 49B1
Auch 18E5
Auchterarder 16F4
Auckland 43E3
Auckland Islands 39G7
Audo mts 34E3
Augsburg 13M6
Augusta 20F6
Augusta 47K5
Augusta 47N3
Auki 41M1
Aurangabad 27G5
Aurich 13K4
Aurillac 18F4
Aurora 46G4
Aurora 47J3
Austin 47I3
Austin 47I3
Austin 46H5
Austintown 48A2
Australia country 40F5
Australian Capital Territory admin. div. 42D5
Austria country 13N7
Autazes 53G4
Auvergne, Monts d' mts 18F4
Auxerre 18F3
Avaré 55A3
Aveiro 19B3
Aveiro 53H4
Avellino 20F4
Aversa 20F4
Avesta 11J6
Avezzano 20E3
Aviemore 16F3
Avignon 18G5
Ávila 19D3
Avilés 19D2
Avoca 42A6
Avola 20F6
Avon r. 15F8
Avon r. 15F8
Avon r. 16F3
Awbārī 32E2
Awe, Loch l. 16D4
Awjilah 33F2
Axminster 15D8
Ayacucho 52D6
Ayacucho 54E5
Ayagoz 27H2
Ayancık 23G8
Ayang 31B5
Aydın 21L6
Aydıncık 21L6
Aylesbury 15G7
Aytos 21L3
Ayutthaya 29C6
Ayvacık 21L5
Ayvalık 21L5
Azaouâd reg. 32C3
Azare 32E3
Azbine 26E4
Azerbaijan country 26D2
Azogues 52C4
Azores terr. 6
Azov 23H7
Azov, Sea of 23H7
Azzaba 20B6
Az Zaqāzīq 33G1
Az Zarqāʾ 33G1
Azzeffâl hills 32B2

B

Baardheere 34E3
Babadag 21M2
Babaeski 21L4
Babahoyo 52C4
Bab al Mandab strait 34E2
Babanusa 33F3
Babati 30D4
Babayevo 22G4
Babayurt 23J8
Bab el Mandeb 34E2
Bacabal 53J4
Bačka Palanka 21H2
Bacău 21L1
Bac Liêu 29C7
Bacolod 29E6
Badajoz 19C4
Baden 31D6
Baden 18I3
Baden-Baden 13L6
Bad Ischl 13N7
Bad Kissingen 13M5
Badou 32C4
Badr Ḩunayn 34D1
Bad Salzungen 13M5
Bad Schwartau 13M4
Badulla 27H6
Bafatá 32B3
Baffin Bay sea 45L2
Baffin Island 45L3
Bafia 32E4
Bafilo 32D4
Bafoussam 32E4
Bāfq 34F1
Bafra 23G8
Bāft 26E4
Bafwasende 34C3
Bagamoyo 35D4
Bagdarin 28B1
Baggera 33F3
Baghdad 33H1
Baghlān 27F3
Bagnois-sur-Cèze
Baicheng 30A3
Baie-Comeau 45L5
Baie-du-Poste 45K4
Baikal, Lake 25L4
Bāilești 21J2
Bainbridge 47J5
Baiquan 30B3
Baird 47H5
Baise 27J4
Baishan 30B4
Baisogala 11M9
Baiyuda Desert 33G3
Baja 21H1
Baja California pen. 46D5
Bajoga 32E3
Bakel 32B3
Baker 46D3
Baker Island terr. 39I1
Baker Lake 45I3
Baker Lake 45I3
Bakersfield 49C3
Bakhmach 23G6
Bakırköy 21M4
Baksan 23I8
Baku 26D2
Balabac Strait strait 29D7
Balaguer 19G3
Balakhna 22I4
Balakliya 23H6
Balakovo 23J5
Balanga 29E6
Balashov 23I6
Balaton, Lake 20G1
Balatonboglár 20G1
Balatonfüred 20G1
Balbina, Represa de resr 53G4
Balchik 21M3
Baldwin 48D2
Baléa 32B3
Balei 28B1
Baleshwar 27H4
Baléyara 32D3
Bali i. 29D8
Bali, Laut sea 29D8
Balige 29C7
Balıkesir 21L5
Balıkpapan 29D8
Balimo 38E2
Balingen 13L6
Balkanabat 26E2
Balkan Mountains 21J3
Balkhash 27H2
Balkhash, Lake 27G2
Ballarat 41J7
Ballé 32C3
Ballina 17C3
Ballina 42F2
Ballinasloe 17D4
Ballycastle 17F2
Ballyclare 17G3
Ballymena 17F3
Ballymoney 17F2
Ballynahinch 17G3
Ballyshannon 17D3
Balranald 42A5
Balsas 53I5
Balta 23F7
Bălți 23E7
Baltic Sea 11J9
Baltimore 48C3
Baltiysk 11J9
Balti 11O8
Balvi 11O8
Balykchy 27H2
Balyksa 23I6
Bam 26E4
Bamaga 41J2
Bamako 32C3
Bamba 32C3
Bambari 34C3
Bamberg 13M6
Bambui 55B3
Bamenda, Penunungan mts 29C8
Banaba i. 38G2
Banagher 17E4
Bananal 53H6
Banas r. 27G4
Banaz 21M5
Banbridge 17F3

Banbury 15F6
Banda, Laut sea 29E8
Banda Aceh 27I6
Bandar-e ʿAbbās 26E4
Bandar-e Lengeh 26E4
Bandar Lampung 29C8
Bandar Seri Begawan 29D7
Bandeira 53I4
Bandiagara 32C3
Bandirma 21L4
Bandon 17B6
Bandon 17D6
Bandundu 34B4
Bandung 29C8
Banes 51I4
Banff 16G3
Banff 44G4
Banfora 32C3
Bangalore 27G5
Bangassou 34C3
Bangka i. 29C8
Bangkok 29C6
Bangkok 29C6
Bangladesh country 27I4
Bangolo 32C4
Bangor 17G3
Bangor 17G3
Bangor 47N3
Bangui 34B3
Bangweulu, Lake 35C5
Banha 33G1
Bani 51J5
Bani Walīd 33E1
Banja Luka 20G2
Banjarmasin 29D8
Banjul 32B3
Banks Peninsula 43D6
Bann r. 17F2
Banská Bystrica 13Q6
Bantry 17C6
Banyo 32E4
Banyuwangi 29D8
Baochang 27K2
Baoding 27K3
Baoji 27J3
Baoqing 30D3
Baotou 27J2
Ba'qūbah 33H1
Baracoa 51J4
Barahona 51J5
Barakaldo 19E2
Baranavichy 11O10
Baranís 33G2
Baraouéli 32C3
Barbacena 55C3
Barbados country 51M6
Barbate 19D5
Barbuda i. 51L5
Barcaldine 41J4
Barcelona 19H3
Barcelona 52F1
Barcelos 52F4
Barclayville 32C4
Barcs 20G2
Bárðarbunga 23J8
Bardejov 23D6
Bareilly 27H4
Barents Sea 24F2
Barentu 33G3
Barham 42B5
Bari 20G4
Barinas 52D2
Bariri 55A3
Barisan, Pegunungan mts 29C8
Barkly East 37H6
Barkly Tableland reg. 41H3
Barkly West 36G5
Barkol 27J2
Barle-le-Duc 18G2
Barlee, Lake salt flat 40D5
Barletta 20G4
Barmer 27G4
Barmouth 15C6
Barnaul 24J4
Barnsley 14F5
Barnstaple 15C7
Barnstaple Bay 15C7
Baro 32D4
Barpeta 27I4
Barquisimeto 52E1
Barra 19C4
Barra i. 16B3
Barra, Sound of sea chan. 16B3
Barraba 42E3
Barra Bonita 55A3
Barra do Bugres 53G7
Barra do Corda 53I5
Barra do Garças 53H7
Barra do Piraí 55C3
Barra Mansa 55B3
Barranqueras 54E3
Barranquilla 52D1
Barreiras 53I6
Barreirinha 53G4
Barreirinhas 53J4
Barreiro 19B4
Barretos 55A3
Barrie 47K3
Barrhead 16E5
Barrow-in-Furness 14D4
Barry 15D7
Barstow 49D3
Bartica 53G2
Bartin 23G8
Bartlesville 47H4
Bartoszyce 13R3
Baruun-Urt 27K2
Barwon r. 42C3
Barysh 23J5
Basarabi 21M2
Basel 18I3
Bashkatovo 23H6
Bashtanka 23G7
Basildon 15H7
Basilan i. 29E7
Basingstoke 15F7
Basra 33H1
Bassano del Grappa 20D2
Bassar 32D4
Bassein 27I5

Basse-Normandie
  admin. reg. 15F9
Basse Santa Su 32B3
Basse-Terre 51L5
Basseterre 51L5
Bass Strait strait 42C7
Bastia 18I5
Bata 32D4
Batabanó, Golfo de b. 51I4
Batagay 25O3
Batangafo 34B3
Batangas 29E6
Batavia 48B1
Bataysk 23H7
Bătdâmbâng 29C6
Batemans Bay 42E5
Batesville 47I4
Bath 15E7
Bathgate 16F5
Bathurst 42D4
Bathurst 45N2
Bathurst Inlet 44H3
Bathurst Island 40G2
Bathurst Island 45I2
Batley 14F5
Batlow 42D5
Batna 32D1
Baton Rouge 47I5
Batouri 33E4
Batticaloa 27H6
Battipaglia 20F4
Battle Creek 47J3
Bat'umi 23I8
Batu Pahat 29C7
Batyrevo 23J5
Baubau 29E8
Bauchi 32D3
Bauru 55A3
Bautzen 13O5
Bavaria state 13M6
Bawku 32C3
Bayamo 51I4
Bayamón 51K5
Bayan 30B3
Bayanhongor 27J2
Bayan Hot 27J3
Bay City 47H6
Bay City 47K3
Bayeux 15G9
Bayındır 21L5
Baykonyr 26F2
Baymak 24G4
Bayombong 29E6
Bayonne 18D5
Bayreuth 13M6
Bayramiç 21L5
Bay Shore 48E2
Bāzārak 23J5
Bazarnyy Karabulak 23J5
Beachy Head 15H8
Beacon 48E2
Beacon Bay 37H7
Beaconsfield 15G7
Beagle Gulf 40F2
Bealanana 35E5
Beaminster 15E8
Beatrice 47H3
Beaufort 42A6
Beaufort Sea 44E2
Beaufort West 36F7
Beaumont 47I5
Beaune 18G3
Beauvais 18F2
Beaver 48A2
Beaver Falls 48A2
Bebedouro 55A3
Bebington 14D5
Beccles 15I6
Bečej 21I2
Béchar 32C1
Beckley 48A4
Bedale 14F4
Bedford 15G6
Bedford 37J5
Bedford 47J4
Bedford 48B4
Bedlington 14F3
Bedworth 15F6
Beenleigh 42F1
Beechworth 42C6
Beenleigh 46H6
Beeville 46H6
Bega 42D6
Behshahr 26E3
Bei'an 30B3
Beihai 27J4
Beijing 27K3
Beira 35D5
Beirut 33G1
Beja 20C6
Béja 20C6
Bejaïa 19I5
Béjar 19D3
Beji 32D3
Bekabad 27F2
Békés 21I1
Békéscsaba 21I1
Bekwai 32C4
Bela 26F4
Bela-Bela 37I3
Bel Air 48C3
Belalcázar 19D4
Belarus country 23E5
Bela Vista 54E2
Bela Vista de Goiás 55A2
Belaya Glina 23I7
Belaya Kalitva 23I6
Belaya Kholunitsa 22K4
Belcher Islands 45K4
Beledweyne 34E3
Belém 53I4
Belev 23H5
Belfast 47N3
Belfast 17G3
Belfast Lough inlet 17G3
Belfort 18H3
Belgaum 27G5
Belgium country 12J5
Belgorod 23H6

Belgrade 21I2
Belinskiy 23I5
Belinyu 29C8
Belize 35B4
Belize 50G5
Belize country 50G5
Bellary 27G5
Bela Unión 54E4
Belledonne mts 18G4
Bellefonte 48C2
Belle Glade 47K6
Belle Isle, Strait of 45M4
Bellevue 46C2
Bellingham 46C2
Bellinzona 18I3
Belluno 20E1
Bellville 36D7
Bell Ville 54D4
Belmont 42E3
Belmonte 55D1
Belmopan 50G5
Belo Campo 55C1
Belo Horizonte 55C2
Beloit 47J3
Belomorsk 22G2
Beloretsk 24G4
Belo Tsiribihina 35E5
Beloye, Ozero l. 22H3
Belozersk 22H3
Batı Mentese Dağları
  mts 21L6
Batı Toroslar mts 21N6
Belyy 22G5
Belyy i. 24H2
Bemidji 47I2
Benavente 19D2
Benbecula i. 16B3
Bend 46C3
Bendigo 42B6
Beneševo 13O6
Benevento 20F4
Bengal, Bay of sea 27I5
Bengbu 27K3
Benghazi 33F1
Bengkulu 29C8
Benguela 35B5
Beni 34C3
Benidorm 19F4
Beni Mellal 32C1
Benin country 32D3
Benin, Bight of g. 32D4
Benin City 32D4
Beni Saf 19F6
Benito Juárez 54D5
Benjamim Constant 52E4
Ben Nevis mt. 16D4
Bennington 48E1
Benoni 37I4
Bentiu 33F4
Bento Gonçalves 55A5
Benton Harbor 47J3
Bentonville 47I4
Benue r. 32D4
Béoumi 32C4
Beppu 31C6
Berat 21H4
Berber 33G3
Berbera 34E2
Berbérati 34B3
Berdyans'k 23H7
Berdychiv 23F6
Berehove 23D6
Berekum 32C4
Berezivka 23F7
Berezne 23E6
Bereznik 24G4
Berezovo 24H3
Berezovo 23J5
Bergama 21L5
Bergamo 20C2
Bergen 11D6
Bergen op Zoom 12J5
Bergerac 18E4
Bergheim (Erft) 13K5
Beringovskiy 25S3
Bering Sea 25S4
Bering Strait strait 44B3
Berkane 19E6
Berkeley 49A2
Berkovitsa 21J3
Berlin 13N4
Bermagui 42E6
Bermejo 52F8
Bermuda terr. 51L2
Bern 18I3
Bernardino de Campos 55A3
Berner Alpen mts 18H3
Beroun 13O6
Berounka r. 13O6
Berrouaghia 19H5
Berry 42E5
Bertolínia 53J5
Bertoua 32E4
Beruri 52F4
Berwick-upon-Tweed 14E3
Beryslav 21O1
Besalampy 35E5
Besançon 18H3
Beslan 23J8
Bessbrook 17F3
Bessonovka 23J5
Bethel Park 48A2
Bethesda 14C5
Bethlehem 37I5
Bethlehem 48D2
Betim 55B2
Betpakdala plain 26G2
Betroka 35E6
Bettiah 27H4
Beverley 14G5
Beverly Hills 49C3
Bexhill 15H8
Beykoz 21M4
Beyla 32C4
Beyneu 26E2
Beypazarı 21N4
Beyşehir 33G1
Bezhanitsy 22F4
Bezhetsk 22H4
Béziers 18F5
Bhamo 27I4
Bhavnagar 27G4

Bhekuzulu 37J4
Bhilwara 27G4
Bhisho 37H7
Bhopal 27G4
Bhubaneshwar 27H4
Bhuj 27F4
Bhutan *country* 27I4
Biała Podlaska 23D5
Białogard 13O4
Białystok 11M10
Biarritz 18D5
Bibai 30F4
Biberach an der Riß 13L6
Bicas 55C3
Bicester 15F7
Bida 32D4
Biddeford 48F1
Bideford 15C7
Bié, Planalto do 35B5
Biel 18H3
Bielawa 13P5
Bielefeld 13L4
Biella 20C2
Bielsko-Biała 13Q6
Biên Hoa 29C6
Biga 21L4
Bigadiç 21M5
Biga Yarımadası *pen.* 21L5
Biggar 46F1
Biggleswade 15G6
Bighorn Mountains 46F3
Bignona 32B3
Big Rapids 47J3
Big Spring 46G5
Big Trout Lake 45I4
Bihać 20F2
Bijār 33H1
Bijeljina 21H2
Bijelo Polje 21H3
Bikaner 27G4
Bikin 30D3
Bila Tserkva 23F6
Bilbao 19E2
Bilecik 21M4
Biłgoraj 23D6
Bilhorod-Dnistrovs'kyy 21N1
Bilibino 25R3
Billericay 15H7
Billingham 14F4
Billings 46F2
Bill of Portland *hd* 15E8
Bilohirs'k 23G7
Bilohir"ya 23E6
Bilovods'k 23H6
Biloxi 47J5
Biltine 33F3
Bilyayivka 21N1
Bimini Islands 47L6
Bindura 35D5
Binghamton 48D1
Bintulu 29D7
Binxian 30B3
Bioco *i.* 32D4
Birao 34C2
Bireun 27I6
Birigüi 55A3
Birjand 26E3
Birkenhead 14D5
Birkirkara 20F7
Birmingham 15F6
Birmingham 47J5
Birnin-Gwari 32D3
Birnin-Kebbi 32D3
Birnin Konni 32D3
Birobidzhan 30D2
Biržai 11N8
Bisbee 46F5
Biscay, Bay of *sea* 18B4
Bishkek 27G2
Bishop Auckland 14F4
Bishop's Stortford 15H7
Biskra 32D1
Bismarck 46G2
Bismarck Archipelago *is* 38E2
Bismarck Sea 38E2
Bissau 32B3
Bistrița 21K1
Bitola 21I4
Bitonto 20G4
Bitterroot Range *mts* 46D2
Biu 32E3
Biwa-ko *l.* 31D6
Biysk 24J4
Bizerte 20C6
Bjästa 10K5
Bjelovar 20G2
Bjerringbro 11F8
Björklinge 11J6
Bjørnøya *i.* 24C2
Bla 32C3
Blackall 38E4
Blackburn 14E5
Black Forest *mts* 13L7
Blackpool 14D5
Blacksburg 48A4
Black Sea 23H8
Blackwater *r.* 17F3
Blagodarnyy 23I7
Blagoevgrad 21J3
Blagoveshchensk 30B2
Blanca, Bahía *b.* 54D5
Blanche, Lake *salt flat* 41H5
Blanes 19H3
Blansko 13P6
Blantyre 35D5
Blayney 42D4
Blenheim 43D5
Blessington Lakes 17F4
Bletchley 15G6
Blida 19H5
Bloemfontein 37H5
Bloomington 47J3
Bloomington 47J4
Bloomsburg 48C2
Bloxham 15F6
Bluefield 48A4
Bluefields 51H6
Blue Mountains 42D4
Blue Nile *r.* 33G3
Blue Ridge 48B4
Blue Ridge *mts* 48A4
Blumenau 55A4
Blyth 14F3
Blytheville 47J4
Bo 32B4
Boa Esperança 55B3
Boa Nova 55C1
Boa Viagem 53K5
Boa Vista 52F3
Bobo-Dioulasso 32C3
Bobrov 23I6
Bobrovytsya 23F6
Bobrynets' 23G6
Boca do Acre 52E5
Bocaiúva 55C2
Bocaranga 34B3
Bocas del Toro 51H7
Bochnia 13R6
Bochum 13K5
Boda 34B3
Bodaybo 25M4
Boden 10L4
Bodmin 15C8
Bodmin Moor *moorland* 15C8
Bodø 10I3
Bodrum 21L6
Boende 33F5
Bogalusa 47J5
Bogandé 32C3
Boggeragh Mountains *hills* 17C5
Bognor Regis 15G8
Bogoroditsk 23H5
Bogorodsk 22I4
Bogotá 52D3
Bogotol 24J4
Boguchany 25K4
Boguchar 23I6
Bogué 32B3
Bo Hai *g.* 27K3
Bohai Wan *b.* 27K3
Bohlokong 37I5
Böhmer Wald *mts* 13N6
Bohodukhiv 23G6
Bohol Sea 29E7
Bohu 27H2
Boise 46D3
Bojnūrd 26E3
Boké 32B3
Bokovskaya 23I6
Bol 33E3
Bolama 32B3
Bolbec 15H9
Bole 27H2
Bolgar 23K5
Bolgatanga 32C3
Bolhrad 21M2
Boli 30C3
Boliden 10L4
Bolintin-Vale 21K2
Bolívar 52C5
Bolivia *country* 52E7
Bolkhov 23H5
Bollnäs 11J6
Bollstabruk 10J5
Bolobo 34B4
Bologna 20D2
Bologoye 22G4
Bol'shakovo 11L9
Bol'shaya Glushitsa 23K5
Bol'shaya Martynovka 23I7
Bol'shevik, Ostrov *i.* 25L2
Bol'shoye Murashkino 22J5
Bol'shoy Kamen' 30D4
Bolton 14E5
Bolu 21N4
Bolvadin 21N5
Bolzano 20D1
Boma 35B4
Bomaderry 42E5
Bombala 42D6
Bomdila 27I4
Bom Jardim de Goiás 55A2
Bom Jesus 55A5
Bom Jesus da Lapa 55C1
Bom Sucesso 55B3
Bon Air 48C4
Bonaire *i.* 51K6
Bonaparte Archipelago *is* 40E2
Bondo 34C3
Bondoukou 32C4
Bone, Teluk *b.* 29E8
Bo'ness 16F4
Bonete, Cerro *mt.* 54C3
Bongaigaon 27I4
Bongandanga 34C3
Bongor 33E3
Boni 32C3
Bonifacio 18I6
Bonifacio, Strait of *strait* 18I6
Bonin Islands 31F8
Bonn 13K5
Bonneville 18H3
Bonnyrigg 16F5
Bontoc 29E6
Bontosunggu 38B2
Boonah 42F1
Booneville 47J5
Boorowa 42D5
Boothia, Gulf of 45J3
Boothia Peninsula 45I2
Bootle 14E5
Bor 21J2
Bor 22J4
Bor 33G4
Borås 11H8
Borāzjān 26E4
Borba 53G4
Borçka 23I8
Bordeaux 18D4
Borden Island 45G2
Bordj Bou Arréridj 19I5
Borgarnes 10□2
Borisoglebsk 23I6
Borisovka 23H6
Borlänge 11I6
Borneo *i.* 29D7
Bornholm *i.* 11I9
Bornova 21L5
Boromo 32C3
Boron 49D3
Borovichi 22G4
Borovoy 10R4
Borovoy 22L3
Borşa 23E7
Borshchiv 23E6
Borūjerd 33H1
Boryslav 23D6
Boryspil' 23F6
Borzna 23G6
Borzya 25M4
Bosnia-Herzegovina *country* 20G2
Bosobolo 34B3
Bosporus *strait* 21M4
Bossangoa 34B3
Bossembélé 34B3
Boston 15G6
Boston 48F1
Botany Bay 42E4
Botevgrad 21J3
Bothnia, Gulf of 11K6
Botlikh 23J8
Botoșani 23E7
Botshabelo 37H5
Botswana *country* 35C6
Bottrop 13K5
Botucatu 55A3
Botuporã 55C1
Bouaflé 32C4
Bouaké 32C4
Bouar 34B3
Bouârfa 32C1
Bouca 34B3
Bougaa 19I5
Bougainville Island 38F2
Bougouni 32C3
Bougtob 32D1
Bouira 19H5
Boujdour 32B2
Boulder 46F3
Boulder City 49E3
Boulogne-Billancourt 18F2
Boulogne-sur-Mer 15I8
Boumerdes 19H5
Bouna 32C4
Boundiali 32C4
Bounty Islands 39H6
Bourail 39G4
Bourg-Achard 15H9
Bourg-en-Bresse 18G3
Bourges 18F3
Bourke 42B3
Bournemouth 15F8
Bou Saâda 19I6
Boutilimit 32B3
Bowling Green 47J4
Bowling Green 47K3
Boyabat 23G8
Boyle 17D4
Bozcaada *i.* 21L5
Bozdoğan 21M6
Bozeman 46E2
Bozoum 34B3
Bozüyük 21N5
Bra 20B2
Brač *i.* 20G3
Bracknell 15G7
Bradenton 47K6
Bradford 14F5
Brady 46H5
Braga 19B3
Bragado 54D5
Bragança 19C3
Bragança 53I4
Bragança Paulista 55B3
Brahin 23F6
Brahmapur 27H5
Brahmaputra *r.* 28B5
Brăila 21L2
Brainerd 47I2
Braintree 15H7
Bramming 11F9
Brampton 14E4
Branco *r.* 52F4
Brandberg *mt.* 35B6
Brande 11F9
Brandenburg 13N4
Brandon 45I5
Braniewo 13Q3
Brantford 48A1
Braxton 42E4
Brasileia 52E6
Brasília 55B1
Brasília de Minas 55B2
Braslaw 11O9
Brașov 21K2
Bratislava 13P6
Bratsk 25L4
Braunau am Inn 13N6
Braunschweig 13M4
Bravo del Norte, Río *r.* 46H6
Brawley 49E4
Bray 17F4
Brazil *country* 53G5
Brazilian Highlands *plat.* 55C2
Brazos *r.* 47H6
Brazzaville 35B4
Brčko 20H2
Břeclav 13P6
Brecon 15D7
Brecon Beacons *reg.* 15D7
Breda 12J5
Bredasdorp 36E8
Bregenz 13L7
Breiðafjörður *b.* 10□2
Bremen 13L4
Bremerhaven 13L4
Brenham 47H5
Brenner Pass *pass* 20D1
Brentwood 15H7
Brescia 20D2
Bressuire 18D3
Brest 11M10
Brest 18B2
Breton Sound *b.* 47J6
Breves 53H4
Brewarrina 42C2
Brewster 48A2
Brezno 13Q6
Bria 34C3
Briançon 18H4
Bridgend 15D7
Bridgeport 48E2
Bridgeton 48D3
Bridgetown 51M6
Bridgnorth 15E6
Bridgwater 15D7
Bridgwater Bay 15D7
Bridlington 14G4
Bridlington Bay 14G4
Bridport 15E8
Bridport 41J8
Brig 18H3
Brigham City 46E3
Brighton 15G8
Brighton 48C1
Brignoles 18H5
Brikama 32B3
Brindisi 20G4
Brisbane 42F1
Bristol 15E7
Bristol 47K4
Bristol 48E2
Bristol 48F2
Bristol Bay 44B4
Bristol Channel *est.* 15C7
British Columbia *prov.* 44F4
British Indian Ocean Territory *terr.* 7
Brits 37H3
Britstown 36F6
Brittany *reg.* 18C2
Brive-la-Gaillarde 18E4
Brixham 15D8
Brno 13P6
Broadford 42B6
Broadstairs 15I7
Brockton 48F1
Brodnica 13Q4
Brody 23E6
Broken Arrow 47H4
Broken Hill 41I6
Brokopondo 53G2
Bromsgrove 15E6
Brønderslev 11F8
Brookhaven 47I5
Brookings 46C3
Brookings 47H3
Brookline 48F1
Brooks Range *mts* 44D3
Broome 40E3
Brosna *r.* 17E4
Brovary 23F6
Brownfield 46G5
Brownsville 47H6
Brownsville 47J4
Brownsville 48B2
Brownwood 46H5
Bruay-la-Bussière 18F1
Bruck an der Mur 13O7
Brugge 12I5
Brumado 55C1
Brumunddal 11G6
Brunei *country* 29D7
Brunflo 10I5
Brunswick 47K5
Brunswick 47N3
Bruntál 13P6
Brusque 55A4
Brussels 12J5
Bryan 47H5
Bryansk 23G5
Bryne 11D7
Bryukhovetskaya 23H7
Brzeg 13P5
Buala 41L1
Bucak 21N6
Bucaramanga 52D2
Buchanan 32B4
Bucharest 21L2
Buckhannon 48A3
Buckhaven 16F4
Buckingham 15G6
Buckingham Bay 41H2
Buda-Kashalyova 23F5
Budapest 21H1
Bude 15C8
Budennovsk 23J7
Buderim 42F1
Buenaventura 52C3
Buenos Aires 54E4
Buerarema 55D1
Buffalo 48B1
Buftea 21K2
Bug *r.* 13S5
Buga 52C3
Bugt 30A2
Buhuşi 21L1
Builth Wells 15D6
Buinsk 23K5
Bujanovac 21I3
Bujumbura 34C4
Bukavu 34C4
Bukittinggi 29C8
Bukoba 34D4
Bülach 18I3
Bulancak 23H8
Bulawayo 35C6
Buldan 21M5
Bulembu 37J3
Bulgan 27J2
Bulgaria *country* 21K3
Bullhead City 49E3
Bulukumba 29E8
Bumba 34C3
Bunbury 40D6
Bundaberg 41K4
Bungay 15I6
Bungendore 42D5
Bunia 34D3
Buôn Ma Thuôt 29C6
Buraydah 34E1
Burbank 49C3
Burco 34E3
Burdur 21N6
Burē 34D2
Bureå 10L4
Burgas 21L3
Burgeo 45M5
Burgersdorp 37H6
Burgess Hill 15G8
Burgos 19E2
Burgundy *reg.* 18G3
Burhaniye 21L5
Buri 55A3
Buritama 55A3
Buriti Alegre 55A2
Buriti Bravo 53J5
Buritirama 53J6
Buritis 55B1
Burkina Faso *country* 32C3
Burley 46E3
Burlington 47I3
Burlington 47M3
Burlington 48B1
Burnie 41J8
Burniston 14G4
Burnley 14E5
Burra 41H6
Bursa 21M4
Būr Safājah 33G2
Burton upon Trent 15F6
Buru *i.* 29E8
Burundi *country* 34C4
Bururi 34C4
Buryn' 23G6
Bury St Edmunds 15H6
Būshehr 26E4
Bushenyi 34D4
Businga 34C3
Buta 34C3
Butare 34C4
Butha Buthe 37I5
Butler 48B2
Butte 46E2
Butuan 29E7
Buturlinovka 23I6
Buurhabaka 34E3
Buxoro 26F3
Buxton 14F5
Buy 22I4
Buynaksk 23J8
Büyükmenderes *r.* 21L6
Buzău 21L2
Buzuluk 24G4
Byala 21K3
Byala Slatina 21J3
Byalynichy 23F5
Byaroza 11N10
Bydgoszcz 13P4
Byerazino 23F5
Byeshankovichy 23F5
Byesville 48A3
Bykhaw 23F5
Bykovo 23J6
Byron Bay 42F2
Byrranga, Gory *mts* 25K2
Bytom 13Q5
Bytów 13P3

C

Caacupé 54E3
Caazapá 54E3
Cabanaconde 52D7
Cabanatuan 29E6
Cabezas 52F7
Cabimas 52D1
Cabinda 35B4
Cabinda *prov.* 35B5
Cabo Frio 55C3
Cabo San Lucas 50C4
Caboolture 42F1
Cabora Bassa, Lake *resr* 35D5
Caborca 46E5
Cabot Strait *strait* 45L5
Caçador 55A4
Čačak 21I3
Cáceres 19C4
Cáceres 53G7
Cacheu 32B3
Cachoeira 55D1
Cachoeira Alta 55A2
Cachoeira do Arari 53I4
Cachoeiro de Itapemirim 55C3
Cacolo 35B5
Caçu 55A2
Caculé 55C1
Čadca 13Q6
Cadereyta 46G6
Cadillac 47J3
Cádiz 19C5
Cádiz, Golfo de *g.* 19C5
Caen 15G9
Caernarfon 15C5
Caernarfon Bay 15C5
Caerphilly 15D7
Caetité 55C1
Cafelândia 55A3
Cagayan de Oro 29E7
Cagliari 20C5
Cagliari, Golfo di *b.* 20C5
Cahir 17E5
Cahors 18E4
Cahul 21M2
Caiapônia 55A2
Cairngorm Mountains 16F3
Cairngorms National Park 16E4
Cairns 41J3
Cairo 33G1
Cajamarca 52C5
Cajuru 55B3
Čakovec 20G1
Calabar 32D4
Calafat 21J3
Calais 18E1
Calama 54C2
Calamocha 19F3
Calandula 35B4
Calapan 29E6
Călărași 21L2
Calbayog 29E6
Calçoene 53H3
Caldas da Rainha 19B4
Caldas Novas 53I7
Caldwell 46D3
Calexico 49E4
Calgary 44G4
Cali 52C3
California *state* 46C3
California, Gulf of 46E5
Callander 16E4
Callao 52C6
Callington 15C8
Caltagirone 20F6
Caltanissetta 20F6
Calulo 35B4
Caluquembe 35B5
Calvi 18I5
Camaçari 55D1
Camacupa 35B5
Camagüey 51I4
Camamu 55D1
Camanongue 35C5
Camapuã 53H7
Camaquã 54F4
Camarillo 49C3
Ca Mau 29C7
Camberley 15G7
Cambodia *country* 29C6
Camboriú 55A4
Camborne 15B8
Cambrai 18F1
Cambrian Mountains *hills* 15D6
Cambridge 15H6
Cambridge 47I2
Cambridge 47K3
Cambridge 48A1
Cambridge 48C3
Cambridge 48F1
Cambridge Bay 45H3
Cambulo 35C4
Cambuquira 55B3
Camden 47I5
Camden 48D3
Cameron Park 49B1
Cameroon *country* 32E4
Cameroun, Mont *vol.* 32D4
Cametá 53I4
Camiri 52F8
Camocim 53J4
Campbell River 46B1
Campbelltown 42E5
Campbeltown 16D5
Campeche 50F5
Campeche, Bahía de *g.* 50F5
Camperdown 42A7
Câmpina 21K2
Campina Grande 53K5
Campinas 55B3
Campina Verde 55A2
Campo 32D4
Campobasso 20F4
Campo Belo 55B3
Campo Belo do Sul 55A4
Campo Grande 54F2
Campo Largo 55A4
Campo Maior 19C4
Campo Maior 53J4
Campo Mourão 54F2
Campos 55C3
Campos Altos 55B2
Campos Novos 55A4
Campos Sales 53J5
Câmpulung 21K2
Câmpulung Moldovenesc 21K1
Çan 21L4
Canada *country* 44H4
Çanakkale 21L4
Canandaigua 48C1
Cananea 46E5
Cañar 52C4
Canary Islands *terr.* 32B2
Canatlán 46G7
Canaveral, Cape 47K6
Canavieiras 55D1
Canberra 42D5
Cancún 51G4
Cândido de Abreu 55A4
Canela 55A5
Canelones 54E4
Canguaretama 53K5
Canguçu 54F4
Canicattì 20E6
Canindé 53K4
Canna *i.* 16C3
Cannes 18H5
Cannock 15E6
Canoas 55A5
Canoinhas 55A4
Cantábrica, Cordillera *mts* 19D2
Cantábrico, Mar *sea* 19C2
Canterbury 15I7
Canterbury Bight *b.* 43C7
Canterbury Plains 43C6
Cần Thơ 29C6
Canton 47J5
Canton 48A2
Canutama 52F5
Canvey Island 15H7
Canyon 46G4
Cao Băng 28C5
Capanema 53I4
Capão Bonito 55A4
Cape Barren Island 41J8
Cape Breton Island 45L5
Cape Coast 32C4
Cape Cod Bay 48F2
Cape Girardeau 47J4
Capelinha 55C2
Capenda-Camulemba 35B4
Cape Town 36D7
Cape Verde *country* 32□
Cape York Peninsula 41I2
Cap-Haïtien 51J5
Capri, Isola di *i.* 20F4
Capricorn Channel 41K4
Caracal 21K2
Caracas 52E1
Caraguatatuba 55B3
Caraí 55C2
Carandaí 55C3
Caransebeş 21J2
Caratinga 55C2
Carauari 52E4
Caravaca de la Cruz 19F4
Caravelas 55D2
Carbondale 48D2
Carbonia 20C5
Carbonita 55C2
Carcaixent 19F4
Carcassonne 18F5
Cárdenas 47K7
Cárdenas 50E4
Cardiff 15D7
Cardigan 15C6
Cardigan Bay 15C6
Cardoso 55A3
Carei 21J1
Carentan 15F9
Cariacica 55C3
Cariamanga 52C4
Caribbean Sea 51H5
Caribou Mountains 44G4
Cariñena 19F3
Carletonville 37H4
Carlisle 14E4
Carlisle 48C2
Carlos Chagas 55C2
Carlow 17F5
Carlsbad 49D4
Carluke 16F5
Carlyle 44H5
Carmagnola 20B2
Carmarthen 15C7
Carmarthen Bay 15C7
Carmaux 18F4
Carmen de Patagones 54D6
Carmichael 49B1
Carmo da Cachoeira 55B3
Carmo do Paranaíba 55B2
Carmona 19D5
Carnac 18C3
Carnarvon 36F6
Carnarvon Range *hills* 40E5
Carnegie, Lake *salt flat* 40E5
Carnot 34B3
Carnoustie 16G4
Carolina 53I5
Caroline Islands 29G7
Caroní *r.* 52F2
Carpathian Mountains 23C6
Carpentaria, Gulf of 41H2
Carpentras 18G4
Carpi 20D2
Carpinteria 49C3
Carrantuohill *mt.* 17C6
Carrara 20D2
Carrickfergus 17G3
Carrick-on-Shannon 17D4
Carrick-on-Suir 17E5
Carrizo Springs 46H6
Carroll 47I3
Carrollton 47J5
Çarşamba 23H8
Carson City 49C1
Cartagena 19F5
Cartagena 52C1
Carthage 47I4
Caruarú 53K5
Carúpano 52F1
Casablanca 32C1
Casa Branca 55B3
Casa Grande 46E5
Casale Monferrato 20C2
Casca 55A5
Cascade Range *mts* 44F5
Cascais 19B4
Cascavel 54F2
Caserta 20F4
Casino 42F2
Casper 46F3
Caspian Lowland 23J7
Caspian Sea *l.* 24F5
Cássia 55B3
Cassiar Mountains 44E3
Cassino 20E4
Castanhal 53I4
Castaños 46G6
Castelfranco Veneto 20D2
Castellón de la Plana 19F4
Castelo Branco 19C4
Castelvetrano 20E6
Castlebar 17C4
Castle Cary 15E7
Castle Douglas 16F6
Castleford 14F5
Castleisland 17C5
Castres 18F5
Castries 51L6
Castro 54B6
Castro 55A4
Castro Alves 55D1
Catacaos 52B5
Cataguases 55C3
Catalão 55B2
Çatalca Yarımadası *pen.* 21M4
Cataluña *aut. comm.* 19G3
Catamarca 54C3
Catanduva 55A3
Catania 20F6
Catanzaro 20G5
Catarman 29E6
Catbalogan 29E6
Catió 32B3
Cat Island 47L7
Catskill Mountains 48D1
Caucaia 53K4
Caucasia 52C2
Caucasus *mts* 24F5
Cauquenes 54B5
Cavan 17E4
Caxias 53J4
Caxias do Sul 55A5
Caxito 35B4
Çay 21N5
Çaycuma 21O4
Çayeli 23I8
Cayenne 53H3
Cayeux-sur-Mer 15I8
Cayman Islands *terr.* 51H5
Cazombo 35C5
Cebu 29E6
Cecina 20D3
Cedar City 49F2
Cedar Rapids 47I3
Ceduna 40G6
Ceerigaabo 34E2
Cegléd 21H1
Celaya 50D4
Celebes *i.* 29E8
Celebes Sea 38C1
Celje 20F1
Celle 13M4
Celtic Sea 12D5
Centereach 48E2
Central *admin. dist.* 37H2
Central, Cordillera *mts* 52C3
Central, Cordillera *mts* 52C6
Central African Republic *country* 34B3
Central City 46H3
Central Range *mts* 38E2
Central Russian Upland *hills* 23H5
Central Siberian Plateau 25M3
Cephalonia *i.* 21I5
Ceres 36D7
Ceres 49B2
Ceres 54D3
Ceres 55A1
Cerignola 20F4
Çerkeş 23G8
Cernavodă 21M2
Cerritos 50D4
Cerro Azul 55A4
Cerro de Pasco 52C6
Cesena 20E2
Cēsis 11N8
České Budějovice 13O6
Českomoravská vysočina *hills* 13O6
Český Krumlov 13O6
Çeşme 21L5
Cessnock 42E4
Cetinje 20H3
Ceuta 19D6
Cévennes *mts* 18F5
Chābahār 26F4
Chachapoyas 52C5
Chad *country* 33E3
Chad, Lake 33E3
Chadan 24K4
Chadron 46G3
Chaeryŏng 31B5
Chaghcharān 26F3
Chagoda 22G4
Chahbounia 19H6
Chajarí 54E4
Chala 52D7
Chalatenango 50G6
Chalkida 21J5
Châlons-en-Champagne 18G2
Chalon-sur-Saône 18G3
Chaman 26F3
Chamba 35D5
Chambersburg 48C3
Chambéry 18G4
Chamonix-Mont-Blanc 18H4
Champagnole 18G3
Champaign 47J3
Champlain, Lake 45K5
Champotón 50F5
Chamzinka 23J5
Chañaral 54B3
Chandigarh 27G3
Chandler 46E5
Chandrapur 27G5
Changbai 30C4
Changchun 30B4
Changde 27K4
Changhŭng 31B6
Changling 30A3
Changsha 27K4
Changting 30C3
Ch'angwŏn 31C6
Changzhou 28D4
Chania 21K7
Channel Islands 15E9
Channel Islands 49C4
Channel-Port-aux-Basques 45M5
Chanthaburi 29C6
Chantilly 18F2
Chaouèn 19D6
Chaozhou 28D5
Chapayevo 26E1
Chapayevsk 23K5
Chapecó 54F3
Chapeltown 14F5
Chaplygin 23H5
Charcas 50D4
Chard 15E8
Charef 19H6
Chārīkār 27F3
Charleroi 12J5
Charles City 47I3
Charleston 47K4
Charleston 47L5
Charleville 17D5
Charleville 41J5
Charleville-Mézières 18G2
Charlotte 47K4
Charlotte Amalie 51L5
Charlottesville 48B3
Charlottetown 45L5
Charlton 42A6
Chartres 18E2
Chase 46D1
Chashniki 23F5
Chasŏng 30B4
Châteaubriant 18D3
Châteaudun 18E2
Châteauroux 18E3
Château-Thierry 18F2
Châtellerault 18E3
Chatham 15H7
Chatham Island 39I6
Chatham Islands 39I6
Chattanooga 47J4
Chaumont 18G2
Chaves 19C3
Chavusy 23F5
Cheadle 15F6
Cheb 13N5
Cheboksary 22J4
Chech'ŏn 31C5
Cheddar 15E7
Cheektowaga 48B1
Chegdomyn 30D2
Chegga 32C2
Chegutu 35D5
Chehalis 46C2
Cheju 31B6
Chekhov 23H5
Chekhov 30F3
Chełm 23D6
Chełmno 13Q4
Chelmsford 15H7
Cheltenham 15E7
Chelva 19F4
Chelyabinsk 24H4
Chemnitz 13N5
Chengde 27K2
Chengdu 27J3
Chennai 27H5
Chenzhou 27K4
Chepén 52C5
Chepstow 15E7
Cher *r.* 18E3
Cherbourg-Octeville 15F9
Cherchell 19H5
Cherdakly 23K5
Cheremkhovo 25L4
Cherepovets 22H4
Chéria 20B7
Cherkasy 23G6
Cherkessk 23I7
Chernigovka 30D3
Chernihiv 23F6
Cherninivka 23H7
Chernivtsi 23E6
Chernogorsk 24K4
Chernyakhiv 23F6
Chernyakhovsk 11L9
Chernyanka 23H6
Chernyshevskiy 25M3
Chernyshkovskiy 23I6
Chernyye Zemli *reg.* 23J7
Chernyy Yar 23J6
Cherry Hill 48D3
Chertkovo 23I6
Cherven Bryag 21K3
Chervonohrad 23E6
Chervyen' 23F5
Cherwell *r.* 15F7
Chesapeake 47L4
Chesapeake Bay 48C3
Chesham 15G7
Cheshunt 15G7
Chester 14E5
Chester 47K5
Chesterfield 14F5
Chesterfield Inlet 45I3
Chester-le-Street 14F4
Chetumal 50G5
Chetwynd 44F4
Cheviot Hills 14E3
Cheyenne 46G3
Chhapra 27H4
Chiang Mai 29B6
Chiang Rai 28B6
Chiautla 50E5
Chiba 31F6
Chicago 47J3
Chichaoua 32C1
Chichester 15G8
Chichibu 31E6
Chickasha 46H4
Chiclana de la Frontera 19C5
Chiclayo 52C5
Chico 46C4
Chicopee 48E1
Chicoutimi 45K5
Chieti 20F3
Chifeng 27K2
Chihuahua 46F6
Chihuahua, Desierto de 45J3
Childers 41K5
Childress 46G5
Chile *country* 54B4
Chile Chico 54B7
Chililabombwe 35C5
Chillán 54B5
Chillicothe 47I4
Chillicothe 47K4
Chilliwack 44F5
Chiloé, Isla de *i.* 54B6
Chilpancingo 50E5
Chiltern Hills 15G7
Chimaltenango 50F6
Chimbas 54C4
Chimborazo *mt.* 52C4
Chimbote 52C5
Chimoio 35D5
China *country* 28B4
Chinandega 50G6
Chincha Alta 52C6
Chinchilla 42E1
Chindo 31B6
Chingola 35C5
Chinguar 35B5
Chinhae 31C6
Chinhoyi 35D5
Chinju 31C6
Chioggia 20E2
Chios 21L5
Chios *i.* 21K5
Chipata 35D5
Chipindo 35B5
Chipinge 35D6
Chippenham 15E7
Chipping Sodbury 15E7
Chirchiq 27F2
Chiredzi 35D6
Chirk 15D6
Chisasibi 45K4
Chișinău 21M1
Chistopol' 22K5
Chita 25M4
Chitinskaya Oblast' *admin. div.* 30A1
Chitose 30F4
Chitradurga 27G5
Chitral 27G3
Chitré 51H7
Chittagong 27I4
Chitungwiza 35D5
Chivasso 20B2
Chkalovsk 22I4
Chlef 19G5
Choiseul *i.* 39F2
Chojnice 13P4
Chókwé 37K3
Cholet 18D3
Choluteca 51G6
Chomutov 13N5
Ch'ŏnan 31B5
Chon Buri 29C6
Chone 52B4
Ch'ongdo 31C6
Ch'ŏngjin 30C4
Ch'ŏngju 31B5
Chŏngp'yŏng 31B5
Chongqing 27J4
Chŏngŭp 31B6
Chŏnju 31B6
Chorley 14E5
Chornobyl' 23F6
Chornomors'ke 21O2
Chortkiv 23E6
Ch'osan 30B4
Chōshi 31F6
Choszczno 13O4
Choybalsan 27K2
Choyr 27J2
Chřiby *hills* 13P6
Christchurch 15F8
Christchurch 43D6
Christiansburg 48A4
Christmas Island *terr.* 29C9
Chrudim 13O6
Chudniv 23F6
Chudovo 22F4
Chuguyevka 30D3
Chuhuyiv 23H6
Chukchi Sea 25T3
Chukhloma 22I4
Chukotskiy Poluostrov *pen.* 25T3
Chula Vista 49D4
Chulucanas 52B5
Chulym 24J4
Chumbicha 54C3
Chumphon 29B6
Ch'unch'ŏn 31B5
Ch'ungju 31B5
Chuquicamata 54C2
Chur 18I3
Churapcha 25O3
Chuxiong 27J4
Cianorte 54F2
Cide 23G8
Ciechanów 13R4
Ciego de Ávila 51I4
Ciénaga 52D1
Cienfuegos 51H4
Cieza 19F4
Cifuentes 19E3
Cilacap 29C8
Cincinnati 47K4
Çine 21M6
Cintalapa 50F5
Cirebon 29C8
Cirencester 15F7
Čitluk 20G3
Citrus Heights 49B1
Città di Castello 20E3
Ciudad Acuña 46G6
Ciudad Altamirano 50D5
Ciudad Bolívar 52F2
Ciudad Camargo 46F6
Ciudad Constitución 46E6
Ciudad del Carmen 50F5
Ciudad Delicias 46F6
Ciudad de Valles 50E4
Ciudad Guayana 52F2
Ciudad Guzmán 50D5
Ciudad Juárez 46F5
Ciudad Mante 50E4
Ciudad Obregón 46F6
Ciudad Real 19E4
Ciudad Río Bravo 46H6
Ciudad Rodrigo 19C3
Ciudad Victoria 50E4
Civitanova Marche 20E3
Civitavecchia 20D3
Çivril 21M5
Clacton-on-Sea 15I7
Clara 17E4
Clare 41H6
Claremont 48E1
Claresholm 46E1
Clarksburg 48A3
Clarksdale 47I5
Clarksville 47I4
Clarksville 47J4
Clearfield 48B2
Clearwater 47K6
Cleburne 47H5
Cleethorpes 14G5
Clermont 41J4
Clermont-Ferrand 18F4
Clevedon 15E7
Cleveland 47I5
Cleveland 47K4
Cleveland 48A2
Cleveland Heights 48A2
Cleveland Hills 14F4
Cleveleys 14D5
Clinton 46H4
Clinton 47I3
Clipperton, Île *terr.* 50C6
Clitheroe 14E5
Cloncurry 41I4
Clonmel 17E5
Clovis 46G5
Clovis 49C2
Cluj-Napoca 21J1
Cluses 18H3
Clwydian Range *hills* 14D5
Clyde *r.* 16E5
Clyde, Firth of *est.* 16E5
Clydebank 16E5
Coachella 49D4
Coalville 15F6
Coari 52F4
Coastal Plain 47I5
Coast Mountains 44F4
Coast Ranges *mts* 49B2
Coatbridge 16E5
Coatesville 48D3
Coatzacoalcos 50F5
Cobar 42B3
Cobden 42A7
Cobh 17D6
Cobija 52E6
Cobourg Peninsula 40G2
Cobram 42B5
Coburg 13M5
Coca 19D3
Coca 52C4
Cocalinho 55A1
Cochabamba 52E7
Cocos 55B1
Cocos Islands *terr.* 29B9
Codajás 52F4
Codlea 21K2
Codó 53J4
Codsall 15E6
Cody 46F3
Coeur d'Alene 46D2
Coffeyville 47H4
Coffs Harbour 42F3
Cognac 18D4
Cohoes 48E1
Cohuna 42B5
Coihaique 54B7
Coimbatore 27G5
Coimbra 19B3
Colac 42A7
Colatina 55C2
Colby 46G4
Colchester 15H7
Coleman 46H5
Coleraine 17F2
Colima 50D5
Coll *i.* 16C4
Collado Villalba 19E3
Collier Bay 40E3
Collinsville 41J4
Colmar 18H2
Colmenar Viejo 19E3
Cologne 13K5
Colombia *country* 52D3
Colombo 27G6
Colomiers 18E5
Colón 51I7
Colón 54D4
Colón 54E4
Colonial Heights 48C4
Colonsay *i.* 16C4
Colorado *r.* 46H6
Colorado *r.* 49F2
Colorado *state* 46F4
Colorado Plateau 46F4
Colorado Springs 46G4
Colquiri 52E7
Colton 49D3
Columbia 47I4
Columbia 47J4
Columbia 47K5
Columbia 48C2
Columbia 48C3
Columbia *r.* 46C2
Columbia, District of *admin. dist.* 48C3
Columbia Mountains 44F4
Columbia Plateau 46D2
Columbus 47H3
Columbus 47J4
Columbus 47J5
Columbus 47K4
Columbus 47K5
Colwyn Bay 14D5
Comacchio 20E2
Comalcalco 50F5
Comănești 21L1
Comilla 27I4
Comitán de Domínguez 50F5
Commack 48E2
Como 20C2
Como, Lake 20C2
Comodoro Rivadavia 54C7
Comoros *country* 35E5
Compiègne 18F2
Comrat 21M1
Conakry 32B4
Conceição da Barra 55D2
Conceição do Araguaia 53I5
Conceição do Mato Dentro 55C2
Concepción 54B5
Concepción 54E2
Conchos *r.* 46G6
Concord 48F1
Concord 49A2
Concordia 46H4
Concordia 54E4
Condeúba 55C1
Condobolin 42C4
Conegliano 20E2
Congleton 14E5
Congo *country* 34B4
Congo *r.* 34B4
Congo, Democratic Republic of the *country* 34C4
Congo Basin 34C4
Congonhas 55C3
Conneaut 48A2
Connecticut *state* 48E2
Connemara *reg.* 17C4
Conroe 47H5
Conselheiro Lafaiete 55C3
Consett 14F4
Constance, Lake 18I3
Constanța 21M2
Constantine 32D1
Contagalo 55C3
Conway 47I4
Coober Pedy 40G5
Cook Inlet *sea chan.* 44C3
Cook Islands *terr.* 39J3
Cookstown 17F3
Cook Strait *strait* 43E5
Cooktown 41J3
Coolamon 42C5
Coolgardie 40E6
Coonabarabran 42D3
Coonamble 42D3
Cooper Creek *watercourse* 41H5
Coos Bay 46C3
Copenhagen 11H9
Copertino 20H4
Copiapó 54B3
Coquimbo 54B3
Corabia 21K3
Coração de Jesus 55B2
Coraki 42F2
Coral Sea 38F3
Coral Sea Islands Territory *terr.* 41K3
Corby 15G6
Corcoran 49C2
Cordele 47K5
Córdoba 19D5
Córdoba 50E5
Córdoba 54D4
Córdoba, Sierras de *mts* 54D4
Cordova 44D3
Corfu *i.* 21H5
Coribe 55B1
Corigliano Calabro 20G5
Corinth 21J6
Corinth 47J5
Corinth, Gulf of *sea chan.* 21J5
Corinto 55B2
Cork 17D6
Çorlu 21L4
Cornélio Procópio 55A3
Corner Brook 45M5
Corner Inlet *b.* 42C7
Corning 48C1
Cornwall 45K5
Coro 52E1
Coroaci 55C2
Coroatá 53J4
Coromandel 55B2
Coromandel Coast 27H5
Coromandel Peninsula 43E3
Corona 49D4
Coronado 49D4
Coronel Fabriciano 55C2
Coronel Oviedo 54E3
Coronel Pringles 54D5
Coronel Suárez 54D5
Corpus Christi 47H6
Corque 52E7
Corrente 53I6
Correntina 55B1
Corrib, Lough *l.* 17C4
Corrientes 54E3
Corrientes, Cabo *c.* 50C4
Corrientes, Cabo *c.* 52C2
Corse, Cap *c.* 18I5
Corsham 15E7
Corsica *i.* 18I5
Corsicana 47H5
Cortegana 19C5
Cortez 46F4
Cortland 48C1
Cortona 20D3
Çoruh *r.* 23I8
Çorum 26C2
Corumbá 53G7
Corumbá de Goiás 55A1
Corvallis 46C3
Corwen 15D6
Cosenza 20G5
Cosne-Cours-sur-Loire 18F3
Costa Blanca *coastal area* 19F4
Costa Brava *coastal area* 19H3
Costa del Sol *coastal area* 19D5
Costa Marques 52F6
Costa Rica 46F7
Costa Rica 53H7
Costa Rica *country* 51H6
Costești 21K2
Cotabato 29E7
Côte d'Ivoire *country* 32C4
Cotonou 32D4
Cotopaxi, Volcán *vol.* 52C4
Cotswold Hills 15E7
Cottbus 13O5
Cottenham 15H6
Cottian Alps *mts* 18H4
Council Bluffs 47H3
Courland Lagoon *b.* 11L9
Courtenay 44F5
Coutances 18D2
Cove Mountains *hills* 48B3
Coventry 15F6
Covilhã 19C3
Covington 48A4
Cowan, Lake *salt flat* 40E6
Cowdenbeath 16F4
Cowes 15F8
Cowra 42D4
Coxim 53H7
Cox's Bazar 27I4
Cozumel 51G4
Cradock 37G7
Craig 46F3
Craigavon 17F3
Craigieburn 42B6
Crailsheim 13M6
Craiova 21J2
Cramlington 14F3
Cranbourne 42B7
Cranbrook 44G5
Cranston 48F2
Crateús 53J5
Crato 53K5
Crawley 15G7
Credenhill 15E6
Crema 20C2
Cremona 20D2
Cres *i.* 20F2
Creston 46D2
Creston 47I3
Crestview 47J5
Creswick 42A6
Crete *i.* 21K7
Crewe 15E5
Criciúma 55A5
Crieff 16F4
Crimea *pen.* 21O2
Cristalândia 53I6
Cristalina 55B2
Crixás 55A1
Črnomelj 20F2
Croatia *country* 20G2
Cromarty Firth *est.* 16E3
Crookston 47H2
Crookwell 42D5
Crosby 14D5
Crotone 20G5
Crowborough 15H7
Crowland 15G6
Crows Nest 42F1
Crozet 48B3
Cruz Alta 54F3
Cruz del Eje 54D4
Cruzeiro 55B3
Cruzeiro do Sul 52D5
Crystal Brook 41H6
Crystal City 46H6
Csongrád 21I1
Cuauhtémoc 46F6
Cuba *country* 51H4
Cubal 35B5
Cubango *r.* 35C5
Cubatão 55B3
Cuchi 35B5
Cuchilla Grande *hills* 54E4
Cúcuta 52D2
Cuddalore 27G5
Cuddapah 27G5
Cuemba 35B5
Cuenca 19E3
Cuenca 52C4
Cuernavaca 50E5
Cugir 21J2
Cuiabá 53G7
Cuillin Hills 16C3
Cuillin Sound *sea chan.* 16C3
Cuiluan 30C3
Culcairn 42C5
Culiacán 46F7
Cullera 19F4
Cullman 47J5
Cullybackey 17F3
Culpeper 48C3
Cumaná 52F1
Cumberland 48B3
Cumberland Plateau 47J4
Cumberland Sound *sea chan.* 45L3
Cumbernauld 16F5
Cumnock 16E5
Cunene *r.* 35B5
Cuneo 20B2
Cunnamulla 42B2
Curaçá 53K5
Curaçao *i.* 51K6
Curicó 54B4
Curitiba 55A4
Curitibanos 55A4
Currais Novos 53K5
Cururupu 53J4
Curvelo 55B2
Cusco 52D6
Cuttack 27H4
Cuxhaven 13L4
Cuyahoga Falls 48A2
Cwmbrân 15D7
Cyangugu 34C4
Cyclades *is* 21K6
Cyprus *country* 33G1
Czech Republic *country* 13O6
Częstochowa 13Q5

D

Da'an 30B3
Dabakala 32C4
Dabola 32B3
Dąbrowa Górnicza 13Q5
Dachau 13M6
Daet 29E6
Dagana 32B3
Dagupan 29E6
Da Hinggan Ling *mts* 30A2
Dahlak Archipelago *is* 33H3
Dakar 32B3
Dākhilah, Wāḥāt ad *oasis* 33F2
Dakoro 32D3
Đakovo 20H2
Dalaba 32B3
Dalain Hob 27J2
Dalälven *r.* 11J6
Dalaman 21M6
Dalandzadgad 27J2
Đa Lat 29C6
Dalbeattie 16F6
Dale City 48C3
Dalhart 46G4
Dali 27J4
Dalian 28E4
Dalizi 30B4
Dalkeith 16F5
Dallas 47H5
Dal'negorsk 30D3
Dal'nerechensk 30D3
Daloa 32C4
Dalton 47K5
Daly City 49A2
Daman 27G4
Damanhūr 33G1
Damascus 33G1
Damaturu 32E3
Dammam 34F1
Dampier 40D4
Dampier Archipelago *is* 40D4
Dampir, Selat *sea chan.* 29F8
Danané 32C4
Đa Năng 29C6
Danbury 48E2
Dandong 31B4
Dangriga 50G5
Danilov 22I4
Danilovka 23J6
Dankov 23H5
Danlí 51G6

Dano 32C3
Danube r. 13Q8
Danube r. 18I2
Danube r. 23F7
Danville 47J3
Danville 47L4
Danville 48C2
Daoukro 32C4
Dapaong 32D3
Dapitan 29E7
Da Qaidam 27I3
Daqing 30B3
Dara 32B3
Dar'ā 33G1
Dārāb 26E4
Darazo 32E3
Dardanelles strait 21L4
Dar es Salaam 35D4
Dargaville 43D2
Darhan 27J2
Darién, Golfo del g. 52C2
Darjiling 27H4
Darling r. 42B3
Darling Downs hills 42D1
Darling Range hills 40D6
Darlington 14F4
Darmstadt 13L6
Darnah 33F1
Daroca 19F3
Darovskoy 22J4
Dartford 15H7
Dartmoor hills 15C8
Dartmouth 15D8
Dartmouth 45L5
Daru 38E2
Darwen 14E5
Darwin 40G2
Daşkäsän 23J8
Daşoguz 26E2
Datça 21L6
Date 30F4
Datong 27K2
Daugava r. 11N8
Daugavpils 11O9
Davao 29E7
Davenport 47I3
Daventry 15F6
Daveyton 37I4
David 51H7
Davis 49B1
Davis Strait strait 45M3
Dawqah 26E5
Dawson Creek 44F4
Dax 18D5
Daylesford 42B6
Dayr az Zawr 33H1
Dayton 47K4
Daytona Beach 47K6
Dazhou 27J3
Dead Sea salt l. 33G1
Deal 15I7
Dean, Forest of 15E7
Deán Funes 54D4
Dearne r. 14F5
Death Valley depr. 49D2
Deauville 15H9
Debar 21I4
Debrecen 21I1
Debre Zeyit 34D3
Decatur 47J4
Decatur 47J5
Deccan plat. 27G5
Deception Bay 42F1
Děčín 13O5
Decorah 47I3
Dédougou 32C3
Dedovichi 22F4
Dee est. 14D5
Dee r. 15D5
Dee r. 16G3
Degema 32D4
Deggendorf 13N6
Dehlorān 33H1
Dej 21J1
De Kalb 47J3
Dékoa 34B3
Delap-Uliga-Djarrit 7
Delareyville 37G4
Delaware r. 48D3
Delaware state 48D3
Delaware Bay 48D3
Delémont 18H3
Delft 12J4
Delfzijl 13K4
Delhi 27G4
Dellys 19H5
Del Mar 49D4
Delmenhorst 13L4
Delnice 20F2
De-Longa, Ostrova is 25Q2
Del Rio 46G6
Delsbo 11J6
Delta 46F4
Demba 35C4
Demidov 23F5
Deming 46E5
Demirci 21M5
Demirköy 21L4
Denakil reg. 33H3
Denbigh 14D5
Dengkou 27J2
Den Helder 12J4
Dénia 19G4
Denison 47H3
Denizli 21M6
Denman 42E4
Denmark country 11F8
Denmark Strait strait 45P3
Denny 16F4
Denpasar 29D8
Denton 47H5
D'Entrecasteaux, Point 40D6
D'Entrecasteaux Islands 41K1
Denver 46F4
Denver 48C2
Deputatskiy 25O3
Dera Ghazi Khan 27G3
Derby 15F6
Derby 48E2
Dereham 15H6
Derg, Lough l. 17D5
Dergachi 23K6
Derhachi 23H6
De Ridder 47I5
Derry 48F1
De Rust 36F7
Derwent r. 14F6
Derwent r. 14G5
Derzhavinsk 26F1
Desē 34D2
Des Moines 47I3
Desna r. 23F6
Desnogorsk 23G5
Dessau 13N5
Dete 35C5
Detmold 13L5
Detroit 47K3
Detroit Lakes 47H2
Deutschlandsberg 13O7
Deva 21J2
Deventer 13K4
Devil's Lake 46H2
Devizes 15F7
Devnya 21L3
Devon Island 45I2
Devonport 41J8
Devrek 21N4
Dewas 27G4
Dewsbury 14F5
Deyang 27J3
Dezfūl 33H1
Dezhneva, Mys c. 25T3
Dezhou 27K3
Dhahran 34F1
Dhaka 27I4
Dhamār 34E2
Dhanbad 27H4
Dhar Adrar hills 32B3
Dhar Oualâta hills 32C3
Dhar Tîchît hills 32C3
Dharwad 27G5
Dhule 27G4
Dhuusa Marreeb 34E3
Diablo, Mount 49B2
Diablo Range mts 49B2
Diamante 54D4
Diamantina 55C2
Diamantina, Chapada plat. 55C1
Diamantino 53G6
Dianópolis 53I6
Diapaga 32D3
Dibaya 35C4
Dibrugarh 27I4
Dickinson 46G2
Didiéni 32C3
Diébougou 32C3
Diéma 32C3
Dieppe 15I9
Dietikon 18I3
Diffa 32E3
Digne-les-Bains 18H4
Dijon 18G3
Dikhil 34E2
Dikili 21L5
Dikson 24J2
Dila 34D3
Dili 29E8
Dillingham 44C4
Dillon 46E2
Dilolo 35C5
Dimapur 27I4
Dimbokro 32C4
Dimitrovgrad 21K3
Dimitrovgrad 23K5
Dinan 18C2
Dinant 12J5
Dinar 21N5
Dinaric Alps mts 20G2
Dindigul 27G5
Dingle Bay 17B5
Dinguiraye 32B3
Dingwall 16E3
Dioïla 32C3
Dionísio Cerqueira 54F3
Diourbel 32B3
Dipayal 27H4
Diré 32C3
Dīrē Dawa 34E3
Dirk Hartog Island 40C5
Dirs 34E2
Discovery Bay 41I7
Distrito Federal admin. dist. 55B1
Ditloung 36F5
Divinópolis 55B3
Divnoye 23I7
Divo 32C4
Dixon 49B1
Dixon Entrance sea chan. 44E4
Diyarbakır 26D3
Djado, Plateau du 32E2
Djambala 34B4
Djelfa 19H6
Djenné 32C3
Djibo 32C3
Djibouti 34E2
Djibouti country 34E2
Djougou 32D4
Djoum 32E4
Dmitriyev-L'govskiy 23G5
Dmitrov 22H4
Dnieper r. 26C2
Dniester r. 23F6
Dniester r. 23F7
Dniprodzerzhyns'k 23G6
Dnipropetrovs'k 23G6
Dno 22F4
Doba 33E4
Dobele 11M8
Doberai, Jazirah pen. 29F8
Doboj 20H2
Dobrich 21L3
Dobrinka 23I5
Dobroye 23H5
Dobrush 23F5
Dodecanese is 21L7
Dodge City 46G4
Dodoma 35D4
Dogondoutchi 32D3
Doğu Menteşe Dağları mts 21M6
Doha 34F1
Dokkum 13J4
Dokshytsy 11O9
Dokuchayevs'k 23H7
Dole 18G3
Dolgellau 15D6
Dolgorukovo 23H5
Dolinsk 30F3
Dolomites mts 20D2
Dolores 54E4
Dolores 54E5
Dolyna 23D6
Domažlice 13N6
Dombóvár 20H1
Domeyko 54B3
Dominica country 51L5
Dominican Republic country 51J5
Domokos 21J5
Dompu 29D8
Don r. 16G3
Don r. 23H7
Donaghadee 17G3
Donald 42A6
Don Benito 19D4
Doncaster 14F5
Dondo 35B4
Donegal 17D3
Donegal Bay 17D3
Donets'k 23H7
Donets'kyy Kryazh hills 23H6
Dongchuan 27J4
Dongfang 27J5
Donggang 31B5
Đông Hơi 29C6
Dongning 30C3
Dongola 33G3
Dongting Hu l. 27K4
Dongying 27K3
Donskoye 23I7
Doomadgee 41H3
Dorchester 15E8
Dordogne r. 18D4
Dordrecht 12J5
Dores do Indaiá 55B2
Dori 32C3
Dorking 15G7
Dornoch Firth est. 16E3
Doro 32C3
Dorogobuzh 23G5
Dorohoi 23E7
Dorrigo 42F3
Dortmund 13K5
Dosso 32D3
Dothan 47J5
Douai 18F1
Douala 32D4
Doubtful Sound inlet 43A7
Douentza 32C3
Douglas 14C4
Douglas 46F3
Douglas 46F5
Douglas 47K5
Dourados 54F2
Douro r. 19B3
Dover 15I7
Dover 48A2
Dover 48D2
Dover 48D3
Dover 48F1
Dover, Strait of strait 15I8
Dovey r. 15D6
Downpatrick 17G3
Doylestown 48D2
Drâa, Hamada du plat. 32C2
Dracena 55A3
Drachten 13K4
Drăgănești-Olt 21K2
Drăgășani 21K2
Draguignan 18H5
Drahichyn 11N10
Drakensberg mts 37I3
Drama 21K4
Drammen 11G7
Drava r. 20H2
Dréan 20B6
Dresden 13N5
Dreux 18E2
Drobeta-Turnu Severin 21J2
Drogheda 17F4
Drohobych 23D6
Droitwich Spa 15E6
Dromore 17F3
Dronfield 14F5
Drummondville 45K5
Druskininkai 11N10
Druzhnaya Gorka 11Q7
Dryanovo 21K3
Duartina 55A3
Dubai 26E4
Dubawnt Lake 45H3
Dubbo 42D4
Dublin 17F4
Dublin 47K5
Dubna 22H4
Dubno 23E6
Dubovka 23J6
Dubovskoye 23I7
Dubrovnik 20H3
Dubrovytsya 23E6
Dubuque 47I3
Dudinka 24J3
Dudley 15E6
Duékoué 32C4
Duero r. 19C3
Dufourspitze mt. 18H4
Dugi Rat 20G3
Duisburg 13K5
Dukathole 37H6
Dukhovnitskoye 23K5
Dulovo 21L3
Duluth 47I2
Dumaguete 29E7
Dumai 27J6
Dumas 46G4
Dumat al Jandal 26C4
Dumbarton 16E5
Dumfries 16F5
Dumyāț 33G1
Dunajská Streda 13P7
Dunakeszi 21H1
Dunaújváros 20H1
Dunayivtsi 23E6
Duncan 46H5
Duncansby Head 16F2
Dundaga 11M8
Dundalk 17F3
Dundalk 48C3
Dundalk Bay 17F4
Dundas 45L5
Dundee 16G4
Dundee 37J5
Dundonald 17G3
Dunedin 43C7
Dunfermline 16F4
Dungannon 17F3
Dungarvan 17E5
Dungeness hd 15H8
Dungiven 17F3
Dungog 42E4
Dungu 34C3
Dungun 29C7
Dunhua 30C4
Dunkirk 18F1
Dunkirk 48B1
Dún Laoghaire 17F4
Dunmore 48D2
Dunmurry 17G3
Dunnet Head 16F2
Dunnville 48B1
Duns 16G5
Dunstable 15G7
Dupnitsa 21J3
Durağan 23G8
Durance r. 18G5
Durango 46F4
Durango 46G7
Durant 47H5
Durazno 54E4
Durban 37J5
Durban-Corbières 18F5
Durbanville 36D7
Durham 14F4
Durham 47L4
Durlești 21M1
Durrës 21H4
Durrington 15F7
Dursunbey 21M5
Dushanbe 27F3
Düsseldorf 13K5
Dutse 32D3
Dutsin-Ma 32D3
Duyun 27J4
Düzce 21N4
Dwarka 27F4
Dyat'kovo 23G5
Dyersburg 47J4
Dymytrov 23H6
Dzaoudzi 35E5
Dzerzhinsk 22I4
Dzhankoy 23G7
Dzhusaly 26F2
Działdowo 13R4
Dzuunmod 27J2
Dzyarzhynsk 11O10

E

Eagle Pass 46G6
Earn, Loch l. 16E4
Eastbourne 15H8
East China Sea 28E4
Easter Island 6
Eastern Cape prov. 37H6
Eastern Desert 33G2
Eastern Ghats mts 27G5
East Falkland i. 54E8
East Frisian Islands 13K4
East Grinstead 15G7
Easthampton 48E1
East Hartford 48E2
East Kilbride 16E5
Eastlake 48A2
Eastleigh 15F8
East Liverpool 48A2
East London 37H7
Eastmain r. 45K4
Easton 48C3
Easton 48D2
East Orange 48D2
East Providence 48F2
East Siberian Sea 25P2
East Timor country 29E8
East York 48B1
Eau Claire 47I3
Ebbw Vale 15D7
Ebebiyin 32E4
Eberswalde-Finow 13N4
Ebetsu 30F4
Eboli 20F4
Ebolowa 32E4
Ebro r. 19G3
Écija 19D5
Eckernförde 13L3
Ecuador country 52C4
Ed 33H3
Eday i. 16G1
Ed Damazin 33G3
Ed Damer 33G3
Ed Debba 33G3
Ed Dueim 33G3
Edéa 32E4
Edéia 55A2
Eden 42D6
Edenderry 17E4
Edessa 21J4
Edinburg 46H6
Edinburgh 16F5
Edirne 21L4
Edmonton 44G4
Edmundston 45L5
Edremit 21L5
Edward, Lake 34C4
Edwards Plateau 46G5
Effingham 47J4
Eger 13R7
Egersund 11E7
Egilsstaðir 10□
Eğirdir 21N6
Egmont, Cape 43D4
Egvekinot 25T3
Egypt country 33G2
Ehen Hudag 27J3
Ehingen (Donau) 13L6
Eifel hills 13K5
Eigg i. 16C4
Eighty Mile Beach 40E3
Eilat 33G2
Eindhoven 12J5
Einsiedeln 18I3
Eirunepé 52E5
Eisenach 13M5
Eisenhüttenstadt 13O4
Eisenstadt 13P7
Ekenäs 11M7
Eksjö 11I8
El Aouinet 20B7
El Arrouch 20B6
Elazığ 26C3
Elba, Isola d' i. 20D3
El'ban 30E2
Elbasan 21I4
El Bayadh 32D1
Elbe r. 13L4
Elbert, Mount 46F4
Elbeuf 15I9
Elbląg 13Q3
El'brus mt. 23I8
Elburz Mountains 26D3
El Cajon 49D4
El Callao 52F2
El Campo 47H6
El Centro 49E4
El Cerro 52F7
Elche-Elx 19F4
Elda 19F4
El'dikan 25O3
El Dorado 47H4
El Dorado 47I5
Eldorado 54F3
Eldorado 55A4
Eldoret 34D3
El Ejido 19E5
Eleuthera i. 47L6
El Fasher 33F3
El Fuerte 46F6
El Geneina 33F3
Elgin 16F3
Elgin 47J3
El Goléa 32D1
Elgon, Mount 26C6
El Hadjar 20B6
El Hank esc. 32C2
Elías Piña 51J5
Elista 23J7
Elizabeth 48D2
Elizabeth City 47L4
Elizabethtown 47J4
El Jadida 32C1
El Jem 20D7
Ełk 13S4
El Kala 20C6
Elk City 46H4
El Kelaâ des Srarhna 32C1
Elkford 46E1
Elk Grove 49B1
Elkhart 47J3
Elkhovo 21L3
Elkins 48B3
Elko 46D3
Elkton 48D3
Ellensburg 46C2
Ellesmere Island 45J2
Ellesmere Port 14E5
Ellicott City 48C3
Elliot 37H6
Ellsworth 47N3
Elmalı 21M6
El Meghaïer 32D1
Elmira 48C1
Elmshorn 13L4
El Muglad 33F3
El Obeid 33G3
El Oued 32D1
El Paso 46F5
El Porvenir 46F5
El Porvenir 51I7
El Prat de Llobregat 19H3
El Progreso 50G5
El Puerto de Santa María 19C5
El Reno 46H4
El Salto 46F7
El Salvador 54C3
El Salvador country 50G6
Elsinore 49D4
El Tarf 20C6
El Tigre 52F2
El'ton 23J6
Elvas 19C4
Elverum 11G6
Ely 15H6
Elyria 47K3
Emba 26E2
Embalenhle 37I4
Embarcación 54D2
Embu 34D4
Emden 13K4
Emet 21M5
Emgwenya 37J3
Emi Koussi mt. 33E3
Emiliano Zapata 50F5
Emirdağ 21N5
eMjindini 37J3
Emmaboda 11I8
Emmaus 48D2
Emmen 13K4
Emmen 18I3
Empangeni 37J5
Empoli 20D3
Emporia 47H4
Emporia 47L4
eMzinoni 37I4
Encarnación 54E3
Encinitas 49D4
Encruzilhada 55C1
Endeavour Strait 41I2
Endicott 48C1
Enerhodar 23G7
Engel's 23J6
England admin. div. 15E6
English Channel strait 15F9
Enid 46H4
Eniwa 30F4
Enköping 11J7
Enna 20F6
Ennis 17D5
Ennis 47H5
Enniscorthy 17F5
Enniskillen 17E3
Enschede 13K4
Ensenada 46D5
Enshi 27J3
Entebbe 34D3
Entre Rios de Minas 55B3
Entroncamento 19B4
Enugu 32D4
Envira 52D5
Ephrata 48C2
Épinal 18H2
Epsom 15G7
Equatorial Guinea country 32D4
Érd 20H1
Erdek 21L4
Erechim 54F3
Ereğli 21N4
Ereğli 33G1
Erenhot 27K2
Erfurt 13M5
'Erg Chech des. 32C2
Ergli 11N8
Erie 48A1
Erie, Lake 48A1
Eritrea country 34D2
Erlangen 13M6
Ermelo 37I4
Ermenek 33G1
Ermoupoli 21K6
Erode 27G5
Erongo admin. reg. 36B1
Er Rachidia 32C1
Ertil' 23I6
Erzgebirge mts 13N5
Erzincan 26C3
Erzurum 26D3
Esbjerg 11F9
Escanaba 47J2
Escárcega 50F5
Eschwege 13M5
Escondido 49D4
Escuinapa 50C4
Escuintla 50F6
Eséka 32E4
Eşfahān 26E3
Esikhawini 37K5
Eskilstuna 11J7
Eskipazar 23G8
Eskişehir 21N5
Eslāmābād-e Gharb 33H1
Eslöv 11H9
Eşme 21M5
Esmeraldas 52C3
Esperance 40E6
Esperanza 46F6
Espinhaço, Serra do mts 55C2
Espinosa 55C1
Espírito Santo state 55C2
Espiritu Santo i. 39G3
Espoo 11N6
Esquel 54B6
Essaouira 32C1
Es Semara 32B2
Essen 13K5
Essequibo r. 53G2
Essex 48C3
Estância 53K6
Estcourt 37I5
Estelí 51G6
Estepona 19D5
Estevan 46G2
Estherville 47I3
Estonia country 11N7
Estrela 55A5
Estrela, Serra da mts 19C3
Estrela do Sul 55B2
Estremoz 19C4
Étampes 18F2
Ethandakukhanya 37J4
Ethiopia country 34D3
Etna, Mount vol. 20F6
Etobicoke 48B1
Etosha Pan salt pan 35B5
Euclid 48A2
Euclides da Cunha 53K6
Eugene 46C3
Euphrates r. 26D3
Euphrates r. 33H1
Eura 11M6
Eureka 46C3
Eureka 46D2
Euroa 42B6
Europa, Île i. 35E6
Europa Point 19D5
Evans City 48A2
Evanston 46E3
Evansville 47J4
Evaton 37H4
Everard Range hills 40G5
Everest, Mount 27H4
Everett 46C2
Everglades swamp 47K6
Evesham 15F6
Évora 19C4
Évreux 18E2
Evvoia i. 21K5
Ewe, Loch b. 16D3
Ewo 34B4
Exe r. 15D8
Exeter 15D8
Exeter 48F1
Exmoor hills 15D7
Exmouth 15D8
Exmouth 40C4
Exmouth Gulf 40C4
Exton 48D2
Extremadura aut. comm. 19D4
Eyasi, Lake salt l. 34D4
Eyemouth 16G5
Eyjafjörður inlet 10□
Eynsham 15F7
Eyre (North), Lake salt flat 41H5
Eyre (South), Lake salt flat 41H5
Eyre Peninsula 41H6
Ezakheni 37J5
Ezhva 22K3
Ezine 21L5

F

Faaborg 11G9
Fabriano 20E3
Fada-N'Gourma 32D3
Faenza 20D2
Făgăraș 21K2
Fagatogo 39I3
Fagersta 11I7
Fairbanks 44D3
Fairfax 48C3
Fairfield 49A1
Fair Head 17F2
Fair Isle i. 16H1
Fairlie 43C7
Fairmont 47I3
Fairmont 48A3
Faisalabad 27G3
Falenki 22K4
Falkenberg 11H8
Falkirk 16F5
Falkland Islands terr. 54E8
Falkland Sound sea chan. 54D8
Falköping 11H7
Fallbrook 49D4
Fallon 46D4
Fall River 48F2
Falmouth 15B8
Falmouth 48C3
False Bay 36D8
Falster i. 11G9
Fălticeni 23E7
Falun 11I6
Famagusta 33G1
Fandriana 35E6
Fangzheng 30C3
Fano 20E3
Faraba 32B3
Farafangana 35E6
Farāfirah, Wāḥāt al oasis 33F2
Farāh 26F3
Faranah 32B3
Fareham 15F8
Farewell, Cape 43D5
Farewell, Cape 45N3
Fargo 47H2
Faribault 47I3
Farmington 46F4
Farmville 48B4
Farnborough 15G7
Farnham 15G7
Faro 19C5
Faro 53G4
Faroe Islands terr. 10□
Farquhar Group is 35F5
Farsund 11E7
Fasano 20G4
Fastiv 23F6
Fatehpur 27H4
Fatick 32B3
Fauske 10I3
Fawley 15F8
Faxaflói b. 10□
Faya 33E3
Fayetteville 47I4
Fayetteville 47L4
Fdérik 32B2
Fear, Cape 47L5
Fécamp 15H9
Federalsburg 48D3
Feijó 52D5
Feira de Santana 55D1
Feldkirch 13L7
Feldkirchen in Kärnten 13O7
Felipe C. Puerto 50G5
Felixlândia 55B2
Felixstowe 15I7
Fenoarivo Atsinanana 35E5
Feodosiya 23G7
Feres 21L4
Fergus Falls 47H2
Fériana 20C7
Ferizaj 21I3
Ferkessédougou 32C4
Fermo 20E3
Fermoselle 19C3
Fernandina Beach 47K5
Fernandópolis 55A3
Ferrara 20D2
Ferrol 19B2
Ferros 55C2
Fès 32C1
Fethiye 21M6
Fetlar i. 16□
Feyzābād 27G3
Ffestiniog 15D6
Fianarantsoa 35E6
Fier 21H4
Fife Ness pt 16G4
Figeac 18F4
Figueira da Foz 19B3
Figueres 19H2
Figuig 32C1
Figuil 33E4
Fiji country 39H3
Filadelfia 54D2
Filey 14G4
Filingué 32D3
Filippiada 21I5
Filipstad 11I7
Fillmore 49C3
Findlay 47K3
Finger Lakes 48C1
Finike 21N6
Finisterre, Cape 19B2
Finland country 10O5
Finland, Gulf of 11M7
Finnmarksvidda reg. 10H2
Finspång 11I7
Firmat 54D4
Firminy 18G4
Fish watercourse 36C5
Fisher Strait 45J3
Fishguard 15C7
Flagstaff 37I6
Flagstaff 46E4
Flamborough Head 14G4
Flattery, Cape 46C2
Fleetwood 14D5
Flekkefjord 11E7
Flen 11J7
Flensburg 13L3
Flinders Island 41J7
Flinders Ranges mts 41H6
Flin Flon 44H4
Flint 14D5
Flint 47K3
Florence 20D3
Florence 46E5
Florence 47J5
Florence 47L5
Florencia 52C3
Flores 50G5
Flores i. 29E8
Flores, Laut sea 29D8
Floresta 53K5
Floriano 53J5
Florianópolis 55A4
Florida 54E4
Florida state 47K5
Florida, Straits of strait 47K7
Florin 49B1
Florina 21I4
Florø 11D6
Foça 21L5
Focșani 21L2
Foggia 20F4
Foix 18E5
Folda sea chan. 10I3
Foligno 20E3
Folkestone 15I7
Follonica 20D3
Fomboni 35E5
Fond du Lac 47J3
Fondi 20E4
Fonte Boa 52E4
Fontur pt 10□
Foraker, Mount 44C3
Forchheim 13M6
Fordham 15H6
Fordingbridge 15F8
Forécariah 32B4
Forest 47J5
Forest Hill 42C5
Forestville 49A1
Forfar 16G4
Forked River 48D3
Forlì 20E2
Formby 14D5
Formiga 55B3
Formosa 54E3
Formosa 55B1
Formoso r. 55A1
Forrest City 47I4
Forssa 11M6
Forster 42F4
Fortaleza 53K4
Fort-de-France 51L6
Fort Dodge 47I3
Fort Edward 48E1
Forth r. 16F4
Forth, Firth of est. 16F4
Fort Lauderdale 47K6
Fort Macleod 46E2
Fort McMurray 44G4
Fort Myers 47K6
Fort Payne 47J5
Fort Pierce 47K6
Fort Portal 34D3
Fort Scott 47I4
Fort Smith 44G3
Fort Smith 47I4
Fort Stockton 46G5
Fort Wayne 47J3
Fort William 16D4
Fort Worth 47H5
Fossano 20B2
Foster 42C7
Fougères 18D2
Foula i. 16□
Foumban 32E4
Fouta Djallon reg. 32B3
Foveaux Strait strait 43A8
Fowler 46G4
Fox Creek 44G4
Foxe Basin g. 45K3
Foyle r. 17E3
Foyle, Lough b. 17E2
Foz do Iguaçu 54F3
Framingham 48F1
Franca 55B3
Francavilla Fontana 20G4
France country 18F3
Franceville 34B4
Francistown 35C6
Frankfort 47K4
Frankfurt am Main 13L5
Frankfurt an der Oder 13O4
Fränkische Alb hills 13M6
Franklin 48B2
Franklin 48F1
Franklin D. Roosevelt Lake resr 46D2
Frankston 42B7
Frantsa-Iosifa, Zemlya is 24G2
Frascati 20E4
Fraser r. 44F5
Fraser r. 45L4
Fraserburgh 16G3
Frauenfeld 18I3
Fray Bentos 54E4
Freckleton 14E5
Fredericia 11F9
Frederick 48C3
Fredericksburg 46H5
Fredericksburg 48C3
Fredericton 45L5
Frederikshavn 11G8
Frederiksværk 11H9
Fredonia 48B1
Fredrikstad 11G7
Freehold 48D2
Freeport 47H6
Freeport City 47L6
Free State prov. 37H5
Freetown 32B4
Freiburg im Breisgau 13K6
Freising 13M6
Freistadt 13O6
Fréjus 18H5
Fremantle 40D6
Fremont 47H3
Fremont 49B2
French Guiana terr. 53H3
French Polynesia terr. 6
French Southern and Antarctic Lands terr. 7
Frenda 19G6
Fresnillo 50D4
Fresno 49C2
Freudenstadt 13L6
Fria 32B3
Frias 54C3
Fribourg 18H3
Friedrichshafen 13L7
Frobisher Bay 45L3
Frohavet b. 10F5
Frolovo 23I6
Frome 15E7
Frome, Lake salt flat 41H6
Frontera 50F5
Fronteras 46F5
Front Royal 48B3
Frosinone 20E4
Frýdek-Místek 13Q6
Fuenlabrada 19E3
Fuerte Olimpo 54E2
Fuerteventura i. 32B2
Fujairah 26E4
Fuji 31E6
Fujin 30C3
Fujinomiya 31E6
Fuji-san vol. 31E6
Fujiyoshida 31E6
Fukuchiyama 31D6
Fukui 31E5
Fukuoka 31C6
Fukushima 31F5
Fulda 13L5
Fullerton 49D4
Fulton 47I4
Fulton 48C1
Funabashi 31E6
Funafuti atoll 39H2
Funchal 32B1
Fundão 19C3
Fundão 55C2
Fundy, Bay of g. 45L5
Funtua 32D3
Furmanov 22I4
Furnas, Represa resr 55B3
Furneaux Group is 41J8
Fürstenwalde 13O4
Fürth 13M6
Furukawa 31F5
Fushun 30A4
Fusong 30B4
Fuyang 27K3
Fuyu 30B3
Fuyu 30B3
Fuyun 27H2
Fuzhou 27K4
Fuzhou 28D5
Fyn i. 11G9
Fyne, Loch inlet 16D5

G

Gaalkacyo 34E3
Gabela 35B5
Gabès 32E1
Gabès, Golfe de g. 32E1
Gabon country 34B4
Gaborone 37G3
Gabrovo 21K3
Gabú 32B3
Gadsden 47J5
Găești 21K2
Gaeta 20E4
Gafsa 20C7
Gagarin 23G5
Gagnoa 32C4
Gagra 23I8
Gainesville 47H5
Gainesville 47K5
Gainesville 47K6
Gainsborough 14G5
Gairdner, Lake salt flat 41H6
Galanta 13P6
Galapagos Islands 52□
Galashiels 16G5
Galați 21M2
Galatina 20H4
Galesburg 47I3
Galeshewe 36G5
Galich 22I4
Galicia aut. comm. 19C2
Gallatin 47J4
Galle 27H6
Gallinas, Punta pt 52D1
Gallipoli 20H4
Gallipoli 21L4
Gällivare 10L3
Gallup 46F4
Galmudug reg. 26D6
Galtee Mountains hills 17D5
Galveston 47I6
Galveston Bay 47I6
Galway 17C4
Galway Bay 17C4
Gamalakhe 37J6
Gambēla 34D3
Gamboma 34B4
Gamleby 11J8
Gäncä 23J8
Ganda 35B5
Gandajika 35C4
Gander 45M5
Gandesa 19G3
Gandhinagar 27G4
Gandia 19F4
Ganganagar 27G4
Gangdisê Shan mts 27H3
Ganges r. 27I4
Ganges, Mouths of the 27H4
Gannan 30A3
Gannett Peak 44H5
Ganye 32E4
Gao 32C3
Gaoua 32C3
Gaoual 32B3
Gap 18H4
Garabogazköl Aýlagy b. 26E2
Garalo 32C3
Garanhuns 53K5
Ga-Rankuwa 37H3
Garbahaarrey 34E3
Garbsen 13L4
Garça 55A3
Garda, Lake 20D2
Garden City 46G4
Gardēz 27F3
Gardner 48F1
Gargždai 11L9
Gariep Dam resr 37G6
Garies 36C6
Garissa 34D4
Garonne r. 18D4
Garoowe 34E3
Garopaba 55A5
Garoua 32E4
Gary 47J3
Garza García 46G6
Gascony reg. 18D5
Gascony, Gulf of 18C5
Gascoyne r. 40C5
Gashua 32E3
Gaspésie, Péninsule de la pen. 47N2
Gastonia 47K4
Gatchina 11Q7
Gateshead 14F4
Gatesville 46H5
Gauteng prov. 37I4
Gavarr 23J8
Gavdos i. 21K7
Gävle 11J6
Gavrilov-Yam 22H4
Gawler 41H6
Gawler Ranges hills 41H6
Gaya 32D3
Gayéri 32D3
Gayndah 41K5
Gayny 22L3
Gaza 26C3
Gaza prov. 37K2
Gaziantep 33G1
Gbarnga 32C4
Gdańsk 13Q3
Gdańsk, Gulf of 13Q3
Gdov 11O7
Gdynia 13Q3
Gedaref 33G3
Geelong 42B7
Gegen Gol 30A2
Geilo 11F6
Gejiu 27J4
Gela 20F6
Gelendzhik 23H7
Gemena 34B3
Gemlik 21M4
General Acha 54D5
General Alvear 54C5
General Juan Madariaga 54E5
General Pico 54D5
General Roca 54C5
General Salgado 55A3
General Santos 29E7
General Villegas 54D5
Geneseo 48C1
Geneva 18H3
Geneva 48C1
Geneva, Lake 18H3
Genk 13J5
Genoa 20C2
Genoa, Gulf of 20C2
Geographe Bay 40D6
Geographe Channel 40C4
George 36F7
George Town 29C7
Georgetown 32B3
Georgetown 46H5
Georgetown 47L5
George Town 51H5
Georgetown 53G2
Georgia country 23I8
Georgia state 47K5
Georgian Bay 45J5
Georgiyevka 27H2
Georgiyevsk 23I7
Gera 13N5
Geral de Goiás, Serra hills 55B1
Geral do Paraná, Serra hills 55B1
Geraldton 40C5
Gerede 23G8
Germany country 13L5
Gerze 23G8
Gettysburg 48C3
Gevgelija 21J4
Geyve 21N4
Ghadāmis 32D1
Ghana country 32C4
Ghanzi 35C6
Ghanzi admin. dist. 36F2
Ghardaïa 32D1
Gharyān 33E1
Ghazal, Bahr el watercourse 33E3
Ghazaouet 19F6
Ghaziabad 27G4
Ghaznī 26F3
Ghent 12I5
Gheorgheni 21K1
Gherla 21J1
Ghisonaccia 18I5
Giaginskaya 23I7
Giannitsa 21J4
Giant's Causeway lava field 17F2
Giarre 20F6
Gibraltar terr. 19D5
Gibraltar, Strait of strait 19C6
Gibson Desert 40E4
Gießen 13L5
Gifu 31E6
Gijón-Xixón 19D2
Gila r. 49E4
Gilbués 53I5
Gilgandra 42D3
Gilgit 27G3
Gillette 46F3
Gillingham 15H7
Gilroy 49B2
Ginosa 20G4
Gioia del Colle 20G4
Gippsland reg. 42B7
Giresun 23H8
Girona 19H3
Gironde est. 18D4
Girvan 16E5
Gisborne 43G4
Gislaved 11H8
Gitarama 34C4
Gitega 34C4
Giulianova 20E3
Giurgiu 21K3
Giyani 37J2
Giza 33G2
Gjakovë 21I3
Gjilan 21I3
Gjirokastër 21I4
Gjøvik 11G6
Glace Bay 45M5
Gladstone 41K4
Glamoč 20G2
Glasgow 16E5
Glasgow 47J4
Glastonbury 15E7
Glazov 22L4
Glendale 46E5
Glendale 49C3
Glen Innes 42E2
Glen More valley 16E3
Glenrothes 16F4
Glens Falls 48E1
Gliwice 13Q5
Globe 46E5
Głogów 13P5
Glomfjord 10H3
Gloucester 15E7
Gloucester 42E3
Gloucester 48F1
Gloversville 48D1
Glubokoye 23I6
Glubokoye 27H1
Gmünd 13O6
Gmunden 13N7
Gniezno 13P4
Goba 34E3
Gobabis 36D2
Gobi Desert 27J2
Gobō 31D6
Gochas 36D3
Godalming 15G7
Godavari r. 27H5
Goiana 53L5
Goianésia 55A1
Goiânia 55A2
Goiás 55A1
Goiás state 55A2
Goio-Erê 54F2
Gökçeada i. 21K4
Gölcük 21M4
Gold Coast 42F2
Golden Bay 43D5
Goldsboro 47L4
Göle 23I8
Goleta 49C3
Gölköy 23H8
Golmud 27I3
Gölpazarı 21N4
Goma 34C4
Gombe 32E3
Gómez Palacio 46G6
Gonaïves 51J5
Gonbad-e Kāvūs 26E3
Gonder 34D2
Gönen 21L4
Gonzales 47H6
Good Hope, Cape of 36D8
Goole 14G5
Goondiwindi 42E2
Göppingen 13L6
Gorakhpur 27H4
Gördes 21M5
Gorē 34D3
Gorey 17F5
Gorgān 26E3
Gorizia 20E2
Gorlice 23D6
Görlitz 13O5
Gorna Oryakhovitsa 21K3
Gornji Milanovac 21I2
Gornji Vakuf 20G3
Gorno-Altaysk 24J4
Gornozavodsk 30F3
Gornyak 24J4
Gornyy 23K6
Gorodets 22I4
Gorodishche 23J5
Gorodishche 23J6
Gorodovikovsk 23I7
Goroka 38E2
Gorokhovets 22I4
Gorom Gorom 32C3
Gorontalo 29E7
Gorshechnoye 23H6
Goryachiy Klyuch 23H7
Gorzów Wielkopolski 13O4
Gosforth 14F3
Goshen 48D2
Gospić 20F2
Gosport 15F8
Gossi 32C3
Gostivar 21I4
Götene 11H7
Gotha 13M5
Gothenburg 11G8
Gotland i. 11K8
Gotse Delchev 21J4
Gōtsu 31D6
Göttingen 13L5
Gouda 12J4
Gouin, Réservoir resr 45K5
Goulburn 42D5
Goundam 32C3
Gouraya 19G5
Gourcy 32C3
Gouré 32E3
Governador Valadares 55C2
Govĭ Altayn Nuruu mts 27I2
Goya 54E3
Göyçay 23J8
Gozo i. 20F6
Graaff-Reinet 36G7
Grabouw 36D8
Gračac 20F2
Grafton 42F2
Grafton 48A3
Graham 46H5
Grahamstown 37H7
Grajaú 53I5
Grampian Mountains 16E4
Granada 19E5
Granada 51G6
Granby 45K5
Gran Canaria i. 32B2
Gran Chaco reg. 54D3
Grand Bahama i. 47L6
Grand Bank 45M5
Grand Banks of Newfoundland sea feature 45M5
Grand-Bassam 32C4
Grand Canyon gorge 49F2
Grand Cayman i. 51H5
Grande, Bahía b. 54C8
Grande Prairie 44G4
Grand Erg de Bilma des. 32E3
Grand Erg Occidental des. 32C1
Grand Erg Oriental des. 32D2
Grandes, Salinas salt marsh 54C4
Grand Falls-Windsor 45M5
Grand Forks 47H2
Grand Island 46H3
Grand Junction 46F4
Grand-Lahou 32C4
Grândola 19B4
Grand Rapids 47I2
Grand Rapids 47J3
Grand Turk 51J4
Grängesberg 11I6
Granja 53J4
Gränna 11I7
Grantham 15G6
Grantown-on-Spey 16F3
Grants 46F4
Grants Pass 46C3
Grantville 48C2
Grão Mogol 55C2
Graskop 37J3
Grasse 18H5
Graus 19G2
Gravataí 55A5
Gravesend 15H7
Gravina in Puglia 20G4
Grays 15H7
Graz 13O7
Great Abaco i. 47L6
Great Australian Bight g. 40F6
Great Bahama Bank sea feature 47L6
Great Barrier Island 43E3
Great Barrier Reef reef 41I2
Great Basin 46D4
Great Bear Lake 44G3
Great Belt sea chan. 11G9
Great Bend 46H4
Great Britain i. 12G4
Great Dividing Range mts 42B6
Greater Antilles is 51H4
Great Exuma i. 47L7
Great Falls 46E2
Great Inagua i. 47M7
Great Karoo plat. 36F7
Great Limpopo Transfrontier Park nat. park 37J2
Great Malvern 15E6
Great Nicobar i. 27I6
Great Ouse r. 15H6
Great Rift Valley valley 34D4
Great Salt Lake 46E3
Great Salt Lake Desert 46E3
Great Sand Sea des. 33F2
Great Sandy Desert 40E4
Great Slave Lake 44G3
Great Stour r. 15I7
Great Torrington 15C8
Great Victoria Desert 40F5
Great Waltham 15H7
Great Yarmouth 15I6
Greece country 21I5
Greeley 46G3
Green Bay 47J3
Green Bay 47J2
Greeneville 47K4
Greenfield 48E1
Greenland terr. 45N2
Greenland Sea 24A2
Greenock 16E5
Green River 46F3
Greensburg 48B2
Greenville 32C4
Greenville 47H5
Greenville 47I5
Greenville 47J5
Greenville 47K5
Greenwich 48E2
Greenwood 47K5
Gregory, Lake salt flat 40F4
Gregory Range hills 40E4
Gregory Range hills 41I3
Greifswald 13N3
Grenå 11G8
Grenada 47J5
Grenada country 51L6
Grenfell 42D4
Grenoble 18G4
Gretna 16F6
Grevena 21I4
Greybull 46F3
Greymouth 43C6
Grey Range hills 42A2
Gribanovskiy 23I6
Griffin 47K5
Griffith 42C5
Grimari 34C3
Grimsby 14G5
Grimshaw 44G4
Grimstad 11F7
Grindavík 10□
Grindsted 11F9
Grmeč mts 20G2
Groblersdal 37I3
Groningen 13K4
Groote Eylandt i. 41H2
Grootfontein 35B5
Groot Swartberge mts 36E7
Grootvloer salt pan 36E5
Grosseto 20D3
Groß-Gerau 13L6
Großglockner mt. 13N7
Grover Beach 49B3
Groznyy 23J8
Grubišno Polje 20G2
Grudziądz 13Q4
Gryazi 23H5
Gryazovets 22I4
Gryfice 13O4
Gryfino 13O4
Guadalajara 19E3
Guadalajara 50D4
Guadalcanal i. 41M1
Guadalquivir r. 19C5
Guadalupe Victoria 46G7
Guadarrama, Sierra de mts 19D3
Guadeloupe terr. 51L5
Guadix 19E5
Guaíba 55A5
Guaíra 54F2
Gualeguay 54E4
Gualeguaychu 54E4
Guam terr. 29G6
Guamúchil 46F6
Guanajuato 50D4
Guanambi 55C1
Guanare 52E2
Guane 51H4
Guangyuan 27J3
Guangzhou 27K4
Guanhães 55C2
Guantánamo 51I4
Guapé 55B3
Guaporé 55A5
Guaporé r. 52E6
Guarabira 53K5
Guaranda 52C4
Guarapari 55C3
Guarapuava 55A4
Guararapes 55A3
Guaratinguetá 55B3
Guaratuba 55A4
Guarda 19C3
Guarujá 55B3
Guasave 46F6
Guatemala 50F6
Guatemala country 50F5
Guaxupé 55B3
Guayaquil 52C4
Guayaquil, Golfo de g. 52B4
Guaymas 46E6
Gubkin 23H6
Gudermes 23J8
Guéckédou 32B4
Guelma 20B6
Guelmine 32B2
Guelph 48A1
Guéret 18E3
Guernsey terr. 15E9
Guérou 32B3
Guider 33E4
Guidonia-Montecelio 20E4
Guiglo 32C4
Guildford 15G7
Guilin 27K4
Guimarães 19B3
Guimarães 53J4
Guinea country 32B3
Guinea, Gulf of 32D4
Guinea-Bissau country 32B3
Güines 51H4
Guiratinga 53H7
Guiyang 27J4
Gujranwala 27G3
Gukovo 23H6
Gulbarga 27G5
Gulbene 11O8
Gulfport 47J5
Guliston 27F2
Gul'kevichi 23I7
Gulu 34D3
Gumare 35C5
Gumel 32D3
Guna 27G4
Gundagai 42D5
Güney 21M5
Gunnison 46F4
Guntakal 27G5
Gunungsitoli 29B7
Gurinhatã 55A2
Gurupá 53H4
Gurupi 53I6
Gur'yevsk 11L9
Gusau 32D3
Gusev 11M9
Gushan 31A5
Gusinoozersk 25L4
Gus'-Khrustal'nyy 22I5
Güstrow 13N4
Gütersloh 13L5
Guwahati 27I4
Guyana country 53G2
Guymon 46G4
Guyra 42E3
G'uzor 26F3
Gvardeysk 11L9
Gwalior 27G4
Gwanda 35C6
Gwardafuy, Gees c. 34F2
Gweru 35C5
Gweta 35C6
Gwoza 32E3
Gydan Peninsula 24I2
Gympie 41K5
Gyöngyös 13Q7
Győr 20G1
Gytheio 21J6
Gyula 21I1
Gyumri 23I8

H

Haapsalu 11M7
Haarlem 12J4
Habbān 34E2
Hachinohe 30F4
Hackensack 48D2
Haddington 16G5
Hadejia 32E3
Haderslev 11F9
Hadhramaut 34E2
Hadyach 23G6
Haeju 31B5
Haenam 31B6
Hagåtña 29E6
Hagen 13K5
Hagerstown 48C3
Hagfors 11H6
Hagi 31C6
Hagueneau 18H2
Haida Gwaii 44E4
Haifa 33G1
Haikou 27K4
Ha'il 26D4
Hailsham 15H8
Hailun 30B3
Hainan Dao i. 27K5
Haiti country 51J5
Hajdúböszörmény 21J1
Hajjah 34E2
Hakodate 30F4
Hakui 31E5
Halaib Triangle terr. 33G2
Halberstadt 13M5
Halden 11G7
Haldensleben 13M4
Halesowen 15E6
Halesworth 15I6
Halifax 14F5
Halifax 45L5
Halle (Saale) 13M5
Hällefors 11I7
Hallein 13N7
Hallsberg 11I7
Halls Creek 40F3
Halmahera i. 29E7
Halmstad 11G8
Hals 11G8
Haltwhistle 14E4
Hamada 31C6
Hamadān 33H1
Hamāh 33G1
Hamamatsu 31E6
Hamar 11G6
Hambantota 27H6
Hamburg 13L4
Hamburg 48L1
Hamden 48E2
Hämeenlinna 11N6
Hameln 13L4
Hamersley Range mts 40D4
Hamhŭng 31B5
Hami 27J2
Hamilton 16E5
Hamilton 43E3
Hamilton 47K4
Hamilton 48B1
Hamilton 51L2
Hamina 11O6
Hamju 31B5
Hamm 13K5
Hammamet 20D6
Hammamet, Golfe de g. 20D6
Hammerfest 10M1
Hammonton 48D3
Hampshire Downs hills 15F7
Hampton 48C4
Hanak 34D1
Hanamaki 31F5
Handan 27F3
Handeni 35D4
Hanford 49C2
Hangayn Nuruu mts 27I2
Hangzhou 28E4
Hangzhou Wan b. 28E4
Hanko 11M7
Hanna 44G4
Hannibal 47I4
Hannover 13L4
Hanöbukten b. 11I9
Hanover 48C4
Hantsavichy 11O10
Hanzhong 27J3
Haparanda 10N4
Happy Valley-Goose Bay 45L4
Haradh 34E1
Haradok 23E6
Haramachi 31F5
Harare 35D3
Harbin 30B3
Hardangerfjorden sea chan. 11D7
Hardap admin. reg. 36C3
Harer 34E3
Hargeysa 34E3
Harima-nada b. 31D6
Harjavalta 11M6
Harleston 15I6
Harlow 15H7
Harney Basin 46C3
Härnösand 10J5
Harper 32C4
Harris, Sound of sea chan. 16B3
Harrisburg 48C2
Harrison 47I4
Harrisonburg 48B3
Harrisonville 47I4
Harrogate 14F5
Hârşova 21L3
Harstad 10J2
Hartberg 13O7
Hartford 48E2
Hartlepool 14F4
Harvey 46G2
Harwich 15I7
Haslemere 15G7
Hasselt 12J5
Hässleholm 11H8
Hastings 15H8
Hastings 43F4
Hastings 46H3
Hastings 47I3
Hatfield 14G5
Hatteras, Cape 47L4
Hattiesburg 47J5
Hat Yai 29C7
Haud reg. 34E3
Haugesund 11D7
Haukeli 11D7
Hauraki Gulf 43E2
Haut Atlas mts 32C1
Haute-Normandie admin. reg. 15I9
Hauts Plateaux 32C1
Havana 51H4
Havant 15G8
Haverfordwest 15C7
Havlíčkův Brod 13O6
Havøysund 10N1
Havre 46F2
Havre Rock i. 41J6
Havza 23G8

I

Iaçu 55C1
Ianca 21L2
Iaşi 21L2
Ibadan 32D4
Ibagué 52C2
Ibaiti 55A3

Hawai'i i. 46□
Hawick 16G5
Hawke Bay 43F4
Haxby 14F4
Hay 42B5
Hay watercourse 41H4
Haymā' 26E5
Hayrabolu 21L4
Hay River 44G3
Hays 46H4
Haysyn 23I6
Hayward 49A2
Haywards Heath 15G8
Hazleton 48D2
Ḥ'a'il 26D4
Hegang 30E3
Heide 13L3
Heidelberg 13L6
Heidelberg 37I4
Heihe 30B2
Heilbronn 13L6
Heiligenhafen prov. 30C3
Heilong Jiang r. 30D2
Heinola 11N6
Hekla vol. 10□²
Horn 13O6
Horn, Cape 54C9
Horncastle 14G5
Hornefors 10K5
Hornsby 42E4
Horodenka 23E6
Horodnya 23F6
Horodok 23D6
Horodok 23E6
Horsens 11F8
Horsham 15G7
Horsham 41I7
Horten 11G7
Hoshiarpur 27G3
Hotan 27I3
Hot Springs 47I5
Houghton 47J2
Houghton le Spring 14F4
Houma 47I6
Houston 47H6
Hovd 27I2
Hove 15G8
Hovmantorp 11I8
Hövsgöl Nuur l. 27J1
Howden 14G5
Howick 37J5
Howland Island terr. 39I1
Howlong 42C5
Höxter 13L5
Hoy i. 16F2
Hoyerswerda 13O5
Hradec Králové 13O5
Hrazdan 23J8
Hrebinka 23G6
Hrodna 23D6
Hsinchu 28E5
Huacho 52C6
Huadian 30B4
Huaibei 27K3
Huaihua 27J4
Huainan 27K3
Huajuápan de León 50E5
Huambo 35B5
Huanan 30C3
Huancavelica 52C6
Huancayo 52C6
Huanren 30B4
Huánuco 52C5
Huaráz 52C5
Huasco 54B3
Hidalgo del Parral 46F6
Hidrolândia 55B2
Highlands 48E2
Highland Springs 48C4
High Level 44G4
High Point 47L4
High Prairie 44G4
High Wycombe 15G7
Higüey 51K5
Hiiumaa i. 11L7
Hijaz reg. 34D1
Hikone 31E6
Hildesheim 13L4
Hillah 33H1
Hillerød 11H9
Hillston 42B4
Hilo 46□
Hilton Head Island 47K5
Hilversum 12J4
Himalaya mts 27G3
Himarë 21I4
Himeji 31D6
Hinckley 15F6
Hindley 14E5
Hindu Kush mts 26F3
Hinesville 47K5
Hinthada 27I5
Hirosaki 30F4
Hiroshima 31D6
Hirson 18G2
Hirtshals 11F8
Hisar 27J4
Hispaniola i. 51J4
Hitachi 31F5
Hitachinaka 31F5
Hjälmaren l. 11I7
Hjørring 11F8
Hlotse 37I5
Hluhhiv 23J6
Hlukhiv 23I6
Hlybokaye 11O9
Ho 32D4
Hobart 41J8
Hobbs 46G5
Ho Chi Minh City 29C6
Hoddesdon 15G7
Hodeidah 34E2
Hódmezővásárhely 21I1
Hof 13M5
Hofors 11J6
Hofsjökull ice cap 10□²
Höganäs 11H8
Hohhot 27K2
Hoh Xil Shan mts 27H3
Hoima 34D3
Hokkaidō i. 30F4
Hokksund 11G7
Holbæk 11H9
Holbrook 46C5
Holdrege 46H3
Holguín 51I4
Hollabrunn 13O6
Hollidaysburg 48B2
Holmes 18H5
Holly Springs 47J5
Hollywood 47K6
Holmestrand 11G7
Holmsund 10L5
Holstebro 11F8
Holt 15I6
Holyhead 14C5
Holyhead Bay 14C5
Holy Island 14C5
Holy Island 14F3
Home Bay 45L3
Homer 48C1

Ibarra 52C3
Ibb 34E2
Iberian Peninsula 19
Ibiá 55B2
Ibiapaba, Serra da hills 53J4
Ibiassucê 55C1
Ibicaraí 55D1
Ibirama 55A4
Ibitinga 55A3
Ibiza 55A3
Ibiza 55A3
Ibiza i. 19G4
Ibotirama 53J6
Ibrā' 26E4
Ibri 26E4
Ica 52C6
Icatu 53J4
Iceland country 10□²
Ichinomiya 31E6
Ichinoseki 31F5
Ichnya 23G6
Ico 53K5
Iconha 55C3
Idah 32D4
Idaho state 46E3
Idaho Falls 46E3
Idar-Oberstein 13K6
Idfu 33G2
Idiofa 35B4
Idlib 33G1
Iepê 55A3
Ifakara 35D4
Ifanadiana 35E6
Ife 32D4
Ifenat 33I3
Iferouâne 32D3
Ifôghas, Adrar des hills 32D3
Iganga 35D4
Igarapava 55B3
Igarka 24J3
Iggesund 11J6
Iglesias 20C5
Igdnangna 11O9
Igoumenitsa 21I5
Iguaí 55C1
Iguala 50E5
Igualada 19G3
Iguape 55B4
Iguatemi 54F2
Iguatu 53K5
Ih Tol Gol 30A2
Ihosy 35E6
Iisalmi 10O5
Iizuka 31C6
Ijebu-Ode 32D4
IJssel r. 13J4
IJsselmeer l. 12J4
Ijuí 54F3
Ikare 32D4
Ikaria i. 21L6
Ikast 11F8
Ikhtiman 21J3
Ikom 32D4
Iksan 31B6
Ikungu 35D4
Ilagan 29E6
Ilām 33H1
Iława 13N4
Ilebo 35C4
Ilemi Triangle terr. 34D3
Ileza 22I3
Ilfeld 13M5
Ilford 15H7
Ilfracombe 15C7
Ilgaz 23G8
Ilha Grande, Represa resr 54F2
Ílhavo 19B3
Ilhéus 55D1
Ilkeston 15F6
Ilkley 14F5
Illapel 54B4
Illéla 32D3
Iller r. 13L6
Illichivs'k 21N1
Illinois r. 47I4
Illinois state 47J4
Illizi 32D2
Ilmen', Ozero l. 22F4
Ilo 52D7
Iloilo 29E6
Ilorin 32D4
Ilovlya 23I6
Iululissat 45M3
Imari 31B6
Imaichi 31E5
Imarra 21L6
Imatra 11P6
Imbituba 55A4
Imbituva 55A4
Imola 20D2
Imperatriz 53I5
Imperia 20C3
Imperial 49E4
Imperial Beach 49D4
Impfondo 34B3
Imphal 27I4
İmroz 21K4
İnarijärvi l. 10O2
Inca 19G3
Inch'ŏn 31B5
Indaal, Loch b. 16C5
Indalsälven r. 10J5
Inda Silasē 34D2
Independence 47I4
Inder 26E2
India country 27G4
Indiana 48B2
Indiana state 47J3
Indianapolis 47J4
Indianola 47I3
Indigirka r. 25P2
Indija 21I2
Indio 49D4
Indonesia country 29D8
Indore 27G4
Indus r. 27G4
Indus, Mouths of the 26F4
İnebolu 23G8
İnegöl 21L4
Inglewood 42E2
Inglewood 49C4
Ingolmells 14F5
Ingolstadt 13M6
Inhambane 35D5
Inhambane prov. 37L2
Inhumas 55A2
Inner Sound sea chan. 16D3
Innisfail 41J3
Innsbruck 13M7
Inongo 34B4
Inowrocław 13J4
In Salah 32D2
Inta 24H3
International Falls 47I1
Inukjuak 45K4
Inuvik 44E3
Invercargill 43B8
Invergordon 16E3
Inverkeithing 16F4
Inverness 16E3
Investigator Group is 40G6
Investigator Strait 41H7
Inyonga 35D4
Inza 23I5
Inzhavino 23I5

Ioannina 21I5
Iola 47H4
Iona i. 16C4
Ionian Islands 21H5
Ios i. 21K6
Iowa state 47I3
Iowa City 47I3
Ipameri 55B2
Ipanema 55C2
Ipatinga 55C2
Ipatovo 23I7
Ipiá 55D1
Ipiranga 55A4
Ipoh 29C7
Iporá 55A2
Ippy 34C3
Ipsala 21L4
Ipswich 15I6
Ipswich 42F1
Ipu 53J4
Iqaluit 45L3
Iquique 54B2
Iquitos 52D4
Irai 54F3
Iraklion 21K7
Iramaia 55C1
Iran country 26E3
Irapuato 50D4
Iraq country 33H1
Irará 55D1
Irati 55A4
Irbid 33G1
Irbit 24H4
Irecê 53J6
Ireland country 17E4
Ireland i. 17
Irgiz 26F2
Irian Jaya reg. 29G8
Irinjalakuda 27G6
Íríri r. 53H4
Irish Sea 17G4
Iritua 53I4
Irkutsk 25L4
Irondequoit 48C1
Iron Mountain 47J2
Irosin 29E6
Irpin' 23F6
Irrawaddy r. 27I5
Irtysh r. 27G1
Irún 19E5
Irvine 16E5
Irvine 49C4
Isa 32D3
Isabela 29E7
Isafjardardjúp est. 10□²
Ísafjördur 10□²
Ise 31E6
İsère r. 18G4
Isernia 20F4
Ise-wan b. 31E6
Iseyin 32D4
Ishikari-wan b. 30F4
Ishinomaki 31F5
Ishioka 31F5
Isil'kul' 24I4
Isipingo 37J5
Isiro 34C3
Iskenderun 33G1
Iskitim 24J4
Islamabad 27G3
Islands, Bay of 43E2
Islay i. 16C5
Isoka 35D5
Isparta 21N5
Isperikh 21L3
Issia 32C4
Issoire 18F4
Istanbul 21M4
İstiaia 21J5
Istres 18G5
Istria pen. 20E2
Itaberá 55A3
Itaberaba 55C1
Itaberaí 55A2
Itabira 55C2
Itabirito 55C3
Itabuna 55D1
Itacajá 53I5
Itacarambi 55B1
Itacoatiara 53G4
Itaeté 55C1
Itaguaçu 55C2
Itaguaí 55C3
Itaí 55A3
Itaiópolis 55A4
Itaituba 53G4
Itajaí 55A4
Itajubá 55B3
Italy country 20E3
Itamarandiba 55C2
Itambacuri 55C2
Itambé 55C1
Itanhaém 55C2
Itaobím 55C2
Itapaci 55A2
Itapajipe 55A2
Itapebi 55D1
Itaperuna 55B3
Itapecuru Mirim 53J4
Itapemirim 55C3
Itaperuna 55C3
Itapetinga 55C1
Itapetininga 55A3
Itapeva 55A3
Itapicuru 53J6
Itapipoca 53K4
Itapira 55B3
Itaporanga 55A3
Itaqui 54E3
Itaúna 55B3
Itaúna 55C3
Itea 21J5
Ithaca 48C1
Itiquira 53H7
Itiruçu 55C1
Itô 31E6
Itu 55C1
Ituaçu 55C1
Ituberá 55D1
Ituiutaba 55A2
Itumbiara 55A2
Itupiranga 53I5
Ituporanga 55A4
Iturama 55A2
Itzehoe 13L4
Ivalo 10O2
Ivanava 11N10
Ivankiv 23F6
Ivano-Frankivs'k 23E6
Ivanovo 22I4
Ivanteyevka 23K5
Ivatsevichy 11N10
Ivaylovgrad 21L4
Ivdel' 24H3
Ivrea 20B2
Ivujivik 45K3
Ivyanets 11O10
Iwaki 31F5
Iwamizawa 30F4
Iwo 32D4
Ixmiquilpán 50E4
Ixtlán 50D4
Ixworth 15I6

Izberbash 23J8
Izhevsk 24G4
Izmayil 21M2
İzmir 21L5
İzmir Körfezi g. 21L5
İzmit 21M4
Iztochni Rodopi mts 21K4
Izumo 31D6
Izyaslav 23E6
Iz'yayu 22M2
Izyum 23H6

J

Jabalpur 27G4
Jablanica 20G3
Jaboatão dos Guararapes 53L5
Jaboticabal 55A3
Jacareí 55B3
Jacarèzinho 55A3
Jacinto 55C2
Jackson 47I5
Jackson 47I5
Jackson 47I4
Jacksonville 47I4
Jacksonville 47K5
Jacksonville 47L5
Jacmel 51J5
Jacobabad 26F4
Jacobina 53J6
Jacunda 53I4
Jaén 19E5
Jaffa, Cape 41H7
Jaffna 27H6
Jagdalpur 27H5
Jaguarão 54F4
Jaguariaíva 55A4
Jaguaripe 55D1
Jahrom 26E3
Jaicós 53J5
Jaipur 27G4
Jaisalmer 27G4
Jajarkot 27H3
Jakarta 29C8
Jakobstad 10M5
Jalālābād 27G3
Jalandhar 27G3
Jales 55A3
Jalgaon 27G4
Jalingo 32E4
Jalna 27G5
Jalpa 50D4
Jalpaiguri 27H4
Jamaica country 51I5
Jamaica Channel 51I5
Jambi 29C8
James r. 46H3
James Bay 45J4
Jamestown 41H6
Jamestown 46H2
Jamestown 48B1
Jammu 27G3
Jāmsā 11N6
Jämsänkoski 10N6
Jamshedpur 27H4
Janaúba 55C1
Janesville 47J3
Januária 55B1
Japan country 31D5
Japan, Sea of 31D5
Japurá r. 52F4
Jaraguá 55A2
Jaraguá do Sul 55A4
Jardinópolis 55B3
Jarocin 13P5
Jarosław 23D6
Jarrettsville 48C3
Jarú 52F6
Järvenpää 11N6
Jäsk 26E4
Jasło 23D6
Jasper 44G4
Jasper 47I5
Jastrzębie-Zdrój 13Q6
Jászberény 21H1
Jataí 55A2
Jaú 55A3
Jauja 52C6
Java i. 29C8
Java, Laut sea 29D8
Jawhar 34E3
Jawor 13P5
Jaya, Puncak mt. 29F8
Jayapura 29G8
Jedburgh 16G5
Jedda 34D1
Jefferson City 47I4
Jeffreys Bay 36B8
Jēkabpils 11N8
Jelenia Góra 13O5
Jelgava 11M8
Jember 29D8
Jena 13M5
Jendouba 20C6
Jennings 47I5
Jequié 55C1
Jequitinhonha 55C2
Jérémie 51J5
Jerez 50D4
Jerez de la Frontera 19C5
Jerome 46E3
Jersey i. 15E9
Jersey City 48D2
Jerumenha 53J5
Jerusalem 33G1
Jervis Bay 42E5
Jervis Bay Territory admin. div. 42E5
Jesenice 20F1
Jesi 20E3
Jessheim 11G6
Jesup 47K5
Jhang Sadar 27G3
Jhansi 27G4
Jharsuguda 27H4
Jiamusi 30C3
Ji'an 27K4
Ji'an 30B4
Jianyang 28D5
Jiaohe 30B4
Jiaozuo 27J3
Jiaxing 28E4
Jiayuguan 27I3
Jieznas 11N9
Jihlava 13O6
Jijel 32D1
Jijiga 34E3
Jilib 34E3
Jilin 30B4
Jima 34D3
Jiménez 46F6
Jiménez 46F7
Jim Thorpe 48D2
Jīnan 28D2
Jindřichův Hradec 13O6
Jingdezhen 28D5
Jinggu 30B5
Jingmen 27J3
Jingyuan 27J3
Jingzhou 27J3
Jinhua 28D5
Jining 27J2
Jining 28D3
Jinja 34D3
Jinotepe 51G6
Jinxi 28D5
Jinzhong 27K3
Jinzhou 27L2
Ji-Paraná 52F6
Jipijapa 52B4
Jiquiriçá 55D1
Jishou 27J4
Jiu r. 21J3
Jiujiang 28D5
Jixi 30D3
Jixian 30C3

Jīzān 34E2
Jizzax 26F2
João Pessoa 53L5
João Pinheiro 55B2
Jodhpur 27G4
Joensuu 10P5
Joetsu 31E5
Jōgeva 11O7
Johannesburg 37H4
John Day 46D3
John o' Groats 16F2
Johnsonburg 48D1
Johnstone 16E5
Johnstown 48D1
Johor Bahru 29C7
Joinville 18G2
Joinville 55A4
Joliet 47J3
Jonava 11N9
Jonesboro 47I5
Jones Sound sea chan. 45J2
Jönköping 11I8
Jonquière 45K5
Joplin 47I4
Jordan 27I4
Jordan country 33G1
Jos 32D4
José de San Martín 54B6
Joseph Bonaparte Gulf 40F2
Jos Plateau 32D4
Jouberton 37H4
Joutseno 11P6
Juan Aldama 46G7
Juan de Fuca Strait strait 44F5
Juan Fernández, Islas is 53I5
Juazeiro 53J5
Juazeiro do Norte 53K5
Juba 33G4
Jubba r. 34E3
Júcar r. 19F4
Juchitán 50E5
Judenburg 13O7
Juigalpa 51G6
Juína 55D3
Juiz de Fora 55C3
Juliaca 52D7
Jumilla 19F4
Junagadh 27G4
Junction City 47I4
Jundiaí 55B3
Juneau 44E4
Junee 42C5
Jungfrau mt. 18H3
Junggar Pendi basin 27G2
Junín 54D4
Juodupė 11N8
Jura i. 16D4
Jura mts 18G4
Jura, Sound of sea chan. 16D5
Jurbarkas 11M9
Jūrmala 11M8
Juruti 53G4
Jussara 55A1
Jutaí 52E5
Jutiapa 50G6
Juticalpa 51G6
Jutland pen. 11F8
Jwaneng 36G3
Jyväskylä 10N5

K

K2 mt. 27G3
Kaarina 11M6
Kabale 34C4
Kabalo 35C4
Kabarega Bight b. 43C5
Kabinda 35C4
Kabong 35C4
Kābul 27F3
Kabwe 35C5
Kachchh, Rann of marsh 27G4
Kachia 32D4
Kachreti 23J8
Kachug 25L4
Kadıköy 21M4
Kadoma 35C5
Kaduna 32D3
Kaduy 22H4
Kaédi 32B3
Kaélé 33E3
Kaesŏng 31B5
Kafanchan 32D4
Kafue 35C5
Kafue r. 35C5
Kaga 31E5
Kaga Bandoro 34B3
Kagoshima 31C7
Kagoshima pref. 31C7
Kahama 35D4
Kahnūj 26E4
Kahramanmaraş 26C3
Kaifeng 27J3
Kainan 31D6
Kaiyuan 30B4
Kaiyuan 30B4
Kajaani 10O4
Kajakı Dam 26F3
Kaka 26F3
Kakamega 34D3
Kakata 32B4
Kakhovka 21O1
Kakinada 27H5
Kakogawa 31D6
Kalabáka 21I5
Kalabo 35C5
Kalach 21I2
Kalach-na-Donu 23I6
Kalajoki 10M4
Kalamaria 21J4
Kalamata 21J6
Kalamazoo 47J3
Kalanchak 21O1
Kalanshiyū ar Ramlī al Kabīr, Sarīr des. 33F1
Kale 21M6
Kalemie 35C4
Kalevala 10Q4
Kalgoorlie 40E6
Kali 20F2
Kalima 34C4
Kalimantan reg. 29D8
Kaliningrad 11L9
Kalininsk 23I6
Kalinkavichy 23F5
Kalispell 46E2
Kalisz 13P5
Kalixälven r. 10M3
Kalkan 21M6
Kallsjön l. 10H5
Kalmar 11I8
Kalmar 11I8
Kalundborg 11G9
Kalush 23D6
Kalyazin 22H4
Kama 34C4
Kama r. 24G4
Kamaishi 31F5
Kamanjab 35B5
Kamchatka Peninsula 25Q4
Kamenjak, Rt 20E2
Kamenka 23J5
Kämen'-na-Obi 24J4
Kamensk-Shakhtinskiy 23I6

Kamensk-Ural'skiy 24H4
Kamina 35C4
Kamloops 44F4
Kampene 34C4
Kâmpóng Cham 29C6
Kâmpóng Saôm 29C6
Kâmpóng Thum 29C6
Kâmpôt 29C6
Kam"yanets'-Podil's'kyy 23E6
Kam"yanka-Buz'ka 23E6
Kamyanyets 11M10
Kämyärän 33H1
Kamyshin 23J6
Kamyzyak 23J7
Kananga 35C4
Kanash 22J5
Kanazawa 31E5
Kanchipuram 27G5
Kandahār 26E3
Kandalaksha 10R3
Kandi 32D3
Kandıra 21M4
Kandos 42D4
Kandy 27H6
Kandyagash 26E2
Kâne'ohe 46□
Kangän 26E4
Kangar 29C7
Kangaroo Island 41H7
Kanggye 30B4
Kangnŭng 31C5
Kangping 30A4
Kaniama 35C4
Kanifing 32B3
Kanin, Poluostrov pen. 22J2
Kankaanpää 11M6
Kankakee 47J3
Kankan 32C3
Kano 32D3
Kanoya 31C7
Kanpur 27H4
Kansas state 46H4
Kansas City 47I4
Kansk 25K4
Kantchari 32D3
Kantemirovka 23H6
Kanyamazane 37J5
Kaohsiung 28E5
Kaolack 32B3
Kapiri Mposhi 35C5
Kapoeta 33G4
Kaposvár 20G1
Kapuskasing 45J5
Kapuvár 20G1
Kapyl' 11O10
Kara 32D4
Karabalyk 26F1
Karabük 23G8
Karacaköy 21M4
Karacasu 21L6
Karachayevsk 23I8
Karachev 23G5
Karachi 26F4
Karaganda 27G2
Karagayly 27G2
Karahallı 21L5
Karaj 26E3
Kara-Köl 27G2
Karakol 27G2
Karakoram Range mts 27G3
Karaman 33G1
Karamanlı 21L5
Karaman 27H2
Karamürsel 21M4
Karas admin. reg. 36C4
Karasburg 36B3
Karasu 21M4
Karasuk 24I4
Karatau 27G2
Karatsu 31C6
Karbalā' 33H1
Karcag 21I1
Karditsa 21I5
Kärdla 11M7
Kareima 33G3
Kareliya, Respublika aut. rep. 10R5
Kargalinskaya 23J8
Kargopol' 22H3
Kariba 35C5
Kariba, Lake resr 35C5
Kariba Dam 35C5
Karimata, Selat strait 29C8
Karksi-Nuia 11N7
Karlıova 23I8
Karlovac 20F2
Karlovy Vary 13N5
Karlsborg 11I8
Karlshamn 11I8
Karlskoga 11I7
Karlskrona 11I8
Karlsruhe 13L6
Karlstad 11H7
Karnal 27G3
Karnobat 21L3
Karoi 35C5
Karonga 35D4
Karpenisi 21I5
Karpogory 22J2
Karratha 40D4
Kars 23I8
Karsava 11O8
Karstan 27J3
Karun r. 33H1
Karvina 13Q6
Karwar 27G5
Karymskoye 25M4
Karystos 21K5
Kasai r. 34C4
Kasama 35D5
Kasane 35C5
Kasese 34D3
Kasevo 11Q4
Kashan 26E3
Kashary 23I6
Kashgar 27G3
Kashira 23H5
Kashiwazaki 31J5
Kasimov 23I5
Kashmir 26E3
Kaskö 11L5
Kasongo 35C4
Kasongo-Lunda 35B4
Kaspiysk 23J8
Kassala 33G3
Kassel 13L5
Kasserine 20C7
Kastamonu 23G8
Kastoria 21I4
Kastsyukovichy 23G5
Kasulu 35C4
Katakwi 34D3
Katanning 40D6
Katerini 21J4
Katete 35D5
Kathmandu 27H4
Katihar 27H4
Katima Mulilo 35C5

Katiola 32C4
Katlehong 37I4
Kato Achaïa 21I5
Katoomba 42E4
Katowice 13Q5
Kātrīnā, Jabal mt. 33G2
Katrine, Loch l. 16E4
Katrineholm 11J7
Katsina 32D3
Katsina-Ala 32D4
Katsuura 31F6
Kattegat strait 11G8
Kaua'i Channel 46□
Kauhajoki 10M5
Kauhava 10M5
Kaunas 11M9
Kaura-Namoda 32D3
Kavadarci 21J4
Kavak 23H8
Kavala 21K4
Kavalerovo 30D3
Kavarna 21L3
Kavīr-e Lūt des. 26E3
Kavīr, Dasht-e des. 26E3
Kawagoe 31E6
Kawaguchi 31E6
Kawasaki 31E6
Kawm Umbū 33G2
Kawthoung 29C6
Kaya 32D3
Kayseri 23H6
Kazakhstan country 26F2
Kazan' 22J5
Kazanlŭk 21K3
Kaz Dağı mts 21L5
Kazincbarcika 23D6
Kazmın 26E3
Kéa i. 21K6
Keady 17F3
Kearney 46H3
Kebili 32D1
Keçiborlu 21N6
Kecskemét 21I1
Kédainiai 11M9
Kedong 30B3
Kędzierzyn-Koźle 13Q5
Keene 48E1
Keetmanshoop 36D4
Keffi 32D4
Keflavík 10□²
Kegen 27G2
Kehra 11N7
Keighley 14F5
Keith 16G3
Keith 41J7
Kelibia 20D6
Kelkit r. 26C2
Kelmė 11M9
Kélo 33E4
Kelowna 44G5
Keluang 29C7
Kem' 10R4
Kemalpaşa 21L5
Kemer 21M6
Kemerovo 24J4
Kemi 10N4
Kempen 13K5
Kempele 10N4
Kempten (Allgäu) 13M7
Kempton Park 37J3
Kendal 14E4
Kendari 29E8
Kendawangan 29D8
Kenema 32B4
Kenge 35B4
Kenhardt 36E5
Kénitra 32C1
Kennewick 46D2
Kenosha 47J3
Kent 48A2
Kentucky state 47K4
Kenya country 34D3
Kenya, Mount 34D3
Keokuk 47I3
Keppel Bay 41K4
Kepsut 21M5
Kerang 42A5
Kerava 11N6
Kerch 23H7
Kerema 38E2
Keren 33G3
Kerewan 32B3
Kericho 34D4
Kerkyra 21H5
Kermadec Islands 39I5
Kermān 26E3
Kermit 46G5
Kerrville 46H5
Keşan 21L4
Keşap 23H8
Kesennuma 31F5
Kestel'ga 10Q4
Keswick 14D4
Keszthely 20G1
Kettering 15G6
Keuruu 10N5
Keyihe 30A2
Key Largo 47K6
Keynsham 15E7
Keyser 48B3
Key West 47K7
Kgalagadi admin. dist. 36E3
Kgalagadi Transfrontier National Park 36C4
Kgatleng admin. dist. 37H3
Kgotsong 37H4
Khabarovsk 30D2
Khabarovskiy Kray admin. div. 30D2
Khairpur 27F4
Khamar-Daban, Khrebet mts 25L4
Khamgaon 27G4
Khamis Mushayt 34E2
Khandyga 25P3
Khanewal 27G3
Khanka, Lake 30D3
Khanpur 27G4
Khanty-Mansiysk 24H3
Kharabali 23J7
Kharagpur 27H4
Kharan 26F4
Kharkiv 23H6
Kharmanli 21K4
Khartoum 33G3
Khasavyurt 23J8
Khāsh 26E4
Khashm el Girba 33G3
Khaskovo 21K4
Khaybar 34D1
Khayelitsha 36B8
Khemis Miliana 19H5
Khenchela 20D7
Khenifra 32C1
Kherson 21O1
Khilok 25M4
Khlevnoye 23H5
Khmel'nyts'kyy 23E6
Khmil'nyk 23E6
Khodoriv 23E6
Kholm 22F4
Khomas admin. reg. 36C2
Khon Kaen 29C6
Khor 30D2
Khorol 23G6
Khorramābād 33H1

Kladno 13O5
Klagenfurt 13O7
Klaipėda 11L9
Klaksvík 10□¹
Klamath r. 44F5
Klamath Falls 46C3
Klatovy 13N6
Klerksdorp 37H4
Kletnya 23G5
Kletskaya 23I6
Klimavichy 23G5
Klimovo 23G5
Klin 22H4
Klintsy 23G5
Ključ 20G2
Kłodzko 13P5
Klosterneuburg 13P6
Kluczbork 13Q5
Klyetsk 11O10
Klyuchevskaya, Sopka vol. 25R4
Knaresborough 14F4
Knighton 15D6
Knittelfeld 13O7
Knjaževac 21J3
Knockmealdown Mountains hills 17D5
Knoxville 47K4
Knysna 36F8
Kōbe 31D6
Koblenz 13K5
Kobryn 11N10
K'obulet'i 23I8
Kočani 21J4
Kočevje 20F2
Kōchi 31D6
Kōchi 31C6
Kochubeyevskoye 23I7
Kodiak 44C4
Kodiak Island 44C4
Kodino 22H3
Kodyma 23F6
Koforidua 32C4
Kōfu 31E6
Køge 11H9
Kohila 11N7
Kohīma 27I4
Kohtla-Järve 11O7
Kokkola 10M5
Kokomo 47J3
Kokosi 37H4
Kokpekty 27H2
Kokshetau 27F1
Kokstad 37I6
Kola 10R2
Kolaka 29E8
Kolding 11F9
Koléa 19H5
Kolhapur 27G5
Kolín 13O6
Kolka 11M8
Kolkata 27G5
Kollam 27G6
Kołobrzeg 13O3
Kolokani 32C3
Kolomna 23H5
Kolomyya 23E6
Kolondiéba 32C3
Kolonedale 38C2
Kolpashevo 24J4
Kolpny 23H5
Koluli 33H3
Kolwezi 35C5
Kolyma r. 25R3
Kolymskiy, Khrebet mts 25R3
Kolyshley 23I5
Komaki 31E6
Komárno 13J7
Komatsu 31E5
Kominternivs'ke 21N1
Komiža 20G3
Komló 20H1
Komotini 21K4
Komsomol'sk 23G6
Komsomol'sk-na-Amure 30E2
Kondoa 35D3
Kondopoga 22G3
Kondrovo 23G5
Kong Christian X Land reg. 45M3
Kong Frederik IX Land reg. 45M3
Kongolo 35C4
Kongoussi 32C3
Kongsberg 11G7
Kongsvinger 11H6
Konin 13Q4
Konosha 22I3
Konotop 23G6
Konstantinovka 30B2
Konstanz 13L7
Konya 33G1
Koper 20E2
Köping 11I7
Koprivnica 20G1
Korablino 23I5
Korçë 21I4
Korčula i. 20G3
Korea Bay g. 31B5
Korea Strait strait 31C6
Korenovsk 23H7
Korets' 23E6
Korfez 21M4
Korhogo 32C4
Kōriyama 31F5
Korkuteli 21N6
Korla 27G2
Körmend 20G1
Koro 32C3
Koro i. 39H3
Korocha 23H6
Korogwe 35D4
Korop 23I6
Korosten' 23E6
Korostyshiv 23E6
Korsakov 30F3
Korsør 11G9
Korsun'-Shevchenkivs'kyy 23F6
Kortrijk 12I5
Koryazhma 22J3
Koryŏng 31C6
Kos 21L6
Kos i. 21L6
Kosan 21B5
Kościan 13P4
Kościerzyna 13P3
Kosciuszko, Mount 42D6
Koshki 23K5
Košice 23D6
Kosŏng 31C5
Kosovo country 21I3
Kostanay 26F1
Kostenets 21J3
Kostinbrod 21J3
Kostomuksha 10Q4
Kostopil' 23E6
Kostroma 22I4
Kostyantynivka 23H6
Koszalin 13O3
Köszeg 20G1
Kota 27G4
Kotabaru 29D8
Kota Bharu 29C7
Kota Kinabalu 29D7
Kotel 21L3
Kotel'nikovo 23I7
Kotel'nyy, Ostrov i. 25O2
Kotido 34D3
Kotka 11O6
Kotlas 22J3
Kotovo 23J6

Kotovsk 23I5
Koudougou 32C3
Koulikoro 32C3
Koumac 39G4
Koundâra 32B3
Koupéla 32C3
Kourou 53H2
Kouroussa 32C3
Koussérі 33E3
Koutiala 32C3
Kouvola 11O6
Kovdor 10Q3
Kovel' 23E6
Kovernino 22I4
Kovrov 22I4
Kovylkino 23I5
Kowanyama 41I3
Köyceğiz 21M6
Kozani 21I4
Kozara *mts* 20G2
Kozelets' 23F6
Kozel'sk 23G5
Kozhikode 27G5
Kozlu 21N4
Koz'modem'yansk 22J4
Kožuf *mts* 21J4
Kozyatyn 23F6
Kpalimé 32D4
Krabi 29B7
Krâchéh 29C6
Kragerø 11F7
Kragujevac 21I2
Kraków 13Q5
Kramators'k 23H6
Kramfors 10J5
Kranidi 21J6
Kranj 20F1
Krāslava 11O9
Krasnaya Gorbatka 22I5
Krasnoarmeysk 23J6
Krasnoarmiys'k 23H6
Krasnoborsk 22J3
Krasnodar 23H7
Krasnodon 23H6
Krasnogorodsk 11P8
Krasnogvardeyskoye 23I7
Krasnohrad 23G6
Krasnohvardiys'ke 23G7
Krasnoperekops'k 23G7
Krasnoslobodsk 23I5
Krasnoyarsk 24K4
Krasnyy 23F5
Krasnyye Baki 22J4
Krasnyy Kholm 22H4
Krasnyy Kut 23J6
Krasnyy Luch 23H6
Krasnyy Lyman 23H6
Krasnyy Yar 23K7
Krasyliv 23E6
Krefeld 13K5
Kremenchuk 23G6
Krems an der Donau 13O6
Kresttsy 22G4
Kretinga 11L9
Kribi 32D4
Kristiansand 11E7
Kristianstad 11I8
Kristiansund 10E5
Kristinehamn 11I7
Kritiko Pelagos *sea* 21K6
Krk *i.* 20F2
Krolevets' 23G6
Kronshtadt 11P7
Kroonstad 37H4
Kropotkin 23I7
Krosno 23D6
Krotoszyn 13P5
Krui 29C8
Krumovgrad 21K4
Krupki 23F5
Kruševac 21I3
Krychaw 23F5
Krymsk 23H7
Kryvyy Rih 23G7
Ksar Chellala 19H6
Ksar el Boukhari 19H6
Ksar el Kebir 19D6
Ksour Essaf 20D7
Kstovo 22J4
Kuala Lipis 29C7
Kuala Lumpur 29C7
Kuala Terengganu 29C7
Kuandian 30B4
Kuantan 29C7
Kubrat 21L3
Kuching 29D7
Kuçovë 21H4
Kudat 29D7
Kufstein 13N7
Kugesi 22J4
Kuhmo 10P4
Kuito 35B5
Kujang 31B5
Kuji 31F4
Kukës 21I3
Kukmor 22K4
Kula 21M5
Kular 25O2
Kuldīga 11L8
Kulebaki 23I5
Kulmbach 13M5
Kŭlob 27F3
Kul'sary 26E2
Kulunda 24I4
Kumagaya 31E5
Kumamoto 31C6
Kumano 31E6
Kumanovo 21I3
Kumasi 32C4
Kumba 32D4
Kumdah 34E1
Kumeny 22K4
Kumertau 24G4
Kumi 31C5
Kumi 33G4
Kumla 11I7
Kumo 32E3
Kumylzhenskiy 23I6
Kungälv 11G8
Kungsbacka 11H8
Kunlun Shan *mts* 27G3
Kunming 27J4
Kunsan 31B6
Kuopio 10O5
Kupang 40E2
Kupiškis 11N9
Kup"yans'k 23H6
Kuqa 27H2
Kurashiki 31D6
Kurayoshi 31D6
Kurchatov 23G6
Kŭrdzhali 21K4
Kure 31D6
Kuressaare 11M7
Kurgan 24H4
Kurganinsk 23I7
Kurikka 10M5
Kuril Islands 30H3
Kurkino 23H5
Kurmuk 33G3
Kurnool 27G5
Kuroiso 31F5
Kurri Kurri 42E4
Kursavka 23I7
Kursk 23H6
Kurskaya 23J7
Kurşunlu 23G8
Kuruman 36F4
Kurume 31C6
Kurunegala 27H6
Kuşadası 21L6
Kushchevskaya 23H7
Kushiro 30G4
Kushmurun 26F1
Kusŏng 31B5
Kütahya 21M5
K'ut'aisi 23I8
Kutjevo 20G2
Kutno 13Q4
Kutu 34B4
Kutztown 48D2
Kuusamo 10P4
Kuusankoski 11O6
Kuvshinovo 22G4
Kuwait 26D4
Kuwait *country* 26D4
Kuybyshev 24I4
Kuybysheve 23H7
Kuybyshevskoye Vodokhranilishche *resr* 23K5
Kuytun 27H2
Kuyucak 21M6
Kuznetsk 23J5
Kuznetsovs'k 23E6
Kuzovatovo 23J5
Kvarnerić *sea chan.* 20F2
Kwale 32D4
KwaMashu 37J5
Kwa Mtoro 35D4
Kwangju 31B6
Kwanobuhle 37G7
Kwatarkwashi 32D3
Kwatinidubu 37H7
KwaZulu-Natal *prov.* 37J5
Kwekwe 35C5
Kweneng *admin. dist.* 36G2
Kwidzyn 13Q4
Kyakhta 25L4
Kyaukpyu 27I5
Kymi 21K5
Kyneton 42B6
Kyogle 42F2
Kyŏngju 31C6
Kyōto 31D6
Kyparissia 21I6
Kyrgyzstan *country* 27G2
Kythira *i.* 21J6
Kyūshū *i.* 31C7
Kyustendil 21J3
Kyzyl 24K4
Kyzylkum Desert 26F2
Kyzyl-Mazhalyk 24K4
Kyzylorda 26F2

L

Laagri 11N7
Laâyoune 32B2
La Banda 54D3
Labasa 39H3
Labé 32B3
Labinsk 23I7
Labouheyre 18D4
Laboulaye 54D4
Labrador *reg.* 45L4
Labrador City 45L4
Labrador Sea 45M3
Lábrea 52F5
Labuhanbilik 27J6
Labuna 29E8
Labytnangi 24H3
La Carlota 54D4
Laccadive Islands 27G5
Lac du Bonnet 47H1
La Ceiba 51G5
Lachlan *r.* 42A5
La Chorrera 51I7
Lachute 45K5
La Ciotat 18G5
Lac La Biche 44G4
Laconia 48F1
La Crosse 47I3
Ladainha 55C2
La Déroute, Passage de *strait* 15E9
Ladik 23G8
Ladoga, Lake 11Q6
Ladysmith 37I5
Lae 38E2
Lafayette 47I5
Lafayette 47J3
Lafia 32D4
Lafiagi 32D4
La Flèche 18D3
La Galite, Canal de *sea chan.* 20C6
Lagan' 23J7
Lagan *r.* 17G3
Lågen *r.* 11G7
Laghouat 32D1
Lago Agrio 52C3
Lagoa Santa 55C2
Lagoa Vermelha 55A5
Lagos 19B5
Lagos 32D4
Lagosa 35C4
La Grande 46D2
La Grande 4, Réservoir *resr* 45K4
La Grange 47J5
La Gran Sabana *plat.* 52F2
Laguna 55A5
Laha 30B2
La Habra 49D4
Lahad Datu 29D7
La Hague, Cap de *c.* 15F9
Lahat 29C8
Laḥij 34E2
Lahore 27G3
Lahti 11N6
Laï 33E4
Laidley 42F1
Laihia 10M5
L'Aïr, Massif de *mts* 32D3
Laishevo 22K5
Laitila 11L6
Laiyang 28E4
Laizhou Wan *b.* 27K3
Lajeado 55A5
Lajes 53K5
Lajes 55A4
La Junta 46G4
La Juventud, Isla de *i.* 51H4
Lake Cargelligo 42C4
Lake Charles 47I5
Lake City 47K5
Lake Havasu City 49E3
Lakehurst 48D2
Lakeland 47K6
Lake Providence 47I5
Lakes Entrance 42D6
Lakeside 48C4
Lakewood 48B1
Lakewood 48D2
Lakhdenpokh'ya 10Q6
Lakota 32C4
Lakselfjorden *sea chan.* 10O1
La Ligua 54B4
Lalín 19B2
La Línea de la Concepción 19D5
Lalitpur 27G4
La Louvière 12J5
Lamar 46G4
La Martre, Lac *l.* 44G3
Lambaréné 34B4
Lambayeque 52C5
Lambert's Bay 36D7
Lambeth 48A1
Lamego 19C3
La Merced 52C6
La Merced 54C3
Lamesa 46G5
La Mesa 49D4
Lamia 21J5
Lammermuir Hills 16G5
Lamont 49C3
Lampang 29B6
Lampazos 46G6
Lamu 34E4
Lancaster 14E4
Lancaster 47K5
Lancaster 48C2
Lancaster 49C3
Lancaster Sound *strait* 45J2
Landeck 13M7
Lander 46F3
Landsberg am Lech 13M6
Land's End *pt* 15B8
Landshut 13N6
Landskrona 11H9
Langenthal 18H3
Langjökull *ice cap* 10□[2]
Langport 15E7
Langres 18G3
Langsa 27I6
Långsele 10J5
Lannion 18C2
Lansing 47K3
Lanxi 30B3
Lanzarote *i.* 32B2
Lanzhou 27J3
Laoag City 29E6
Lao Cai 27J4
Laojunmaio 27I3
Laon 18F2
La Oroya 52C6
Laos *country* 29C6
Laotougou 30C4
Lapa 55A4
La Palma 51I7
La Palma *i.* 32B2
La Paz 46E7
La Paz 50G6
La Paz 52E7
La Paz 54E4
La Pérouse Strait *strait* 30F3
La Plata 54E4
La Plata, Río de *sea chan.* 54E4
Lappeenranta 11P6
Lappland *reg.* 10K3
Lâpseki 21L4
Laptev Sea 25N2
Lapua 10M5
La Quiaca 54C2
L'Aquila 20E3
La Quinta 49D4
Larache 19C6
Laramie 46F3
Laranjal Paulista 55B3
Laranjeiras do Sul 54F3
Larba 19H5
Laredo 46H6
Largs 16E5
L'Ariana 20D6
La Rioja 54C3
La Rioja *aut. comm.* 19E2
Larisa 21J5
Larne 17G3
La Rochelle 18D3
La Roche-sur-Yon 18D3
La Romana 51K5
La Ronge 44H4
La Ronge, Lac *l.* 44H4
Larvik 11G7
Las Cruces 46F5
La Serena 54B3
Las Heras 54C4
Las Palmas de Gran Canaria 32B2
La Spezia 20C2
Las Tablas 51H7
Las Termas 54D3
Las Tunas 51I4
Las Varas 50C4
Las Varillas 54D4
Las Vegas 46F4
Las Vegas 49E2
Latacunga 52C4
Latakia 33G1
La Teste-de-Buch 18D4
Latina 20E4
La Tuque 47M2
Latvia *country* 11N8
Lauchhammer 13N5
Laudio 19E2
Launceston 15C8
Launceston 41J8
Laurel 47J5
Laureldale 48D2
Laurel Hill *hills* 48B3
Laurinburg 47L5
Lausanne 18H3
Lautoka 39H3
Laval 18D2
La Vall d'Uixó 19F4
La Vega 51J5
Lavras 55B3
Lawra 32C3
Lawrence 47H4
Lawrence 48F1
Lawrenceburg 47J4
Lawton 46H5
Lazarev 30F1
Lazarevac 21I2
Lázaro Cárdenas 50D5
Lazdijai 11M9
Leamington Spa, Royal 15F6
Leatherhead 15G7
Lebanon 47I4
Lebanon 48C2
Lebanon 48E1
Lebanon *country* 33G1
Lebedyan' 23H5
Lębork 13P3
Lebowakgomo 37I3
Lebrija 19C5
Lebu 54B5
Lecce 20H4
Lecco 20C2
Lechaina 21I6
Le Creusot 18G3
Le Crotoy 15I8
Ledesma 19D3
Ledmozero 10R4
Leeds 14F5
Leek 15E5
Leesburg 48C3
Leesville 47I5
Leeuwarden 13J4
Leeuwin, Cape 40D6
Leeward Islands 51L5
Lefkada 21I5
Lefkada *i.* 21I5
Lefkimmi 21I5
Legnago 20D2
Legnica 13P5
Le Havre 15H9
Lehmo 10P5
Leibnitz 13O7
Leicester 15F6
Leiden 12J4
Leigh 14E5
Leigh Creek 41H6
Leighton Buzzard 15G7
Leipzig 13N5
Leiria 19B4
Leirvik 11D7
Leizhou Bandao *pen.* 27J4
Le Kef 20C6
Leksand 11I6
Lelystad 12J4
Le Mans 18E2
Le Mars 47H3
Leme 55B3
Lemmon 46G2
Lemoore 49C2
Le Murge *hills* 20G4
Lemvig 11F8
Lena *r.* 25N2
Lenham 15H7
Lenine 23G7
Leningradskaya 23H7
Leningradskaya Oblast' *admin. div.* 11R7
Leningradskiy 25S3
Leninsk 23J6
Leninskiy 23H5
Leninsk-Kuznetskiy 24J4
Leninskoye 30D3
Lens 18F1
Lensk 25M3
Lenti 20G1
Lentini 20F6
Léo 32C3
Leoben 13O7
Leominster 15E6
Leominster 48F1
León 19D2
León 50D4
León 51G6
Leongatha 42B7
Leonidio 21J6
Leonidovo 30F2
Leonora 40E5
Leopoldina 55C3
Lepontine, Alpi *mts* 18I3
Le Puy-en-Velay 18F4
Lerala 37H2
Léré 32C3
Lerma 19E2
Le Roy 48C1
Lerum 11H8
Lerwick 16□
Lesbos *i.* 21K5
Les Cayes 51J5
Leshan 27J4
Leshukonskoye 22J2
Leskovac 21I3
Lesosibirsk 24K4
Lesotho *country* 37I5
Lesozavodsk 30D3
L'Espérance Rock *i.* 39I5
Les Sables-d'Olonne 18D3
Lesser Antilles *is* 51K6
Lesser Caucasus *mts* 23I8
Lesser Slave Lake 44G4
Leszno 13P5
Letchworth Garden City 15G7
Lethbridge 44G5
Leticia 52E4
Letnerechenskiy 22G2
Le Touquet-Paris-Plage 15I8
Letterkenny 17E3
Leuchars 16G4
Leuven 12J5
Levanger 10G5
Levashi 23J8
Levelland 46G5
Leven 14G5
Leven, Loch *l.* 16F4
Lévêque, Cape 40E3
Leverkusen 13K5
Levice 13Q6
Levittown 48D2
Levittown 48E2
Lev Tolstoy 23H5
Lewes 15H8
Lewis, Isle of *i.* 16C2
Lewisburg 48C2
Lewis Range *mts* 46E2
Lewiston 46D2
Lewiston 46F2
Lewistown 46F2
Lewistown 48C2
Lexington 46H3
Lexington 47K4
Lexington 48B4
Lezhë 21H4
L'gov 23G6
Lhasa 27I4
Lianyungang 28D4
Liaodong Wan *b.* 27L2
Liaoning *prov.* 30A4
Liaoyang 30A4
Liaoyuan 30B4
Liaozhong 30A4
Libenge 34B3
Liberal 46G4
Liberec 13O5
Liberia 51G6
Liberia *country* 32C4
Libourne 18D4
Libreville 34A3
Libya *country* 33E2
Libyan Desert 33F2
Libyan Plateau 33F1
Licata 20E6
Lichfield 15F6
Lichinga 35D5
Lichtenburg 37H4
Lida 11N10
Lidköping 11H7
Liebig, Mount 40G4
Liechtenstein *country* 18I3
Liège 13J5
Lieksa 10Q5
Lienz 13N7
Liepāja 11L8
Liezen 13O7
Liffey *r.* 17F4
Lifford 17E3
Lightning Ridge 42C2
Ligurian Sea 18I5
Lika *reg.* 20F2
Likasi 35C5
Likhoslavl' 22G4
Lilla Edet 11H7
Lille 18F1
Lillehammer 11G6
Lillestrøm 11G7
Lilongwe 35D5
Lima 47K3
Lima 48C1
Lima 52C6
Lima Duarte 55C3
Liman 23J7
Limavady 17F2
Limbaži 11N8
Limeira 55B3
Limerick 17D5
Limmen Bight *b.* 41H2
Limnos *i.* 21K5
Limoeiro 53K5
Limoges 18E4
Limon 46G4
Limoux 18F5
Limpopo *prov.* 37I2
Limpopo *r.* 37K3
Limpopo National Park 37J2
Linares 19E4
Linares 46H7
Linares 54B5
Lincoln 14G5
Lincoln 47H3
Lincoln 47J3
Lincoln 54D4
Lindau (Bodensee) 13L7
Linden 53G2
Lindi 35D4
Lindian 30B3
Line Islands 6
Linfen 27K3
Lingen (Ems) 13K4
Lingga, Kepulauan *is* 29C8
Linhares 55C2
Linhe 27J2
Linjiang 30B4
Linköping 11I7
Linkou 30C3
Linlithgow 16F5
Linnhe, Loch *inlet* 16D4
Lins 55A3
Linxi 27K2
Linxia 27J3
Linyi 27K3
Linz 13O6
Lion, Golfe du *g.* 18F5
Lipetsk 23H5
Lipova 21I1
Lira 34D3
Lisala 34C3
Lisbon 19B4
Lisburn 17F3
Lishu 30B4
Lisieux 18E2
Liski 23H6
Lismore 42F2
Lithgow 42E4
Lithuania *country* 11M9
Litoměřice 13O5
Little Andaman *i.* 27I5
Little Belt *sea chan.* 11F9
Little Cayman *i.* 51H5
Little Falls 47I2
Littlefield 46G5
Littlehampton 15G8
Little Minch *sea chan.* 16B3
Little Rock 47I5
Liupanshui 27J4
Liuzhou 27J4
Livadeia 21J5
Livermore 49B2
Liverpool 14E5
Liverpool 42E4
Liverpool Plains 42E3
Liverpool Range *mts* 42D3
Livingston 16F5
Livingston 46E2
Livingston 47I5
Livingstone 35C5
Livno 20G3
Livny 23H5
Livorno 20D3
Livramento do Brumado 55C1
Lizard Point 15B9
Ljubljana 20F1
Ljungby 11H8
Ljusdal 11J6
Llandovery 15D7
Llandudno 14D5
Llanelli 15C7
Llangollen 15D6
Llano Estacado *plain* 46G5
Llanos *plain* 52E2
Llantrisant 15D7
Llay 15D5
Lleida 19G3
Lobatse 37G3
Loberia 54E5
Lobito 35B5
Lobos 54E5
Lochy, Loch *l.* 16E4
Lockerbie 16F5
Lock Haven 48C2
Lockport 48B1
Lodeynoye Pole 22G3
Lodi 20C2
Lodi 49B1
Lodja 34C4
Łódź 13Q5
Lofoten *is* 10H2
Log 23I6
Logan 46E3
Logan, Mount 44D3
Logatec 20F2
Logroño 19E2
Loimaa 11M6
Loire *r.* 18C3
Loja 19D5
Loja 52C4
Løkken 10F5
Loknya 22F4
Lokoja 32D4
Lokossa 32D4
Lokot' 23G5
Lolland *i.* 11G9
Lom 21J3
Lomas de Zamora 54E4
Lombok *i.* 40D1
Lombok, Selat *sea chan.* 29D8
Lomé 32D4
Lomond, Loch *l.* 16E4
Lomonosov 11P7
Lompoc 49B3
Łomża 13S4
London 15G7
London 47K4
London 48A1
Londonderry 17E3
Londonderry, Cape 40F2
Londrina 55A3
Longa, Proliv *sea chan.* 25S2
Long Ashton 15E7
Long Beach 49C4
Long Branch 48E2
Long Eaton 15F6
Longford 17E4
Long Island 48E2
Long Island Sound *sea chan.* 48E2
Longjiang 30A3
Longmeadow 48E1
Long Melford 15H6
Longmont 46F3
Long Point Bay 48A1
Longreach 41I4
Longtown 14E3
Longview 47I5
Long Xuyên 29C6
Longyan 28D5
Longyearbyen 24C2
Lönsboda 11I8
Lons-le-Saunier 18G3
Lop Buri 29C6
Lop Nur *salt flat* 27I2
Lorain 45J5
Lorca 19F5
Lord Howe Island 41L6
Lorena 55B3
Loreto 53I5
Lorient 18C3
Lorn, Firth of *est.* 16D4
Lorrain, Plateau 18H2
Los Alamos 46F4
Los Angeles 49C3
Los Ángeles 54B5
Los Banos 49B2
Los Chonos, Archipiélago de *is* 54A6
Los Juríes 54D3
Los Mochis 46F6
Lossiemouth 16F3
Los Teques 52E1
Lostwithiel 15C8
Los Vilos 54B4
Lot *r.* 18E4
Lota 54B5
Louangnamtha 28C5
Louangphabang 29C6
Loubomo 35B4
Louga 32B3
Loughborough 15F6
Loughrea 17D4
Loughton 15H7
Louisiade Archipelago *is* 41K2
Louisiana *state* 47I5
Louisville 47J4
Loukhi 10R3
Loulé 19B5
Loum 32D4
Louny 13N5
Lourdes 18D5
Louth 14G5
Loutra Aidipsou 21J5
Lovech 21K3
Loviisa 11O6
Lovington 46G5
Lowell 48F1
Lower Hutt 43E5
Lower Lough Erne *l.* 17E3
Lowestoft 15I6
Łowicz 13Q4
Loxton 41I6
Loyauté, Îles *is* 39G4
Loyew 23F6
Loznica 21H2
Lozova 23H6
Luanda 35B4
Luanshya 35C5
Luau 35C5
Luba 32D4
Lubaczów 23D6
Lubango 35B5
Lubao 35C4
Lubartów 23D6
Lubbock 46G5
Lübeck 13M4
Lubin 13P5
Lublin 23D6
Lubny 23G6
Lubumbashi 35C5
Lucala 35B4
Lucapa 35C4
Lucca 20D3
Luce Bay 16E6
Lucélia 55A3
Lucena 19D5
Lucena 29E6
Lučenec 13Q6
Lucera 20F4
Lucerne 18I3
Luchegorsk 30D3
Luckenwalde 13N4
Lucknow 27H4
Lüdenscheid 13K5
Lüderitz 36B4
Ludhiana 27G3
Ludvika 11I6
Ludwigsburg 13L6
Ludwigshafen am Rhein 13L6
Ludza 11O8
Luebo 35C4
Luena 35B5
Lufkin 47I5
Luga 11P7
Lugano 18I3
Lugo 19C2
Lugo 20D2
Lugoj 21I2
Luhans'k 23H6
Lukhovitsy 23H5
Lukovit 21K3
Łuków 23D6
Lukoyanov 23J5
Luleå 10M4
Luleälven *r.* 10M4
Lüleburgaz 21L4
Lumberton 47L5
Lumbrales 19C3
Lumezzane 20D2
Lund 11H9
Lundy *i.* 15C7
Lune *r.* 14E4
Lüneburg 13M4
Lunéville 18H2
Luninyets 11O10
Lunsar 32B4
Luobei 30C3
Luohe 27K3
Luoyang 27K3
Lupane 35C5
Lupeni 21J2
Lurgan 17F3
Lusaka 35C5
Lusambo 35C4
Lushnjë 21H4
Lutherstadt Wittenberg 13N5
Luton 15G7
Luts'k 23E6
Lutzville 36D6
Luwero 34D3
Luwuk 29E8
Luxembourg 13K6
Luxembourg *country* 13K6
Luxor 33G2
Luza 22J3
Luzhou 27J4
Luziânia 55B2
Luzon *i.* 29E6
Luzon Strait *strait* 29E5
L'viv 23E6
Lyakhavichy 11O10
Lycksele 10K4
Lydd 15H8
Lyel'chytsy 23F6
Lyepyel' 11P9
Lyme Bay 15E8
Lyme Regis 15E8
Lymington 15F8
Lynchburg 48B4
Lynn 48F1
Lyon 18G4
Lyozna 23F5
Lysekil 11G7
Lyskovo 22J4
Lys'va 24G4
Lysychans'k 23H6
Lysyye Gory 23J6
Lytham St Anne's 14D5
Lyuban' 11P10
Lyubim 22I4
Lyudinovo 23G5

M

Ma'ān 33G1
Maastricht 13J5
Mabaruma 52G2
Mablethorpe 14H5
Mabopane 37I3
Macaé 55C3
Macajuba 55C1
Macao 27K4
Macapá 53H3
Macará 52C4
Macarani 55C1
Macas 52C4
Macau 53K5
Macclesfield 14E5
Macdonnell Ranges *mts* 40G4
Macduff 16G3
Macedonia *country* 21I4
Maceió 53K5
Macenta 32C4
Macerata 20E3
Machachi 52C4
Machakos 34D4
Machala 52C4
Machilipatnam 27H5
Machiques 52D1
Machu Picchu *tourist site* 52D6
Machynlleth 15D6
Măcin 21M2
Macintyre Brook *r.* 42E2
Mackay 23H8
Mackay 41J4
Mackenzie *r.* 44E3
Mackenzie Bay 44E3
Mackenzie Mountains 44E3
Macksville 42F3
Maclean 42F2
Macomb 47I3
Mâcon 18G3
Macon 47I4
Macon 47K5
Madadeni 37J4
Madagascar *country* 35E6
Madan 21K4
Madang 38E2
Madaoua 32D3
Madeira *r.* 52G4
Madeira *terr.* 32B1
Madera 46F6
Madgaon 27G5
Madingou 35B4
Madison 47H3
Madison 47I3
Madison 47J4
Madison Heights 48B4
Madisonville 47J4
Madona 11O8
Madra Dağı *mts* 21L5
Madrakah 33G2
Madre, Laguna *lag.* 47H6
Madre del Sur, Sierra *mts* 50D5
Madre Occidental, Sierra *mts* 46F6
Madre Oriental, Sierra *mts* 46G6
Madrid 19E3
Madurai 27G6
Maebashi 31E5
Maevatanana 35E5
Mafadi *mt.* 36I5
Mafeteng 37H5
Maffra 42C6
Mafinga 35D4
Mafra 55A4
Magabeni 37J6
Magadan 25Q4
Magangué 52D2
Magaria 32D3
Magas 23J8
Magdagachi 30B1
Magdalena 46E5
Magdeburg 13M4
Magellan, Strait of 54B8
Maggiore, Lake 20C2
Magherafelt 17F3
Maghnia 19F6
Maghull 14E5
Magnitogorsk 24G4
Magnolia 47I5
Mago 30F1
Magta' Lahjar 32B3
Magwe 27I4
Mahābād 33H1
Mahajanga 35E5
Mahalapye 37H2
Mahalevona 35E5
Mahanoro 35E5
Maha Sarakham 27J5
Mahd adh Dhahab 34E1
Mahdia 19G6
Mahdia 20D7
Mahdia 53G2
Mahenge 35D4
Mahilyow 23F5
Mahón 19I4
Maicao 52D1
Maidenhead 15G7
Maidstone 15H7
Maiduguri 32E3
Maine *state* 47N2
Maine, Gulf of 45L5
Mainland *i.* 16F1
Mainland *i.* 16□
Maintirano 35E5
Mainz 13L5
Maitland 42E4
Maizuru 31D6
Majene 29D8
Majorca *i.* 19H4
Makabana 34B4
Makale 29D8
Makanchi 27H2
Makarov 30F2
Makar'yev 22I4
Makassar 29D8
Makassar, Selat *strait* 29D8
Makat 26E2
Makeni 32B4
Makgadikgadi *depr.* 35C6
Makhachkala 23J8
Makinsk 27G1
Makiyivka 23H6
Makkah 34D1
Makokou 34B3
Maksatikha 22G4
Makunguwiro 35D5
Makurdi 32D4
Malabar Coast 27G5
Malabo 32D4
Malacca, Strait of *strait* 29B7
Maladzyechna 11O9
Málaga 19D5
Malaita *i.* 39G2
Malakal 33G4
Malanje 35B4
Mälaren *l.* 11J7
Malargüe 54C5
Malatya 26C3
Malawi *country* 35D5
Malaya Vishera 22G4
Malāyer 33H1
Malaysia *country* 29C7
Malbork 13Q3
Maldives *country* 27G6
Maldon 15H7
Maldon 42B6
Maldonado 54F4
Male 7
Malgobek 23J8
Malhada 55C1
Mali *country* 32C3
Malili 38C2
Malindi 34E4
Malin Head 17E2
Malkara 21L4
Mallawī 33G2
Mallét 55A4
Mallow 17D5
Malmédy 13K5
Malmesbury 15E7
Malmesbury 36D7
Malmö 11H9
Malmyzh 22K4
Maloshuyka 22H3
Maloyaroslavets 23H5
Malta 11O8
Malta *country* 20F7
Malta Channel 20F6
Maltby 14F5
Maluku, Laut *sea* 29E8
Malung 11H6
Maluti Mountains 37I5
Malvern 47I5
Malyn 23F6
Malyye Derbety 23J7
Mamadysh 22K5
Mamelodi 37I3
Mamfe 32D4
Mamoré *r.* 52E6
Mamou 32B3
Mamuju 38B2
Man 32C4
Man, Isle of *terr.* 14C4
Manacapuru 52F4
Manacor 19H4
Manado 29E7
Managua 51G6
Manakara 35E6
Manama 34F1
Mananara Avaratra 35E5
Mananjary 35E6
Manassas 48C3
Manaus 52F4
Manavgat 33G1
Manchester 14E5
Manchester 48C3
Manchester 48E2
Manchester 48F1
Mandal 11E7
Mandalay 27I4
Mandalgovĭ 27J2
Mandan 46G2
Mandeville 51I5
Mandritsara 35E5
Mandsaur 27G4
Mandurah 40D6
Manduria 20G4
Mandya 27G5
Manevychi 23E6
Manfredonia 20F4
Manga 32C3
Manga 55C1
Mangai 34B4
Mangalia 21M3
Mangalore 27G5
Mangaung 37H5
Mangotsfield 15E7
Mangualde 19C3
Manhattan 47H4
Manhica 37K3
Manhuaçu 55C3
Manicouagan, Réservoir *resr* 45L4
Maniitsoq 45M3
Manila 29E6
Manilla 42E3
Manisa 21L5
Manistee 47J3
Manitoba *prov.* 45I4
Manitoba, Lake 45I4
Manitowoc 47J3
Manizales 52C2
Manja 35E6
Mankato 47I3
Mankono 32C4
Mannar, Gulf of 27G6
Mannheim 13L6
Mannington 48A3
Manp'o 30B4
Manresa 19G3
Mansa 35C5
Mansa Konko 32B3
Mansfield 15F5
Mansfield 42C6
Mansfield 47J3
Mansfield 47K3
Manta 52B4
Manteca 49B2
Mantena 55C2
Mantes-la-Jolie 18E2
Mantiqueira, Serra da *mts* 55B3
Mantoudi 21J5
Mäntsälä 11N6
Mänttä 10N5
Mantua 20D2
Manturovo 22J4
Manuel Ribas 55A4
Manuel Vitorino 55C1
Manukau 43E3
Manyas 21L4
Manyoni 35D4
Manzanillo 50D5
Manzanillo 51I4
Manzhouli 27K2
Manzini 37J4
Mao 33E3
Maokeng 37H4
Maple Creek 46F2
Maputo 37K3
Maputo *prov.* 37K3
Maputsoe 37H5
Maqteïr *reg.* 32B2
Maquela do Zombo 35B4
Maraã 52E4
Marabá 53I5
Maracaibo 52D1
Maracaibo, Lake 52D2
Maracaju 54E2
Maracás 55C1
Maracay 52E1
Maradi 32D3
Marajó, Ilha de *i.* 53H4
Marand 26D3
Marañón *r.* 52D4
Marau 55D1
Marbella 19D5
Marble Hall 37I3
Marburg 37J6
Marburg an der Lahn 13L5
Marcali 20G1
March 15H6
Marcona 52C7
Mardan 27G3
Mar del Plata 54E5
Mardin 33H1
Maree, Loch *l.* 16D3
Margate 15I7
Margherita Peak 34C3
Marg'ilon 27G2
Marhanets' 23G7
Mariana 55C3
Marianna 47I5
Marianna 47J5
Ma'rib 34E2
Maribor 20F1
Mariehamn 11K6
Mariental 36C3
Mariestad 11H7
Marietta 47K5
Marietta 48A3
Marignane 18G5
Mariinsk 24J4
Mariinskiy Posad 22J4
Marijampolė 11M9
Marília 55A3
Marín 19B2
Marina 49B2
Mar"ina Horka 11P10
Marinette 47J2
Maringá 55A3
Marinha Grande 19B4
Marion 47J3
Marion 47K3
Marion 47K4
Marion 47L5
Maritime Alps *mts* 18H4
Mariupol' 23H7
Marīvān 33H1
Marka 34E3
Market Deeping 15G6
Market Harborough 15G6
Market Weighton 14G5
Markovo 25S3
Marks 23J6
Marmande 18E4
Marmara, Sea of *g.* 21M4
Marmaris 21M6
Marne *r.* 18F2
Marne-la-Vallée 18F2
Maroantsetra 35E5
Marondera 35D5
Maroochydore 42F1
Maroua 33E3
Marovoay 35E5
Marquesas Islands 6
Marquês de Valença 55C3
Marquette 47J2
Marra, Jebel *mt.* 33F3
Marra, Jebel *plat.* 33F3
Marrakech 32C1
Marsá al 'Alam 33G2
Marsabit 34D3
Marsala 20E6
Marsá Maṭrūḩ 33F1
Marseille 18G5
Marshall 47H3
Marshall 47I4
Marshall 47I5
Marshall Islands *country* 6
Marshalltown 47I3
Märsta 11J7
Martapura 29D8
Martigny 18H3
Martin 13Q6
Martinho Campos 55B2
Martinique *terr.* 51L6
Martinsburg 48C3
Martinsville 47L4
Martos 19E5
Martuk 26E1
Maruim 53K6
Mary 26F3
Maryborough 41K5
Maryland *state* 48C3
Marysville 49B1
Maryville 47I3
Maryville 47K4
Masai Steppe *plain* 35D4
Masaka 34D4
Masan 31C6
Masasi 35D5
Mascara 19G6
Mascote 55D1
Maseru 37H5
Mashhad 26E3
Masilo 37H5
Masindi 34D3
Masjed-e Soleymān 33H1
Mask, Lough *l.* 17C4
Mason City 47I3
Massa 20D2
Massachusetts *state* 48E1
Massachusetts Bay 48F1
Massafra 20G4
Massango 35B4
Massawa 33G3
Massenya 33E3
Massif Central *mts* 18F4
Massillon 48A2
Massina 32C3
Mastaksay 23K6
Masterton 43E5
Mastung 26F4
Mastūrah 34D1
Masty 11N10
Masuda 31C6
Masvingo 35D6
Masvingo *prov.* 37J1
Matabeleland South *prov.* 37I1
Matadi 35B4
Matagalpa 51G6
Matam 32B3
Matamey 32D3
Matamoros 46G6
Matamoros 47H6
Matane 47N2
Matanzas 47K7
Mataram 29D8
Mataró 19H3
Matā'utu 39I3
Matehuala 50D4
Matemanga 35D5
Matera 20G4
Mateur 20C6
Mathura 27G4
Mati 29E7
Matias Cardoso 55C1
Matías Romero 50E5
Matlock 15F5
Mato Grosso *state* 55A1
Mato Grosso, Planalto do *plat.* 53H7
Matosinhos 19B3
Mato Verde 55C1
Matsue 31D6
Matsumoto 31E5
Matsuyama 31D6
Matterhorn *mt.* 18H4
Matterhorn *mt.* 46D3
Maturín 52F2
Matwabeng 37H5
Mauchline 16E5
Maui *i.* 46□
Maun 35C5
Maunatlala 37H2
Mauritania *country* 32B3
Mauritius *country* 7
Mavinga 35C5
Mawlamyaing 27I5
Mawqaq 33H2
Mayagüez 51K5
Maya Mountains 50G5
Maybole 16E5
Maych'ew 34D2
Mayenne 18D2
Maykop 23I7
Maymanah 26F3
Mayna 23J5
Mayotte *terr.* 35E5
Mayskiy 23J8
Mazara del Vallo 20E6
Mazār-e Sharīf 26F3
Mazatlán 50C4
Mažeikiai 11M8
Mazyr 23F5
Mbabane 37J4
Mbahiakro 32C4
Mbaïki 34B3
Mbale 34D3
Mbalmayo 32E4
Mbandaka 34B4
M'banza Congo 35B4
Mbarara 33G5
Mbari *r.* 34C3
Mbeya 35D4
Mbinga 35D5
Mbombela 37J3
Mbouda 32E4
Mbour 32B3
Mbuji-Mayi 35C4
Mburucuyá 54E3
McAlester 47H5
McAllen 46H6
McCall 46D3
McCook 46G3
Mchinga 35D4
McKinley, Mount 44C3
McMinnville 46C2
McPherson 46H4
Mdantsane 37H7
M'Daourouch 20B6
Mead, Lake *resr* 49E2
Meadville 48A2
Meaux 18F2
Mecca 34D1
Mechanicsville 48C4
Mechelen 12J5
Mecheria 32C1
Mecklenburger Bucht *b.* 13M3
Medan 27I6
Médéa 19H5
Medellín 52C2
Medenine 32E1
Medford 46C3
Medford 48E2
Medgidia 21M2
Media 48D3
Mediaş 21K1
Medicine Bow Mountains 46F3
Medicine Hat 44G4
Medina 34D1
Medina 55C2
Medina de Rioseco 19D3
Mediterranean Sea 20D6
Medvedevo 22J4
Medvezh'yegorsk 22G3
Meekatharra 40D5
Meerut 27G4
Megalopoli 21J6
Meiganga 33E4
Meihekou 30B4
Meiktila 27I4
Meiningen 13M5
Meißen 13N5
Meixi 30C3
Meizhou 28D5
Mek'elē 34D2
Mékhé 32B3
Meknès 32C1
Mekong *r.* 27J4
Mekong *r.* 29C6
Melaka 29C7
Melbourne 42B6
Melbourne 47K6
Melenki 23I5
Melilla 19E6
Melitopol' 23G7
Melk 13O6
Melksham 15E7
Melo 54F4
Melrose 16G5
Melton 42B6
Melton Mowbray 15G6
Melun 18F2
Melville Bay 41H2
Melville Island 40G2
Melville Island 45H2
Memmingen 13M7
Memphis 47I4
Mena 23G6
Mena 47I5
Mende 18F4
Mendefera 33G3
Mendeleyevsk 22L5
Mendi 38E2
Mendip Hills 15E7
Mendoza 54C4
Menemen 21L5
Menongue 35B5
Mentawai, Kepulauan *is* 29B8
Menton 18H5
Menzel Bourguiba 20C6
Menzel Temime 20D6
Meppen 13K4
Meqheleng 37H5
Merano 20D1
Merauke 29G8
Merced 49B2
Mercedes 54E3
Mercedes 54E4
Mercês 55C3
Mere 15E7
Merefa 23H6
Mergui Archipelago *is* 27I5
Mérida 19C4
Mérida 50G4
Mérida 52D2
Meriden 48E2
Meridian 47J5
Mérignac 18D4
Merimbula 42D6
Merowe 33G3
Merredin 40D6
Merrill 47J2
Mersa Fatma 33H3
Mersey *est.* 14E5
Mersin 33G1
Merthyr Tydfil 15D7
Merzig 13K6
Mesa 46E5
Mesagne 20G4
Mesolongi 21I5
Mesquita 55C2
Messina 20F5
Messina, Strait of *strait* 20F5
Messini 21J6
Mestre 20E2
Meta *r.* 52E2
Metán 54C3
Methuen 48F1
Metlaoui 32D1
Metu 34D3
Metz 18H2
Meuse *r.* 12J5
Mevagissey 15C8
Mexicali 49E4
Mexico *country* 50D4
Mexico, Gulf of 47H6
Mexico City 50E5
Meyersdale 48B3
Mezdra 21J3
Mezen' 22J2
Mezen' *r.* 22J2
Mezhdurechensk 22K3
Mezhdurechensk 24J4
Mezőtúr 21I1
Miami 47I4
Miami 47K6
Miami Beach 47K6
Mīāndowāb 33H1
Miandrivazo 35E5
Mianwali 27G3
Mianyang 27J3
Marinarivo 35E5
Miass 24H4
Michalovce 23D6
Michigan *state* 47J2
Michigan, Lake 47J3
Michurinsk 23I5
Micronesia, Federated States of *country* 29G7
Middelburg 12I5
Middelburg 37I3
Middelfart 11F9
Middle River 48C3
Middlesbrough 14F4
Middletown 48D2
Middletown 48E2
Midland 46G5
Midland 47L3
Midleton 17D6
Miðvágur 10□[1]
Mielec 23D6
Miercurea-Ciuc 21K1
Mieres 19D2
Miguel Auza 46G7
Mihara 31D6
Mikhaylov 23H5
Mikhaylovka 23I6
Mikhaylovka 30D4
Mikhaylovskoye 24I4
Mikkeli 11O6
Milan 20C2
Milas 21L6
Milazzo 20F5
Mildenhall 15H6
Mildura 41I6
Miles 42E1
Miles City 46F2
Milford 48F1
Milford Haven 15B7
Milford Sound *inlet* 43A7
Miliana 19H5
Mil'kovo 25Q4
Millau 18F4
Milledgeville 47K5
Mille Lacs, Lac des *l.* 45I5
Millerovo 23I6
Millmerran 42E1
Millville 48D3
Milpitas 49B2
Milton Keynes 15G6
Milwaukee 47J3
Mīnāb 26E4
Minahasa, Semenanjung *pen.* 29E7
Minas 27J6
Minas 54E4
Minas Gerais *state* 55B2
Minas Novas 55C2
Minatitlán 50F5
Mindanao *i.* 29E7
Mindelo 32□
Minden 13L4
Minden 47I5
Mindoro *i.* 29E6
Mindouli 34B4
Minehead 15D7
Mineola 48E2
Mineral'nyye Vody 23I7
Mineral Wells 46H5
Minerva 48A2
Mingäçevir 23J8
Minglanilla 19F4
Mingoyo 35D5
Mingshui 30B3
Minna 32D4
Minneapolis 47I3
Minnesota *state* 47I2
Minorca *i.* 19H3
Minot 46G2
Minsk 11O10
Mińsk Mazowiecki 13R4
Minusinsk 24K4
Mirabela 55B2
Miraí 55C3
Miramar 54E5
Miramichi 45L5
Miranda 54E2
Miranda de Ebro 19E2
Mirandela 19C3
Mirandola 20D2
Mirassol 55A3
Mirboo North 42C7
Miri 29D7
Mirim, Lagoa *l.* 54F4
Mirnyy 25M3
Mirpur Khas 27F4
Miryang 31C6
Mirzapur 27H4
Miskolc 23D6
Miṣrātah 33E1
Mission Viejo 49D4
Mississauga 48B1
Mississippi *r.* 47J6
Mississippi *state* 47J5
Missoula 46E2
Missouri *r.* 47I4
Missouri *state* 47I4
Mistassini, Lac *l.* 45K4
Mistelbach 13P6
Mitchell 41J5
Mitchell 46H3
Mitchell *r.* 41I3
Mitchelstown 17D5
Mito 31F5
Mitrovicë 21I3
Mitú 52D3
Mitumba, Chaîne des *mts* 35C5
Miura 31E6
Miyako 31F5
Miyakonojō 31C7
Miyazaki 31C7
Miyazu 31D6
Miyoshi 31D6
Mizen Head 17C6
Mizhhir"ya 23D6
Mizusawa 31F5
Mjölby 11I7
Mkata 35D4
Mladá Boleslav 13O5
Mladenovac 21I2
Mława 13R4
Mlungisi 37H6
Mmabatho 37G3
Moanda 34B4
Moberly 47I4
Mobile 47J5
Mobile Bay 47J5
Moçambique 35E5
Mocha 34E2
Mochudi 37H3
Mocimboa da Praia 35E5
Mocoa 52C3
Mococa 55B3
Mocuba 35D5
Modder *r.* 37G5
Modena 20D2
Modesto 49B2
Moe 42C7
Moelv 11G6

Moffat 16F5
Mogadishu 34E3
Mogi-Mirim 55B3
Mogocha 25M4
Mogoditshane 37G3
Mohács 20H2
Mohale's Hoek 37H6
Mohammadia 19G6
Mohoro 35D4
Mohyliv Podil's'kyy 23E6
Moinesti 21L1
Mo i Rana 10I3
Mojave Desert 49D3
Moji das Cruzes 55B3
Mokhotlong 37I5
Moknine 20D7
Mokopane 37I3
Mokp'o 31B6
Mokrous 23J5
Mokshan 23J5
Molde 10E5
Moldova country 23F7
Moldovei de Sud, Cîmpia plain 21M1
Molepolole 37G3
Molétai 11J9
Molfetta 20G4
Molina de Aragón 19F3
Mollendo 52D7
Mölnlycke 11H8
Molong 42D4
Molopo watercourse 36E5
Moloundou 33E4
Moluccas is 29E8
Mombaça 53K5
Mombasa 34D4
Momchilgrad 21K4
Mompós 52D2
Møn i. 11H9
Monaco country 18H5
Monadhliath Mountains 16E3
Monaghan 17F3
Monastir 20D7
Monastyrshchina 23F6
Monbetsu 30F3
Moncalieri 20B2
Monchegorsk 10R3
Mönchengladbach 13K5
Monclova 46G6
Moncton 45L5
Mondlo 37I4
Mondoví 20B2
Mondragone 20E4
Monfalcone 20E2
Monforte de Lemos 19C2
Mongbwalu 34D3
Mông Cai 27J4
Mongo 33E3
Mongolia country 27J2
Monkey Bay 35D5
Monmouth 15E7
Monopoli 20G4
Monreal del Campo 19F3
Monreale 20E5
Monroe 47I5
Monrovia 32B4
Mons 12I5
Montana 21J3
Montana state 46F2
Montargis 18F3
Montauban 18E4
Mont Blanc mt. 18H4
Montbrison 18G4
Montceau-les-Mines 18G3
Mont-de-Marsan 18D5
Monte Alegre 53H4
Monte Alegre de Goiás 55B1
Monte Alegre de Minas 55A2
Monte Azul 55C1
Monte Azul Paulista 55A3
Montebelluna 20E2
Monte-Carlo 18H5
Monte Cristi 51J5
Montego Bay 51I5
Montélimar 18G4
Montemorelos 46H6
Montemor-o-Novo 19B4
Montenegro country 20I3
Monterey 49B2
Monterey Bay 49A2
Montería 52C2
Monteros 54C3
Monterrey 46G6
Monte Santo 53K6
Montes Claros 55C2
Montesilvano 20F3
Montevarchi 20D3
Montevideo 54E4
Montgomery 47J5
Montgomery 48A3
Monthey 18I3
Monticello 48D2
Montilla 19D5
Montluçon 18F3
Montmagny 45K5
Monto 42D6
Montpelier 47M3
Montpellier 18F5
Montréal 45K5
Montrose 16G4
Montrose 46F4
Mont-St-Aignan 15I9
Montserrat terr. 51L5
Monywa 27I4
Monza 20C2
Moora 40D6
Moorhead 47F3
Mooroopna 42B6
Moose Jaw 44H4
Mopipi 35C6
Mopti 32C3
Moquegua 52D7
Mora 11J3
Mora 33E3
Morada Nova 53K5
Moramanga 35E5
Morar, Loch l. 16D4
Moray Firth b. 16E3
Mordovo 23J5
Morecambe 14E4
Morecambe Bay 14D4
Morella 19F3
Morena, Sierra mts 19C5
Moreni 21K2
Moreton Valley 49D4
Morgan City 47I6
Morganton 47K4
Morgantown 48B3
Morges 18I3
Morioka 31G5
Morisset 42E4
Morki 23K5
Morlaix 18C2
Morley 14F5
Mornington Island 41H3
Morocco country 32C1
Morogoro 35D4
Moro Gulf 29E6

Morombe 35E6
Mörön 27J2
Morondava 35E6
Morón de la Frontera 19D5
Moroni 35C4
Moroto 34D3
Morozovsk 23I6
Morpeth 14F3
Morrinho 55A2
Morrinson 47K4
Morristown 48D2
Morrisville 48D1
Morro do Chapéu 53J6
Morshanka 23J5
Morteros 54D4
Mortlake 42A7
Moruya 42E5
Morvern reg. 16D4
Morwell 42C7
Mosbach 13L6
Moscow 22H5
Moscow 46D2
Moselle r. 18H2
Moses Lake 46D2
Moshi 34D4
Mosjøen 10H4
Mosonmagyaróvár 13P7
Mosquitos, Golfo de los b. 51I7
Moss 11H7
Mossel Bay 36F8
Mossley 14E5
Mössman 41J3
Mossoró 53K5
Most 13N5
Mostaganem 19G6
Mostar 20G3
Mostovskoy 23I7
Mosul 33H1
Motala 11J7
Motherwell 16F5
Motilla del Palancar 19F4
Motril 19E5
Motru 21J2
Mottama, Gulf of 27I5
Motul 50G4
Mouila 34B4
Moulins 18F3
Moultrie 47K5
Moundou 33E4
Moundsville 48A3
Mountain Home 46D3
Mountain Home 47I4
Mount Darwin 35D5
Mount Gambier 41I7
Mount Hagen 38E2
Mount Holly 48D3
Mount Isa 41H4
Mount Magnet 40D5
Mountmellick 17E4
Mount Morris 48C1
Mount Pleasant 47I5
Mount Pleasant 47I5
Mount Pleasant 48B2
Mount's Bay 15B8
Mount Shasta 46C3
Mount Vernon 46C2
Mount Vernon 47I4
Moura 17H9
Moura 41J4
Mourdi, Dépression du depr. 33F3
Mourdiah 32C3
Mourne Mountains hills 17F3
Mouscron 12I5
Mouydir, Monts du plat. 32D2
Moyeni 37H6
Moyobamba 52C5
Mozambique country 35D6
Mozambique Channel strait 35E6
Mozdok 23J8
Mozhaysk 23H5
Mozhga 22L4
Mpanda 35D4
Mpika 35D5
Mpumalanga prov. 37I4
Mpwapwa 35I6
M'Saken 20D7
Mstislaw 23F5
Mtathta 37I6
Mtsensk 23H5
Mtwara 35E5
Mubende 34D3
Mubi 32E3
Muconda 35C5
Mucuri 55C2
Mudanjiang 30C3
Mudanya 21M4
Mudurnu 21M4
Nal'chik 23J8
Nallıhan 21N4
Namahadi 37I4
Namangan 27G2
Nambour 42F1
Nambucca Heads 42F3
Nam Dinh 29C5
Namib Desert 36B3
Namibe 35B5
Namibia country 35B6
Nampa 46D3
Nampala 32C3
Nampo 31B5
Nampula 35D5
Namsos 10I4
Namtsy 25N3
Namtu 27I4
Namur 12J5
Namwŏn 31B6
Nan 29C6
Nanaimo 44F5
Nanao 31E5
Nancha 30C3
Nanchang 27J3
Nanchong 27J3
Nancy 18H2
Nanded 27G5
Nanga Eboko 32E4
Nangalangwa 35D4
Nanjing 28D1
Nan Ling mts 27K4
Nanning 27J4
Nanortalik 45N3
Nanping 28D5
Nansei-shotō is 28E3
Nantes 18D3
Nanticoke 48A1
Nanticoke 48D2
Nantong 28E1
Nantucket Sound g. 48F2
Nantwich 15E5
Nanuque 55C2
Nanyang 27K3
Nanyuki 34D3
Napa 49A1
Napier 43G3
Naples 47K6
Naples 20F4
Napo r. 52D4
Naracoorte 41I7
Naranjal 52C4
Narbonne 18F5
Nardò 21I5
Nares Strait strait 45K2
Narimanov 23J7
Narmada r. 26F4
Narni 20E3

Phuket 29B7
Piacenza 20C2
Piatra Neamţ 21L1
Picardie admin. reg. 15J9
Picardy reg. 18E2
Picauville 15F9
Picayune 47J5
Pichanal 54E2
Pichilemu 54B4
Pickering 14G4
Picos 53J5
Pico Truncado 54C7
Picton 42E5
Piedade 55B3
Piedras Negras 46G6
Pieksämäki 10O5
Pielinen l. 10P5
Piemonte 19B2
Pieštany 13J6
Pietermaritzburg 37J5
Pigg's Peak 37J3
Pihlajavesi l. 10P6
Pikalevo 22G4
Pikeville 47K4
Piła 13P4
Pilar 54E3
Pilar 54E4
Pil'na 22J3
Pimenta Bueno 52E6
Pinamar 54E5
Pinarhisar 21L4
Piñas 52C4
Pínçzów 13R5
Pindaí 55J3
Pindamonhangaba 55B3
Pindus Mountains 21I5
Pine Bluff 47J5
Pinega 22J2
Pinerolo 20B2
Pinetown 37J5
Pingdingshan 27K3
Pingxiang 27J4
Pingxiang 27K4
Pinhal 55B3
Pinheiro 53I4
Pinjarra 40D6
Pinsk 11O10
Pionki 13R5
Piotrków Trybunalski 13Q5
Piracanjuba 55A2
Piracicaba 55B3
Piracununga 55B3
Piracuruca 53J4
Piraeus 21J6
Piraí do Sul 55A4
Piraju 55A3
Pirajuí 55A3
Piranhas 53H7
Piranhas r. 53K5
Pirapora 55B2
Pirenópolis 55A1
Pires do Rio 55A2
Piripiri 53J4
Pirmasens 13K6
Pisa 20D3
Pisco 52C6
Pisek 13O6
Pissis, Cerro 54C3
Pisté 50G4
Pistoia 20D3
Pitanga 55A4
Pitangui 55B2
Pitcairn Islands terr. 6
Piteå 10L4
Piterka 23J5
Piteşti 21K2
Pitkyaranta 22F3
Pitlochry 16F4
Pittsburg 48B2
Pittsfield 48F1
Pittsworth 42E1
Piumhí 55B3
Piura 52B5
Pivka 20F2
Pixley 49C3
Placentia 49B1
Plácido de Castro 52E6
Plainfield 48F2
Plainview 46G5
Planaltina 55B1
Planura 55A3
Plaquemine 47I5
Plasencia 17C3
Plato 52D2
Platte r. 46H3
Plattsburgh 47M3
Plauen 13N5
Plavsk 23H5
Playas 52C4
Pleasantville 48D3
Plenty, Bay of g. 43F3
Plesetsk 22J3
Pleven 21K3
Pljevlja 21H3
Płock 13Q4
Ploieşti 21L2
Plovdiv 21K3
Plungė 11L9
Plymouth 15C8
Plymouth 47J3
Plymouth 48F2
Plymouth (abandoned) 51L5
Plynlimon hill 15D6
Plzeň 13N6
Pô 32C3
Po r. 20E2
Pocatello 46E3
Pochayiv 23E6
Pochep 23E6
Pochinki 23J5
Pochinok 23G5
Pola de Siero 19C2
Polatsk 11P9
Polessk 11L9
Police 13O4
Polkowice 13P5
Polohy 23H7
Polokwane 37I2
Polonne 23E6
Põlva 11O7
Polyarny 10R2
Polyarny 25S3
Polyarnyye Zori 10R3
Polygyros 21I4
Pomeranian Bay 13O3

Pomezia 20E4
Pomona 49D3
Pomorie 21L3
Prachatice 13O6
Prachuap Khiri Khan 29B6
Prado 55D2
Prague 13O5
Praia 32J4
Prainha 53H4
Prairie du Chien 47I3
Prata 55A2
Prata r. 55A2
Prato 20D3
Pratt 46H4
Prechistoye 22I4
Preiji 11O8
Preniai 11J9
Přerov 13P6
Prescott 46G5
Preševo 21I3
Presidencia Roque
Sáenz Peña 54D3
Presidente Dutra 53J5
Presidente Olegário 55B2
Presidente Prudente 55A3
Presidente Venceslau 55A3
Prešov 23D6
Prespa, Lake 21I4
Presque Isle 47N2
Preston 14E5
Prestwick 16E5
Pretoria 37I3
Preveza 21I5
Pribilof Islands 44A4
Priboj 21H3
Price 46E4
Priekule 11L8
Priekuļi 11N8
Prienai 11M9
Prievidza 13Q6
Prijedor 21H3
Prijepolje 21H3
Prilep 21I4
Primorsky Kray admin. div. 30D3
Primorsko-Akhtarsk 23H7
Prince Albert 44H4
Prince Charles Island 45K3
Prince Edward Island prov. 45L5
Prince George 44F4
Prince of Wales Island 45I2
Prince Rupert 44E4
Princess Charlotte Bay 41I2
Princeton 47I6
Princeton 48A4
Princeton 48D2
Prince William Sound b. 44D3
Priozersk 11Q6
Pripet r. 23I7
Pripet Marshes 23E6
Pristinë 21I3
Privas 18G4
Privlaka 20F2
Privolzhsk 22I4
Privolzhskiy 23J6
Privol'zh'ye 23K5
Priyutnoye 23I7
Prizren 21I3
Professor van
Blommestein Meer resr 53G3
Prokhladny 23I8
Prokop'yevsk 24J4
Prokuplje 21I3
Proletarsk 23I7
Promissão 55A3
Propriá 53K6
Provadiya 21L3
Provence reg. 18G5
Providence 48F2
Providenya 25T3
Provo 46E3
Prudentopolis 55A4
Pruszków 13R4
Prut r. 23F7
Pryluky 23F6
Prymors'k 23H7
Przemyśl 23D6
Pskov 11P8
Pskov, Lake 11O7
Pskovskaya Oblast'
admin. div. 11P8
Ptolemaïda 21I4
Ptuj 20F1
Pucallpa 52D5
Puch'ŏn 31B5
Pudong 28E4
Pudozh 22H3
Pudsey 14F5
Puducherry 27G5
Puebla 50E5
Pueblo 46G4
Puente Genil 19D5
Puerto Ángel 50E5
Puerto Armuelles 51I7
Puerto Ayacucho 52E2
Puerto Baquerizo
Moreno 52□
Puerto Barrios 50G5
Puerto Cabello 52E1
Puerto Cabezas 51H6
Puerto Carreño 52E2
Puerto Inírida 52E3
Puerto Lempira 51H5
Puerto Limón 51H6
Puertollano 19D4
Puerto Madryn 54C6
Puerto Maldonado 52E6
Puerto Montt 54B6
Puerto Natales 54B8
Puerto Peñasco 46E5
Puerto Plata 51J5
Puerto Princesa 29D7
Puerto Rico 54E3
Puerto Rico terr. 51K5
Puerto Santa Cruz 54C8
Puerto Supe 52C6
Puerto Vallarta 50C4
Pukapuka 23K3
Pukekohe 43C7
Pula 20E2
Pulaski 48A4
Pullman 46D2
P'ungsan 30C4
Pune 27G4
Púnghŏ 31C4
Punta Alta 54D5
Punta Arenas 54B8
Punta del Este 54F4
Punta Gorda 51H6
Puntarenas 51H6
Puntland reg. 34E3
Puponga 43C5
Purmerend i. 34E2
Puri 27H5
Purus r. 52F4
Puruehŏn 30C4
Puryŏng 30C4
Pusan 31C6
Pushchino 22H3
Pushkin 11Q7
Pushkino 11Q8
Pushkinskiye Gory 11P8
Putian 28D5
Putao 29B7
Putorana Plato 52D1
Putumayo r. 52D4
Pwllheli 15C6
Pyaozerskiy 10Q4
Pyatigorsk 23I7
P''yatykhatky 23G6
Pye 27I5
Pyetrykaw 23F5
Pyinmana 27I5
Pyin-U-Lwin 27I4
Pyle 15D7
Pylos 21I6
P'yŏktong 30B4
Pyŏnggang 31B5
P'yŏngsong 31B5
P'yŏngt'aek 31B5
P'yŏngyang 31B5
Pyrenees mts 19H2
Pyrgos 21I6
Pyryatyn 23G6
Pytalovo 11O8

Q
Qacha's Nek 37I6
Qaidam Pendi basin 27I3
Qaqortoq 45N3
Qarshi 26F3
Qatar country 34F1
Qattara Depression 33F2
Qax 23I8
Qazax 23J8
Qazvin 33H1
Qeqertarsuup Tunua b. 45M3
Qeydār 33H1
Qian'an 30B3
Qilian Shan mts 27I3
Qīnā 33G2
Qing'an 30B3
Qingdao 28E4
Qinggang 30B3
Qingyuan 30B4
Qinhuangdao 27K3
Qinzhou 27J4
Qionghai 27K5
Qiqihar 30A3
Qitaihe 30C3
Qom 26E3
Qo'qon 27G2
Qorveh 33H1
Quang Ngai 29C6
Quantock Hills 15D7
Qu'Appelle r. 44H4
Quanta Sant'Elena 20C5
Queanbeyan 42D5
Québec 45K5
Québec prov. 45K4
Queen Charlotte
Sound sea chan. 44F4
Queen Elizabeth
Islands 45I1
Queen Maud Land reg. 56C6
Queenscliff 42B7
Queensland state 42B1
Queenstown 41J8
Queenstown 43B7
Quelimane 35D5
Quelpart i. 28F4
Quesnel 44F4
Quetta 26F3
Quetzaltenango 50F6
Quezon City 29E6
Quibala 35B5
Quibdó 52C2
Quillabamba 52D6
Quillacollo 52E7
Quilmes 54E4
Quilpué 54B4
Quimbele 35B4
Quimper 18B3
Quimperlé 18C3
Quincy 47I4
Quincy 48F1
Quinto 19F3
Quirimbas, Parque
Nacional das nat. park 35E5
Quirindi 42E3
Quirinópolis 55A2
Quitilipi 54D3
Quito 52C4
Quixadá 53K4
Quixeramobim 53K5
Qujing 27J4
Quorn 41I6
Qŭrghonteppa 27F3
Quy Nhơn 29C6
Quzhou 28D5

R
Raahe 10N4
Raasay i. 16C3
Raasay, Sound of
sea chan. 16C3
Raba 29D8
Rabat 32C1
Rabaul 38F2
Rabocheostrovsk 22G2
Rach Gia 29C7
Racibórz 13P5
Racine 47I3
Rădăuţi 23E7
Radcliff 47J4
Radford 48A4
Radnevo 21L3
Radom 13R5
Radomsko 13Q5
Radomyshl 23F6
Radviliškis 11M9
Radwāyina 23E6
Radzyń Podlaski 13R5
Rafaela 54D4
Rafsanjān 26E3
Ragusa 20F6
Raha 29E8
Rahachow 23F5
Rahimyar Khan 27G4
Raichur 27G5
Raigarh 27H4
Rainier, Mount vol. 46C2
Raisio 11M6
Rajahmundry 27H5
Rajkot 27G4
Rajshahi 27H4
Rakitnoye 23G6
Rakovski 21K3
Rakvere 11O7
Raleigh 47L4
Ramādī 33H2
Rame Head 15C8
Râmnicu Sărat 21L2
Râmnicu Vâlcea 21K2
Ramon' 23H6
Ramona 49D4
Ramotswa 37G3
Rampur 27G4
Ramree 29A5
Ramsey 14G4
Ramsey 48D2
Ramsgate 15I7
Ramygala 11N9
Ranaghat 27H4
Rancagua 54B4
Ranchi 27H4

Randalstown 17F3
Randers 11G8
Råneå 10M4
Rangoon 27I5
Rangpur 27H4
Rannoch, Loch l. 16E4
Ranong 29B7
Rantauprapat 29B7
Rapallo 20C2
Rapid City 46G3
Rapla 11N7
Rarotonga i. 6
Ras Dejen mt. 34D2
Raseiniai 11M9
Rasht 26D3
Rasony 11P9
Rasskazovo 23I5
Ratanda 37I4
Rat Buri 29B6
Rathenow 13N4
Rathfriland 17F3
Rathlin Island 17F2
Ratnagiri 27G5
Raton 46G4
Rauch 54E5
Raul Soares 55C3
Rauma 11L6
Raurkela 27H4
Ravenna 20E2
Ravenna 48A3
Ravensburg 13L7
Ravi r. 27G3
Rawicz 13P5
Rawlins 46F3
Rawson 54C6
Rayagada 27H5
Raychikhinsk 30C2
Rayleigh 15H7
Raymond Terrace 42E4
Raymondville 46H6
Razgrad 21L3
Razlog 21J4
Reading 15G7
Reading 48D2
Rebiana Sand Sea des. 33F2
Recherche, Archipelago
of the is 40E6
Rechytsa 23F5
Recife 53L5
Recife, Cape 37G8
Recklinghausen 13K5
Reconquista 54E3
Red r. 47I5
Red Bank 48D2
Red Bluff 46C3
Redcar 14F4
Red Cliffs 41I6
Red Deer 44G4
Redding 46C3
Redditch 15F6
Redenção 53H5
Redlands 49D3
Red Oak 47H3
Red Sea 34D1
Redwood City 49A2
Ree, Lough l. 17E4
Reedley 49C2
Regensburg 13N6
Reggane 32D2
Reggio di Calabria 20F5
Reggio nell'Emilia 20D2
Reghin 21K1
Regina 44H4
Registro 55B3
Rehoboth 36C2
Rehoboth Bay 48D3
Reigate 15G7
Reinbek 13M4
Reindeer Lake 45H4
Relizane 19G6
Rembang 29D8
Renfrew 16F5
Rengo 54B4
Reni 21M2
Renmark 41I6
Rennes 18D2
Reno 46C3
Reo 32C3
Reserva 55A4
Resistencia 54E3
Reşiţa 21I2
Resplendor 55C2
Retalhuleu 50F6
Retford 14G5
Rethymno 21K7
Réunion terr. 7
Reus 19G3
Reutlingen 13L6
Revillagigedo, Islas is 50B5
Rewa 27H4
Rexburg 46E3
Reykjavík 10□
Reynosa 46H6
Rēzekne 11O8
Rheine 13J4
Rhine r. 13K5
Rhine r. 18J2
Rhinelander 47J2
Rho 20C2
Rhode Island state 48F2
Rhodes 21M6
Rhodes i. 21M6
Rhodope Mountains 21J4
Rhône r. 18G5
Rhondda 19D5
Rhyl 14D5
Riachão 53I5
Riacho de Santana 55C1
Riacho dos Machados 55C1
Riau, Kepulauan is 29C7
Ribas do Rio Pardo 55A3
Ribble r. 14E5
Ribe 11F9
Ribeira 19B3
Ribeirão Preto 55B3
Ribeiralta 52E6
Ribniţa 23F7
Rîbniţa 23F7
Richards Bay 37K4
Richfield 46E4
Richland 46C2
Richmond 42E2
Richmond 47K4
Richmond 48C4
Richmond 49A1
Ridgecrest 49D3
Riesa 13N5
Rietavas 11L9
Rieti 20E3
Riga 11N8
Riga, Gulf of 11M8
Rijau 32D3
Rijeka 20F2
Rikuzen-takata 31F5
Rila mts 21J3
Rilleux-la-Pape 18G4
Rimavská Sobota 13R6
Rimini 20E2
Rimouski 45L5
Rimsdale 16F2
Ringkøbing 11F8
Ringsted 11G9
Ringwood 15F8
Ringwood 42B6

Rio Azul 55A4
Riobamba 52C4
Rio Bonito 55C3
Rio Branco 52E5
Rio Brilhante 54F2
Rio Casca 55C3
Rio Claro 55B3
Rio Cuarto 54D4
Rio de Contas 55C1
Rio de Janeiro 55C3
Rio de Janeiro state 55C3
Rio do Sul 55A4
Río Gallegos 54C8
Rio Grande 50C4
Rio Grande 54F4
Rio Grande r. 46H6
Rio Grande City 46H6
Rio Grande do Sul state 55A5
Riohacha 52D1
Rioja 52C5
Río Lagartos 50G4
Rio Largo 53K5
Riom 18F4
Rio Novo 55C3
Rio Pardo de Minas 55C1
Rio Preto 55C3
Rio Rancho 46F4
Rio Verde 55A2
Rio Verde de Mato
Grosso 53H7
Ripky 23F6
Ripley 15F5
Ripon 14F4
Risca 15D7
Rişor 11F7
Riva del Garda 20D2
Rivas 51G6
Rivera 54E4
River Cess 32C4
Riverhead 48E2
Riverside 49D4
Riverview 45I5
Rivière-du-Loup 45L5
Rivne 23E6
Rivungo 35C5
Riyadh 34E1
Rize 23I8
Roade 15G6
Road Town 51L5
Roanne 18F3
Roanoke 48B4
Roanoke Rapids 47L4
Roaring Spring 48B2
Roatán 51G5
Robertson 36D7
Robertsport 32B4
Roberval 45K5
Robinson Ranges hills 40D5
Robinvale 41I6
Rocha 54F4
Rochdale 14E5
Rochefort 18D4
Rochegda 22I3
Rochester 15H7
Rochester 42B6
Rochester 47I3
Rochester 48C1
Rochford 15H7
Rockford 47J3
Rockhampton 41K4
Rockingham 40D6
Rock Island 47I3
Rockland 48F1
Rocky Mountains 46F3
Rodeio 55A4
Rodez 18F4
Rodniki 22I4
Roeselare 12I5
Rohnert Park 49A1
Rohrbach in
Oberösterreich 13N6
Roja 11M8
Rojas 54D4
Rokiskis 11N9
Rokytne 23E6
Rolândia 55A3
Rolim de Moura 52F6
Rolla 47I4
Roman 21L1
Romania country 21K2
Romans-sur-Isère 18G4
Romblon 29E6
Rome 20E4
Rome 48D1
Romford 15H7
Romilly-sur-Seine 18F2
Romny 23G6
Romodanovo 23I5
Romorantin-Lanthenay 18E3
Romsey 15F8
Ronda 19D5
Rondon 55B2
Rondonópolis 53H7
Rønne 11I9
Rønne 13L3
Roosendaal 12I5
Roquefort 18D4
Roraima, Mount mt. 52F2
Rosa, Monte mt. 20B2
Rosans 18G4
Rosário 53J4
Rosario 46D5
Rosário 53J4
Rosário do Sul 54F4
Rosário Oeste 53G6
Roscoff 18C2
Roscommon 17D4
Roscrea 17E5
Roseau r. 48F1
Roseau 51L5
Roseburg 46C3
Rosenberg 47I6
Rosenheim 13N7
Roseto degli Abruzzi 20F3
Rosetown 44H4
Roseville 49B1
Rosewood 42F1
Rosh Pinah 36C3
Rosignano Marittimo 20D3
Roşiori de Vede 21K2
Roskilde 11H9
Roslavl' 23G5
Rossano 20F5
Rosso 32B3
Ross-on-Wye 15E7
Rossosh' 23H6
Ross Sea 56D6
Rostock 13N3
Rostov 22H4
Rostov-na-Donu 23H7
Rosvík 10L4
Rota 19C5
Rothbury 14F3
Rotherham 14F5
Rothes 16F3
Rotorua 43F4
Rotterdam 12J5
Rottweil 13L6
Roubaix 18F1
Rouen 18E2
Rousay i. 16F1
Rovaniemi 10N3
Roven'ki 23H6
Rovereto 20D2
Rovigo 20D2
Rovinj 20E2
Rovnoye 23J6

Royston 15G6
Rozdil'na 21N1
Rtishchevo 23I5
Ruabon 15D6
Ruahine Range mts 43F5
Rub' al Khālī des. 34E2
Rubtsovsk 24J4
Ruda Śląska 13Q5
Rudnaya 30D3
Rudnya 23I5
Rudny 26F1
Rudol'fa, Ostrov i. 24G1
Rufiji r. 35D4
Rufino 54D4
Rufisque 32B3
Rugby 15F6
Rugeley 15F6
Rügen i. 13N3
Ruhengeri 34C4
Ruhnu i. 11M8
Rui Barbosa 55C1
Ruipa 35D4
Ruiz 50C4
Rüjiena 11N8
Rukwa, Lake 35D4
Rum i. 16C4
Ruma 21H2
Rumāh 34E1
Rumbek 33F4
Rumphi 35D5
Runcorn 14E5
Runde 35B5
Rusape 35D5
Ruse 21K3
Rushden 15G6
Rushworth 42B6
Russellville 47I4
Russian Federation
country 24I3
Russkiy Kameshkir 23J5
Rust'avi 23J8
Rustenburg 37H3
Ruston 47I5
Rutherglen 42C6
Ruthin 15D5
Rutland 48E1
Ruza 22H4
Ruzayevka 23J5
Ružomberok 13Q6
Rwanda country 34C4
Ryan, Loch b. 16D5
Ryazan' 23H5
Ryazhsk 23I5
Rybinsk 22H4
Rybinskoye
Vodokhranilishche
resr 51L6
Rybnik 13Q5
Rybnoye 23H5
Ryde 15H8
Rye 15H8
Ryl'sk 23G6
Ryn-Peski des. 23K7
Ryukyu Islands 31B8
Rzeszów 23D6
Rzhaksa 23I5
Rzhev 22G4

S
Saale r. 13M5
Saalfeld 13N5
Saarbrücken 13K6
Saaremaa i. 11M7
Saarenkylä 10N3
Saarijärvi 10N5
Saarlouis 13K6
Šabac 21H2
Sabadell 19H3
Sabae 31E6
Sabará 55C2
Sabbah 33E2
Sabinas 46G6
Sabinas Hidalgo 46G6
Sable, Cape 45L5
Sabón Kafi 32D3
Sabzevār 26E3
Sachs'on 31C6
Sacramento 49B1
Sacramento r. 49B1
Sacramento Mountains 46F5
Sada 37H2
Sádaba 19F2
Salgótarján 13Q6
Şahbuz 23I8
Safi 32C1
Safonovo 23G5
Safranbolu 23G8
Saga 31C6
Sagami-nada g. 31E6
Sagar 27G4
Saginaw Bay 47K3
Sagres 19B5
Sagua la Grande 47K7
Sahagún 19D2
Sahara des. 32D3
Sahel reg. 32C3
Sahuayo 50D4
Saïda 19G6
Saijō 31C6
Saiki 31C6
Saikai 11P6
Sal'sk 23I7
Salta 54C3
Saltash 15C8
Saltcoats 16E5
Saltillo 46G6
Salt Lake City 46E3
Salto 54E4
Salto 55B3
Salton Sea salt l. 49E4
Salvador 55D1
Salwah 34F1
Salween r. 27I5
Salzburg 13N7
Salzgitter 13M4
Samar i. 29E6
Samara 23K5
Samarinda 29D8
Samarqand 26F3
Samarra' 33H1
Sambalpur 27H4
Sambava 35F5
Sambir 23D6
Samborombón, Bahía b. 54E5
Samch'ok 31C5
Samīrah 34E1
Same 34D4
Samoa country 39I3
Samokov 21J3
Samos 21L6
Samos i. 21L6
Samothraki i. 21K4
Sampit 29D8
Samsun 23H8
Sana r. 20G2
Şan'ā' 34E2
Sanandaj 33H1
San Andrés 51H6

San Antonio 54B4
San Antonio Oeste 54D6
San Benedetto del
Tronto 20E3
San Bernardino 49D3
San Bernardo 54B4
San Buenaventura 46G6
San Carlos 52E2
San Carlos 54C5
San-Jean, Lac l. 45K5
San Carlos de
Bariloche 54B6
San Carlos de Bolívar 54D5
San Clemente 49D4
San Cristóbal 52D2
San Cristóbal 54B4
San Cristóbal de las
Casas 50F5
Sancti Spíritus 51I4
Sandakan 29D7
Sandanski 21J4
Sandnes 11D7
Sandnessjøen 10H3
Sandomierz 23D6
Sandoway 27I5
Sandviken 11G6
Sandvika 11G7
Sandy 15G6
Sanford 47K6
Sanford 48F1
San Fernando 19C5
San Fernando 29E5
San Fernando 46H7
San Fernando 51L6
San Fernando 54B4
San Fernando de Apure 52E2
Sanford 47K6
San Francisco 49A2
San Francisco 54D4
San Francisco Bay inlet 49A2
San Gabriel Mountains 49C3
Sanger 49C3
San Giovanni in Fiore 20G5
San Jorge, Golfo de g. 54C7
San Jose 49B2
San José 51H7
San José de Buenavista 29E6
San Jose de Comondú 46E6
San José del Guaviare 52D3
San José de Mayo 54E4
San Juan 51K5
San Juan 54C4
San Juan Bautista 54E3
San Juan de los Morros 52E2
San Juan Mountains 46F4
San Justo 54D4
San Lázaro 54D2
Sankt Gallen 18I3
Sankt Pölten 13O6
Sankt Veit an der Glan 13O7
San Lorenzo 54D4
San Lorenzo 54D4
San Lucas 49E4
San Luis 49E4
San Luis Obispo 49B3
San Luis Potosí 50D4
San Marcos 46H6
San Marino 20E3
San Marino country 20E3
San Martín 54C4
San Martín de los
Andes 54B6
San Mateo 49A2
San Matías, Golfo g. 54D6
San Miguel 50G6
San Miguel de
Tucumán 54C3
San Nicolás de los
Arroyos 54D4
San Pablo 29E6
San-Pédro 32C4
San Pedro 54D2
San Pedro Channel 49C4
San Pedro de las
Colonias 46G6
San Pedro de Macorís 51K5
San Pedro de
Ycuamandyyú 54E2
San Pedro Sula 50G5
San Rafael 49A2
San Rafael 54C4
San Remo 20B3
San Salvador 50G6
San Salvador de Jujuy 54C2
San Sebastián 19E2
San Sebastián de los
Reyes 19E3
San Severo 20F4
Santa Ana 49D4
Santa Ana 50G6
Santa Barbara 49C3
Santa Barbara Channel 49B3
Santa Bárbara d'Oeste 55B3
Santa Catalina, Gulf of 49D4
Santa Catarina state 55A4
Santa Clara 51I4
Santa Clarita 49C3
Santa Cruz 52E7

Santa Cruz 53K5
Santa Cruz Cabrália 55D2
Santa Cruz del Sur 51I4
Santa Cruz de Tenerife 32B2
Santa Cruz do Sul 54F3
Santa Fe 46F4
Santa Fe 54D4
Santa Fé do Sul 55A3
Santa Helena 53I4
Santa Helena de Goiás 55A2
Santa Inês 53I4
Santa Maria 49B3
Santa Maria da Vitória 55C3
Santa Maria da Suaçuí 55C2
Santa Maria Madalena 55C3
Santa Monica 49C3
Santa Monica Bay 49C4
Santana 55C1
Santander 19E2
Sant'Antioco 20C5
Santa Quitéria 53J4
Santarém 19B4
Santarém 53H4
Santa Rosa 49A1
Santa Rosa 54D5
Santa Rosa de Copán 50G6
Santa Rosalía 46E6
Santee 49D4
Santiago 18I7
Santiago 46F4
Santiago 51I6
Santiago 54B4
Santiago de
Compostela 19B2
Santiago de Cuba 51I4
Santiago del Estero 54D3
San Jordi, Golf de g. 19G3
Santo Amaro 55D1
Santo Amaro de
Campos 55C3
Santo Anastácio 55A3
Santo André 55B3
Santo Ângelo 54F3
Santo António 32D4
Santo Antônio da
Platina 55A3
Santo Antônio de Jesus 55D1
Santo Antônio do Içá 52E4
Santo Domingo 51K5
Santorini i. 21K6
Santos 55B3
Santos Dumont 55C3
Santo Tomé 54E3
São Borja 54E3
São Carlos 55B3
São Domingos 55B1
São Félix 53H5
São Félix 55D1
São Fidélis 55C3
São Francisco 55C2
São Francisco r. 55C3
São Francisco de Paula 55A5
São Francisco do Sul 55A4
São Gabriel 54F4
São Gonçalo 55C3
São Gonçalo do Abaeté 55B2
São Gonçalo do
Sapucaí 55B3
São Gotardo 55B2
São João da Barra 55C3
São João da Boa Vista 55B3
São João da Madeira 19B3
São João da Ponte 55C2
São João do Paraíso 55C1
São João do Rei 55B3
São João do Paraíso 55C1
São José 55A4
São José da Laje 55A5
São José do Rio Preto 55A3
São José dos Campos 55B3
São José dos Pinhais 55A4
São Leopoldo 55A5
São Lourenço 55B3
São Luís 53J4
São Luís de Montes
Belos 55A2
São Manuel 55A3
São Mateus 55D2
São Mateus do Sul 55A4
São Miguel do Tapuio 53J5
São Paulo 55B3
São Paulo state 55A3
São Paulo de Olivença 52E4
São Pedro da Aldeia 55C3
São Raimundo Nonato 53J5
São Romão 55B2
São Roque 55B3
São Salvador 55B3
São Sebastião 55B3
São Sebastião do
Paraíso 55B3
São Simão 55A3
São Simão 55B3
São Tomé and Príncipe
country 32D4
São Vicente 55B3
Sapanca 21N4
Sapouy 32C3
Sapozhok 23I5
Sapporo 30F4
Sapucaí r. 55B3
Sapulpa 54C3
Saqqez 33H1
Saraburi 29C6
Saragt 26F3
Sarajevo 20H3
Sarakash 24G4
Saraktash 24G4
Saran 24H4
Saranac r. 47M3
Saransk 23J5
Sarapul 23K4
Sarasota 47K6
Saratoga 49B2
Saratov 23J6

Saratovskoye
Vodokhranilishche
resr 23J5
Sarävän 26F4
Saray 21L4
Sarayköy 21M6
Sardinia i. 20C4
Sardoba 27G3
Sári 33E4
Sárköy 21L4
Sarıçam 21M5
Sarıkamış 21M4
Sarıkaraağaç 21N5
Sárköy 21L4
Sarnen 18I3
Sarny 23E6
Saros Körfezi b. 21L4
Sarpsborg 11G7
Sarrebourg 18H2
Sárvár 20G1
Saryarka plain 27G1
Sasebo 31C6
Saskatchewan prov. 44H4
Saskatchewan r. 44H4
Saskatoon 44H4
Sasolburg 37H4
Sasovo 23J5
Sassandra 32C4
Sassari 20C4
Sassnitz 13N3
Satpura Range mts 27G4
Satu Mare 23D7
Saucillo 46F6
Sauda 11E7
Sauðárkrókur 10□
Saudi Arabia country 34E1
Sault Sainte Marie 45J5
Sault Sainte Marie 47K2
Saumalkol' 26F1
Saumur 18D3
Saurimo 35C4
Sava r. 20I2
Savalou 32D4
Savannah 47K5
Savannah r. 47K5
Savannakhét 29C6
Savanna-la-Mar 51I5
Sävar 10L5
Savaştepe 21L5
Savona 20C2
Savonlinna 10P6
Sävsjö 11I8
Sawel 43J7
Sawu, Laut sea 40E1
Saxilby 14G5
Saxmundham 15I6
Saynshand 27K2
Sayreville 48D2
Scapa Flow inlet 16F2
Scarborough 14G4
Scarborough 51L5
Schaffhausen 18I3
Schärding 13N6
Schenectady 48E1
Schio 20D2
Schleswig 13L3
Schönebeck (Elbe) 13M4
Schwäbische Alb mts 13L7
Schwäbisch Hall 13L6
Schwandorf 13N6
Schwarzenberg 13N5
Schwaz 13M7
Schwedt an der Oder 13O4
Schweinfurt 13M5
Schwerin 13M4
Sciacca 20E6
Scicli 20F6
Scone 16F4
Scone 42E4
Scotland admin. div. 16
Scottsbluff 46G3
Scottsboro 47J5
Scranton 48D2
Scunthorpe 14G5
Scutari, Lake 21H3
Seaford 15H8
Seaham 14G4
Searcy 47I4
Seattle 46C2
Sebba 32D3
Sebeş 21J2
Sebezh 11P8
Sebring 47K6
Sechelt 44F5
Sechura 52B5
Secunda 37I4
Sedalia 47I4
Sedan 18G2
Sédrata 20B6
Šeduva 11M9
Sefadu 32B4
Sefare 37H2
Seferihisar 21L5
Segamat 29C7
Segezha 22J3
Ségou 32C3
Séguéla 32C4
Seguin 46H6
Seine r. 15H9
Seine, Baie de b. 15J9
Seine, Val de valley 26D4
Sejny 11M9
Sekayu 29C8
Sekondi 32C4
Sek'ot'a 34D2
Selby 14G5
Selebi-Phikwe 35C6
Sélibabi 32B3
Selizharovo 22G4
Selkirk 16G5
Selkirk 45I4
Selkirk Mountains 44G4
Selma 47J5
Sel'tso 23G5
Selty 22L4
Selvas reg. 52D5
Selwyn Mountains 44E3
Semarang 29D8
Semeru vol. 29D8
Semey 24J4
Semiluki 23H6
Seminole 46G5
Semnan 26E3
Sena Madureira 52E5
Sendai 30F5
Sendai 31C7

Senegal country 32B3
Senftenberg 13O5
Sengerema 34D4
Sengiley 23J5
Senhor do Bonfim 53J6
Senlis 18F2
Senqu r. 37H6
Sensuntepeque 50G6
Senta 21I2
Senwabarwana 37I2
Seoul 31B5
Sep'o 31B5
Sept-Îles 45L4
Serafimovich 23I6
Seram i. 29E8
Seram, Laut sea 29F8
Serbia country 21I3
Serdobsk 23I5
Seremban 29C7
Serenje 35D5
Sergach 22J5
Sergiyev Posad 22H4
Serik 33G1
Sernur 22J4
Serowe 37H2
Serpukhov 23H5
Serra 55C3
Serra Talhada 53K5
Serres 21J4
Serrinha 53K6
Sêrro 55C2
Sertanópolis 55A3
Sertãozinho 55B3
Sertolovo 11Q6
Serule 35C6
Seryshevo 30C2
Sestri Levante 20C2
Sestroretsk 11P6
Sète 18F5
Sete Lagoas 55B2
Sétif 32D1
Seto 31E6
Settat 32C1
Settle 14E4
Setúbal 19B4
Setúbal, Baía de b. 19B4
Sevan 23J8
Sevan, Lake 23J8
Sevastopol' 23G7
Sevenoaks 15H7
Severn r. 15E7
Severnaya Dvina r. 22I2
Severnaya Zemlya is 25L1
Severnyy 24H3
Severodvinsk 22H2
Severomorsk 10R2
Severo-Yenisseyskiy 24K3
Severskaya 23H7
Severskiy Donets r. 23I7
Sevilla 52C3
Seville 19D5
Seward 44D3
Seychelles country 7
Seymchan 25Q3
Seymour 47J4
Sfântu Gheorghe 21K2
Sfax 20D7
Shaftesbury 15E7
Shahdol 27H4
Shahr-e Kord 26E3
Shahrisabz 26F3
Shakhovskaya 22G4
Shakhty 23I7
Shakhun'ya 22J4
Shaki 32D4
Shalakusha 22I3
Shali 23J8
Shalkar 26E2
Shamrock 46G4
Shandong Bandao pen. 28E4
Shanghai 28E4
Shangzhi 30B3
Shanhe 30B3
Shannon est. 17D5
Shannon r. 17D5
Shannon, Mouth of the 17C5
Shantou 28D5
Shaoyang 27I4
Shapinsay i. 16G1
Shaqra' 33H2
Sharjah 26E4
Sharkawshchyna 11O9
Shark Bay 40C5
Sharon 48C2
Shar'ya 22J4
Shashemenē 34D3
Shatki 23I5
Shatsk 23I5
Shatura 23H5
Shawano 47J4
Shawnee 47H4
Shchekino 23H5
Shchel'yayur 22L2
Shchigry 23H6
Shchors 23F6
Shchuchyn 11N10
Shebekino 23H6
Sheberghān 26F3
Sheboygan 47J3
Shebunino 30F3
Sheerness 15H7
Sheffield 14F5
Sheksna 22H4
Shelburne Bay 41I2
Shelbyville 47J4
Shenandoah Mountains 48B3
Shendam 32D4
Shenkursk 22I3
Shenshu 30C3
Shentala 23K5
Shenyang 30A4
Shepetivka 23E6
Shepparton 42B6
Sheppey, Isle of i. 15H7
Sherbrooke 45K5
Sheridan 46E3
Sherman 47H5
's-Hertogenbosch 12J5
Sherwood Forest reg. 15F5
Shetland Islands 16□
Shetpe 26E2
Sheyenne r. 46H2
Shibata 31I5
Shibin al Kawm 33F1
Shijiazhuang 27K3
Shikoku i. 31D6
Shildon 14F4
Shiliguri 27H4
Shillong 27I4
Shilovo 23I5
Shimada 31E6
Shimanovsk 30B1
Shimonoseki 31C6
Shin, Loch l. 16E2
Shipunovo 24J4
Shiyan 27K3

Shizuishan 27J3
Shizuoka 31E6
Shklow 23F5
Shkodër 21H3
Shōbara 31D6
Shoshong 37H2
Shostka 23G6
Shpakovskoye 23I7
Shpola 23J6
Shreveport 47J5
Shrewsbury 15E6
Shuangcheng 30B3
Shuangliao 30A4
Shuangyang 30B4
Shuangyashan 30C3
Shubarkudyk 26E2
Shulan 30B4
Shumen 21L3
Shumerlya 22J5
Shumilina 23F5
Shuya 22I4
Shuya 22I4
Shymkent 27F2
Shyroke 23G7
Šiauliai 11M9
Šibasa 37J2
Šibenik 20F3
Siberia reg. 25M3
Sibi 26F4
Sibiu 21K2
Sibolga 29B7
Sibu 29D7
Sibut 34B3
Sichuan Pendi basin 27J4
Sicilian Channel 20E6
Sicily i. 20F5
Sicuani 52D6
Sidi Aïssa 19H6
Sidi Ali 19G5
Sidi Bel Abbès 19F6
Sidi Bouzid 20C7
Sidi Kacem 32C1
Sidlaw Hills 16F4
Sidmouth 15D8
Sidney 46G2
Sidney 46G3
Sidney 47K3
Sidon 33G1
Siedlce 11M10
Siegen 13L5
Siena 20D3
Sieradz 13Q5
Sierra Grande 54C6
Sierra Leone country 32B4
Sierra Madre Mountains 49B3
Sierra Vista 46E5
Sierre 18H3
Sig 19F6
Sighetu Marmației 23D7
Sighișoara 21K1
Sigli 27I5
Sigulda 11N8
Siguiri 32C3
Sihanoukville 29C6
Siilinjärvi 10O5
Sikar 27G4
Sikasso 32C3
Sikeston 47J4
Sikhote-Alin' mts 30D4
Šilalė 11M9
Šile 21M4
Siljan l. 11I6
Šilkeborg 11F8
Sillamäe 11O7
Šilutė 11L9
Silvânia 55A2
Silver City 46F5
Silver Spring 48C3
Simav 21M4
Simcoe 48A1
Simcoe, Lake 45K5
Simeonovgrad 21K3
Simferopol' 23G7
Simi Valley 49C3
dimleu Silvaniei 21J1
Simplício Mendes 53J5
Simpson Desert 41H4
Simrishamn 11I9
Sincelejo 52C2
Sindelfingen 13L6
Sındırgı 21M5
Sindou 32C3
Sines 19B5
Singa 33G3
Singapore 29C7
Singapore country 29C7
Singida 35D4
Singkawang 29C7
Singleton 42E4
Siniscola 20C4
Sinjai 29E8
Sinnamary 53H2
Sinop 23H2
Sinop 53G6
Sinp'a 30B4
Sinp'o 31C4
Sinsang 31B5
Sint Eustatius i. 51L5
Sint Maarten i. 51L5
Sint-Niklaas 12J5
Sintra 19B4
Sinŭiju 31B4
Siófok 20H1
Sion 18H3
Sioux City 47H3
Sioux Falls 47H3
Siping 30B4
Sir Edward Pellew Group is 41H3
Şırjan 26F4
Sirsa 27G4
Sirte 33E1
Sirte, Gulf of 33E1
Sisak 20G2
Sitapur 27H4
Siteki 37J4
Sittard 12K5
Sittingbourne 15H7
Sittwe 27I4
Sivas 23H2
Sivasli 21M5
Sivrihisar 21N5
Śiwah, Wāḥāt oasis 33F2
Siyabuswa 37I3
Sjenica 21I3
Sjöbo 11H9
Skadovs'k 23G7
Skagafjörður inlet 10□²
Skagen 11G8
Skagerrak strait 11F8
Skara 11H7
Skarżysko-Kamienna 13R5
Skawina 13Q6
Skegness 14H5
Skellefteå 10L4
Skellefteälven r. 10L4
Skelmersdale 14E5
Ski 11G7

Skien 11F7
Skierniewice 13R5
Skikda 20B6
Skipton 14E5
Skive 11F8
Skjern 11F9
Skopin 11F9
Skopje 21I4
Skovorodino 30A1
Skowhegan 47N3
Skuodas 11L8
Skurup 11H9
Skutskär 11J6
Skvyra 23F6
Skye i. 16C3
Skyros 21K5
Slagelse 11G9
Slantsy 11P7
Slatina 21K2
Slave Coast 32D4
Slavgorod 24I4
Slavonski Brod 20H2
Slavuta 23E6
Slavutych 23F6
Sławno 13P3
Slavyanka 30C4
Slavyansk-na-Kubani 23H7
Sleaford 15G5
Sleat, Sound of sea chan. 16D3
Slieve Bloom Mountains hills 17E5
Slieve Donard hill 17G3
Sligo 17D3
Sligo Bay 17D3
Slippery Rock 48A2
Sliven 21L3
Slobodskoy 22K4
Slobozia 21L2
Slonim 11N10
Slough 15G7
Slovakia country 13Q6
Slovenia country 20F2
Slovenj Gradec 20F1
Slov"yans'k 23H6
Słupsk 13P3
Slutsk 11O10
Slyudyanka 27J1
Smallwood Reservoir 45L4
Smalyavichy 11P9
Smarhon' 11O9
Smederevo 21I2
Smederevska Palanka 21I2
Smidovich 30D2
Smila 23F6
Smithton 41J8
Smithtown 42F3
Smolensk 23F5
Smolyan 21K4
Snake r. 46D2
Snake River Plain 46E3
Snares Islands 39G6
Snettisham 15H6
Snežnik mt. 20F2
Snizort, Loch b. 16C3
Snowdon mt. 15C5
Snowy r. 42D6
Snowy Mountains 42C6
Snyder 46G5
Soanierana-Ivongo 35E5
Sobinka 22I5
Sobral 53J4
Sochi 23H8
Sŏch'ŏn 31B5
Society Islands 6
Socorro 46F5
Socorro 52C2
Socorro 55B3
Socotra i. 26E5
Sodankylä 10O3
Söderhamn 11J6
Söderköping 11J7
Södertälje 11J7
Sodo 34D3
Soest 12L5
Sogne 21I4
Søgne 11E7
Sognefjorden inlet 11D6
Söğüt 21N4
Soissons 18F2
Sokal' 23E6
Sokch'o 31C5
Söke 21M6
Sokhumi 23I8
Sokodé 32D4
Sokol 22I4
Sokolo 32C3
Sokoto 32D3
Sokyryany 23E6
Solana Beach 49D4
Solapur 27G5
Soledad 49C4
Solenoye 23I7
Solginskiy 22I4
Soligalich 22I4
Solihull 15F6
Solikamsk 24G4
Sol'-Iletsk 24G4
Solingen 12K5
Sollefteå 10J5
Solna 11J7
Solnechnogorsk 22H4
Solnechnyy 30E2
Solo r. 29D8
Solomon Islands country 39G2
Solomon Sea 38F2
Solothurn 18H3
Solov'yevsk 30B1
Sol"tsy 22F4
Solwezi 35C5
Solway Firth est. 16F6
Soma 21M5
Somalia country 34E3
Somaliland reg. 34E3
Sombor 21H2
Somero 11M6
Somerset 15E7
Somerset 48B3
Somerset Island 45I2
Somerset West 36D8
Somersworth 48F1
Somerville 48D2
Sŏnbong 30C4
Sŏnch'ŏn 31B5
Sondags r. 37G7
Sønderborg 11F9
Søndre Strømfjord 45M3
Sondrio 20C1
Songea 35D5
Songhua Hu resr 30B4
Songjianghe 30B4
Songkhla 29C7
Sŏngnam 31B5
Songo 35D5
Songwan 30B3
Sonkovo 22H4
Sonneberg 13M5
Sonoran Desert 49F4
Sonqor 33H1
Sopot 13Q3
Sopron 20G1
Sora 20E4
Söråker 10J5
Sorel 47M2
Soria 19E3
Soroca 23F6
Sorocaba 55B3

Sorong 29F8
Soroti 34D3
Sorrento 20F4
Sorsogon 29E6
Sortavala 10Q6
Sŏsan 31B5
Soshanguve 37I3
Sosnogorsk 22L3
Sosnovka 23I5
Sosnovyy Bor 11P7
Sosnowiec 13Q5
Soubré 32C4
Soufrière 51L6
Soufrière vol. 51L6
Sougueur 19G6
Souk Ahras 20B6
Souk el Arbaâ du Rharb 32C1
Soul-sur-Mer 18D4
Soure 53I4
Sour el Ghozlane 19H5
Sousa 53K5
Sousse 20D7
South Africa, Republic of country 36F5
Southampton 15F8
South Anston 14F5
South Australia state 40G6
South Bend 47J3
South Carolina state 47K5
South China Sea 29D6
South Dakota state 46G3
South Downs hills 15G8
South-East admin. dist. 37J3
Southend-on-Sea 15H7
Southern admin. dist. 36G3
Southern Alps mts 43G6
Southern Ocean ocean 40C7
Southern Uplands hills 16E5
South Georgia i. 54I8
South Georgia and the South Sandwich Islands terr. 54I8
South Harris pen. 16B3
South Island 43D7
South Korea country 31B5
South Lake Tahoe 49B1
Southminster 15H7
South Mountains hills 48C3
South Pacific Ocean ocean 41L5
Southport 14D5
South Ronaldsay i. 16G2
South Shields 14F3
South Sudan country 33F3
South Taranaki Bight b. 43E4
South Uist i. 16B3
South West Cape 43A8
Southwold 15I6
Soutpansberg mts 37I2
Sovetsk 11L9
Sovetsk 22I4
Sovetskaya Gavan' 30F2
Sovetskiy 24H3
Sovetskiy 24H3
Sovety's'kyy 23G7
Soweto 37H4
Spain country 19E3
Spalding 15G6
Spanish Town 51I5
Sparks 46D4
Spartanburg 47K5
Sparti 21J6
Spas-Demensk 23G5
Spas-Klepiki 23I5
Spassk-Dal'niy 30D3
Spassk-Ryazanskiy 23I5
Spencer 47H3
Spencer Gulf est. 41H6
Spennymoor 14F4
Sperrin Mountains hills 17E3
Spetses i. 21J6
Spey r. 16F3
Spijkenisse 12J5
Spilsby 14H5
Spirovo 22H4
Spišská Nová Ves 23D6
Spittal an der Drau 13N7
Split 20G3
Spokane 46D2
Spoleto 20E3
Spratly Islands 29D6
Springbok 36C5
Springdale 47I4
Springe 46G4
Springfield 47I4
Springfield 47J4
Springfield 47K4
Springfield 48E1
Spring Hill 47K6
Spring Valley 48D2
Srebrenica 21I2
Sredets 21L3
Srednyy Khrebet mts 25Q4
Sredna Gora 21L3
Sredneuralsk 21J3
Srednyaya Akhtuba 23I6
Sretensk 25M4
Sri Aman 29D7
Sri Lanka country 27H6
Sri Jayewardenepura Kotte 27H6
Srinagar 27G3
Srivardhan 27G5
Stade 13L4
Stadskanaal 13K4
Staffa i. 16C4
Stafford 15E6
Staines 15G7
Stakhanov 23H6
Stalbridge 15E8
Stalham 15I6
Stalowa Wola 23D6
Stamford 15G6
Stamford 48E2
Standerton 37I4
Stanger 37J5
Stanley 14F4
Stanley 54E9
Stannington 14F3
Stanovoye Nagor'ye mts 30A1
Stanovoy Khrebet mts 25N4
Stanthorpe 42E2
Stanton 15H5
Starachowice 13R5
Staraya Russa 22F4
Stara Zagora 21K3
Stargard Szczeciński 13O4
Staritsa 22G4
Starkville 47J5

Starobil's'k 23H6
Starogard Gdański 13Q4
Starokostyantyniv 23E6
Starominskaya 23H7
Staroshcherbinovskaya 23H7
Staryy Darohi 23F5
Staryy Oskol 23H6
State College 48C2
Statesboro 47K5
Staunton 48B3
Stavanger 11D7
Staveley 14F5
Stavropol' 23I7
Stavropol'skaya Vozvyshennost' hills 23I7
Steamboat Springs 46F3
Steinkjer 10G4
Steinkopf 36C5
Stellenbosch 36D7
Stendal 13M4
Stenungsund 11G7
Stephenville 46H5
Stepnoye 23J6
Sterkfontein Dam resr 37I5
Sterling 46G3
Sterlitamak 24G4
Stevenage 15G7
Stewart Island 43A8
Steynsburg 37G6
Steyr 13O6
Stikine River 44E4
Stillwater 47H4
Stilton 15G6
Štip 21J4
Stirling 16F4
Stjørdalshalsen 10G5
Stockholm 11K7
Stockport 14E5
Stockton 49B1
Stockton-on-Tees 14F4
Stoke-on-Trent 15E5
Stokesley 14F4
Stolac 20G3
Stolberg 12K5
Stolin 11O11
Stone 15E6
Stonehaven 16G4
Storm Lake 47H3
Stornoway 16C2
Storozhynets' 23E6
Storrs 48E2
Storsjön i. 10J4
Storuman r. 10J4
Stourbridge 15E6
Stourport-on-Severn 15E6
Stowbtsy 11O10
Stowmarket 15H6
Strabane 17E3
Strakonice 13N6
Stralsund 13N3
Strand 36D8
Strangford Lough inlet 17G3
Stranraer 16D6
Strasbourg 18H2
Stratford 15C8
Stratford 48A1
Stratford-upon-Avon 15F6
Strathspey valley 16F3
Stratton 15C8
Straubing 13N6
Strawberry 48A1
Street 15E7
Strehaia 21J2
Strenči 11N8
Stromboli, Isola i. 20F5
Strömstad 11G7
Stronsay i. 16G1
Stroud 15E7
Struer 11F8
Struga 21I4
Strugi-Krasnyye 11P7
Struma r. 21J4
Strumica 21J4
Struthers 48A2
Strydenburg 36F5
Stryy 23D6
Stupino 23H5
Sturgis 46G3
Sturt Creek watercourse 29E9
Sturt Plain 40G3
Sturt Stony Desert 41I5
Stutterheim 37H7
Stuttgart 13L6
Stuttgart 47J5
Suakin 33G3
Subotica 21H1
Sucha Beskidzka 13Q6
Suceava 23E7
Sucre 52E7
Sudak 23G7
Sudan country 33F3
Sudbury 15H6
Sudd swamp 33F4
Sudety mts 13O5
Sudislavl' 22I4
Sudogda 22I5
Sueca 19F4
Suez 33G2
Suez, Gulf of 33G2
Suez Canal 33G1
Suffolk 47L4
Suhl 13M5
Şuhut 33G2
Sühbaatar 27J1
Sui r. 15E5
Suifenhe 30C3
Suihua 30B3
Suileng 30B3
Suir r. 17E5
Suizhou 27K3
Sukabumi 29C8
Sukagawa 31F5
Sukhinichi 23G5
Sukhona r. 22I3
Sukkur 27F4
Sulaiman Range mts 27F3
Sulaymānīyah 33H1
Sullana 52B4
Sulmona 20E3
Sulphur Springs 47H5
Sulu Archipelago is 29E7
Sulu Sea 29D7
Sumatra i. 29B7
Sumba i. 40E1
Sumba, Selat sea chan. 29D8
Sumbawa i. 40D1
Sumbawabesar 29D8
Sumbawanga 35D4
Sumbe 35B5
Sumburgh Head 16□
Šumperk 13P6
Sumqayıt 26D2
Sumter 47K5
Sumy 23G6
Sunbury 48C2
Sunch'ŏn 31B5
Sunch'ŏn 31B6
Sunda, Selat sea chan. 29C8
Sunderland 14F4
Sundridge 47K2
Sundsvall 10J5
Sunndalsøra 10F5

Sunnyside 46D2
Sunwang 49A2
Suntar 25M3
Suoyarvi 22G3
Superior 47J2
Superior, Lake 47J2
Süq ash Shuyūkh 33H1
Şūr 26E4
Surabaya 29D8
Surakarta 29D8
Surat 27G4
Surat Thani 29B7
Surazh 23G5
Surdulica 21J3
Surgut 24I3
Surigao 29E7
Surin 29C6
Suriname country 53G3
Sürmene 23I8
Surovikino 23I6
Surskoye 23J5
Surtsey i. 10□³
Susaki 31D6
Susanville 46C3
Susuman 25P3
Susurluk 21M5
Sutherland 36E6
Sutter 49B1
Sutton 15H6
Sutton Coldfield 15F6
Sutton in Ashfield 15F5
Suva 39H3
Suvorov 23I5
Suwa 31E5
Suwałki 11M9
Suwŏn 31B5
Suzaka 31E5
Suzdal' 22I4
Suzhou 28E4
Suzuka 31E6
Svalbard terr. 24C2
Svatove 23I6
Svecha 22J4
Švenčionys 11O9
Svendborg 11G9
Sverdlovs'k 23I6
Sveti Nikole 21I4
Svetlograd 23I7
Svetly 11L9
Svetlyy Yar 23I6
Svilengrad 21L4
Svishtov 21K3
Svitava 13P6
Svobodnyy 30C2
Svyetlahorsk 23F5
Swadlincote 15F6
Swains Island atoll 39I3
Swakopmund 36B4
Swale r. 14F4
Swanage 15F8
Swan Hill 42A5
Swanley 15H7
Swansea 15D7
Swansea Bay 15D7
Swaziland country 37J4
Sweetwater 46G5
Świdnica 13P5
Świdwin 13O4
Świebodzin 13O4
Świecie 13Q4
Świnoujście 13N4
Switzerland country 18H3
Syeverodonets'k 23H6
Sydney 42E4
Syeverodonets'k 23H6
Syktyvkar 22K3
Sylhet 27I4
Synel'nykove 23G6
Syracuse 20F6
Syracuse 48C1
Syrdar'ya r. 26F2
Syria country 33G1
Syrian Desert 33G1
Syumsi 22K4
Syzran' 23K5
Szczecin 13O4
Szczecinek 13P4
Szczytno 11L10
Szeged 21I1
Székesfehérvár 20H1
Szeksárd 20H1
Szentes 21I1
Szentgotthárd 20G1
Szigetvár 20G1
Szolnok 21I1
Szombathely 20G1

T

Taagga Duudka reg. 34E3
Tābah 34E1
Tabatinga 52E4
Tabatinga 55A3
Tabligbo 32D4
Tábor 13O6
Tabora 35D4
Tabou 32C4
Tabríz 26D3
Tabūk 26C4
Tāby 11K7
Tacheng 27H2
Tachov 13N6
Tacloban 29E6
Tacna 52D7
Tacoma 46C2
Tacuarembó 54E4
Tadcaster 14F5
Tademaït, Plateau du 32D2
Tadjourah 34E2
Tadmur 33G1
Taegu 31C6
Taejŏn 31B6
T'aepaek 31C5
Tafi Viejo 54C3
Taganrog 23H7
Taganrog, Gulf of 23H7
Tagus r. 19B4
Tahiti i. 6
Tahlequah 47I4
Tahoua 32D3
Tai'an 27K3
T'ainan 28E5
Taipei 28E5
Taiping 29C7
T'aitung 28E5
Taiwan country 28E5
Taiwan Strait strait 28D5
Taiyuan 27K3
Ta'izz 34E2
Tajikistan country 27G3
Tak 29B6
Takāb 33H1
Takahashi 31D6
Takamatsu 31D6

Takaoka 31E5
Takapuna 43E3
Takayama 31E5
Takefu 31E6
Takhemaret 19G6
Takikawa 31F3
Taklimakan Desert 27H3
Takum 32D4
Talachyn 23F5
Talara 52B4
Talavera de la Reina 19D4
Talaya 25Q3
Talca 54B5
Talcahuano 54B5
Taldom 22H4
Taldykorgan 27G2
Tallahassee 47K5
Tallulah 47I5
Taloyoaz 23I6
Talsi 11M8
Tamala 23I5
Tamale 32C4
Tamano 31D6
Tamanrasset 32D2
Tambacounda 32B3
Tambov 23I5
Tambovka 30C2
Tampa 47K6
Tampere 11M6
Tampico 50E4
Tamsweg 13N7
Tamworth 15F6
Tamworth 42E3
Tana r. 34D4
Tana, Lake 34D2
Tanabi 55A3
Tanabe 31D6
Tanami Desert 40G3
Tanch'ŏn 31C4
Tanda 32C4
Tăndărei 21L2
Tandil 54E5
Tandrage 17F3
Tanezrouft reg. 32C2
Tanga 35D4
Tanganyika, Lake 35C4
Tangará 55A4
Tangerang 29D8
Tanggula Shan mts 27H3
Tangier 19D6
Tangra Yumco salt l. 27H3
Tanjungbalai 29B7
Tanjungpandan 29C7
Tanjungredeb 29D7
Tanjungselor 29D7
Tanout 32D3
Țânțâ 33F1
Tan-Tan 32B2
Tanzania country 35D4
Taonan 30A3
Taourirt 32C1
Tapachula 50F6
Tapajós r. 53G4
Tapauá 52E5
Taperoá 55D1
Taquara 55A5
Taquari 55A5
Taquaritinga 55A3
Tarakan 29D7
Taraklı 21N4
Taranto 20G4
Taranto, Golfo di g. 20G4
Tarapoto 52C5
Tarascon 18F5
Tarauacá 52D5
Taraz 27F2
Tarbes 18E5
Tarcoola 41H6
Tarfaya 32B2
Târgoviște 21K2
Targuist 19D6
Târgu Jiu 21J2
Târgu Mureş 21K1
Târgu Neamţ 21L1
Târgu Secuiesc 21L1
Tarif 34E1
Tarija 52E8
Tarim Basin 27H3
Tarime 34D4
Tarko-Sale 24I3
Tarkwa 32C4
Tarlac 29E6
Tărnăveni 21K1
Tarnobrzeg 23D6
Tarnogskiy Gorodok 22I3
Tarnów 23D6
Tarnowskie Góry 13Q5
Taroudannt 32C1
Tarrafal 32□
Tarragona 19G3
Tarsus 33G1
Tartăr 21J2
Tartu 11O7
Tashir 23J8
Taskala 23K6
Tasköprü 23I2
Tasman Bay 43D5
Tasman Mountains 43D5

T'bilisi 23J8
Tbilisskaya 23I7
Tchamba 32D4
Tchibanga 34B4
Tchollirė 33E4
Tczew 13Q3
Te Anau, Lake 43A7
Teapa 50F5
Tébrat 32D3
Tébessa 20C7
Tébourba 20C6
Tecate 49D4
Techiman 32C4
Tecka 54B6
Tecpan 50D5
Tecuala 50C4
Tecuci 21L2
Tees r. 14F4
Tefenni 21M6
Tegucigalpa 51G6
Tehrān 26E3
Tehuacán 50E5
Tehuantepec, Gulf of 50F5
Teignmouth 15D8
Teixeiras 55C3
Teixeira Soares 55A4
Tejen 26F3
Tekax 50G4
Tekirdağ 21L4
Télagh 19F6
Télatai 32D3
Tel Aviv-Yafo 33G1
Telemaco Borba 55A4
Telford 15E6
Télimélé 32B3
Tel'novskiy 30F2
Telšiai 11M9
Temba 37I3
Tembagapura 38D2
Temecula 49D4
Temirtau 27G1
Temnikov 23I5
Temora 42C5
Temple 47H5
Temryuk 23H7
Temuco 54B5
Tena 52C4
Tenali 27H5
Tenbury Wells 15E6
Tenby 15C7
Tendō 31F5
Ténéré du Tafassâsset des. 32E2
Tenerife i. 32B2
Ténès 19G5
Tengréla 32C3
Tenkeli 25P2
Tenkodogo 32C3
Tennant Creek 40G3
Tennessee r. 47J4
Tennessee state 47J4
Tenosique 50F5
Tenterfield 42F2
Teodoro Sampaio 55B4
Teófilo Otoni 55C2
Tepatitlán 50D4
Tepic 50C4
Teploye 23H5
Teramo 20E3
Terang 42A7
Terebovlya 23E6
Teresina 53J5
Teresópolis 55C3
Teriberka 22H1
Termini Imerese 20E6
Termiz 26F3
Termoli 20F4
Ternate 29E7
Terni 20E3
Ternopil' 23E6
Terra Bella 49C3
Terrace 44E4
Terracina 20E4
Teruel 19F3
Teseney 34D2
Tessaoua 32D3
Teshio 31F3
Tetiyiv 23F6
Tetovo 21I3
Tetyushi 23K5
Tétouan 19D6
Teutonia 55A5
Teuva 29D7
Tewantin 41K5
Texarkana 47I5
Texas state 46H5
Texas City 47I6
Teyateyaneng 37I5
Teykovo 22I4
Tezu 27I4
Thaba Nchu 37I5
Thaba-Tseka 37I5
Thabong 37H4
Thai Binh 29C5
Thailand country 29C6
Thailand, Gulf of 29C6
Thai Nguyên 29C5
Thakèk 29C6
Thamaga 37G3
Thames est. 15H7
Thames r. 15H7
Thandwè 27I5
Thanet, Isle of pen. 15I7
Thanh Hoa 29C6
Thanjavur 27G6
Thar Desert 27F4
Thasos i. 21K4
Thaton 27I5
Thayetmyo 27I5
The Bahamas country 51J4
The Dalles 46C2
The Entrance 42E4
The Fens reg. 15G6
The Gambia country 32B3
The Gulf 26E4
The Hague 12J4
The Minch sea chan. 16C2
The North Sound sea chan. 16G1
Thermaikos Kolpos g. 21J4
The Solent strait 15F8
Thessaloniki 21J4
Thetford 15H6
Thetford Mines 47M2
Thiers 18F4
Thief River Falls 47H2
Thika 34D4
Thimphu 27I4
Thionville 18H2
Thirsk 14F4
Thiruvananthapuram 27G6
Thisted 11F8
Thomasville 47K5
Thornbury 15E7
Thornhill 16F5
Thornton 15E5
Thousand Oaks 49C3
Three Kings Islands 43D2

Thun 18H3
Thunder Bay 45J5
Thurles 17E5
Thurso 16F2
T'ianet'i 23J8
Tianjin 27K3
Tianqiaoling 30C4
Tianshui 27J3
Tiaret 19G6
Tiassalé 32C4
Tibagi 55A4
Tibati 32E4
Tiber r. 20E4
Tibesti mts 33E2
Tibet, Plateau of 27H3
Tibro 11I7
Ticehurst 15H7
Ticul 50G4
Tielt 12I5
Tieling 30A4
Tien Shan mts 27G2
Tierra del Fuego, Isla Grande de i. 54B9
Tiétar, Valle de valley 19D3
Tifton 47K5
Tighenciului, Dealurile hills 21M2
Tighina 21M1
Tignère 32E4
Tigris r. 33H1
Tijuana 49D4
Tikhoretsk 23I7
Tikhvin 22G4
Tikrīt 33H1
Tiksi 25N2
Tilburg 12J5
Tilbury 15H7
Tilemsès 32D3
Tilos i. 21M6
Timaru 43C7
Timashevsk 23H7
Timbaúba 53L5
Timber Lake 46G3
Timbuktu 32C3
Timişoara 21I2
Timmins 45J5
Timon 53J5
Timor i. 40F1
Timor Sea 40F2
Tinaca Point 29E7
Tindouf 32C2
Tingri 27H4
Tinian i. 38D1
Tinos i. 21K6
Tinos i. 21K6
Tînțareni 23H8
Tipitapa 51G6
Tipperary 17D5
Tiracambu 53I4
Tiranë 21H4
Tiraspol 21M1
Tire 21L5
Tiree i. 16C4
Tiros 55B2
Tirschenreuth 13N5
Tiruchirappalli 27G5
Tirupati 27G6
Tisa r. 21I2
Tissemsilt 19G6
Titao 32C3
Titicaca, Lake 52E7
Titu 21K2
Titusville 47K6
Tivat 21H3
Tiverton 15D8
Tivoli 20E4
Tizimín 50G4
Tizi Ouzou 19I5
Tiznit 32C2
Tlaxcala 50E5
Tlemcen 19F6
Tlokweng 37G3
Toamasina 35E5
Toba 31E6
Tobago i. 53G1
Tobermory 16C4
Tobi i. 38C2
Tobol r. 24I4
Tobol'sk 24H4
Tobruk 33E1
Tocantinópolis 53I5
Tocantins r. 53I4
Tocantins state 55A1
Toccoa 47K5
Tocopilla 54B2
Tocumwal 42B5
Togo country 32D4
Tojala 11M6
Tokarevka 23I6
Tokat 23H2
Tokelau terr. 39I2
Tokmak 23H7
Tokmok 27G2
Tokoza 37I4
Tokushima 31D6
Tokyo 31F6
Tôlañaro 35E6
Toledo 47K3
Toledo 19D4
Toledo 55A4
Toliara 35E6
Tolitoli 29E7
Tolmachevo 11P7
Toluca 50E5
Tol'yatti 23K5
Tomakomai 30F4
Tomar 19B4
Tomari 30F3
Tomaszów Lubelski 23D6
Tomaszów Mazowiecki 13R5
Tombua 35A5
Tomelilla 11H9
Tomelloso 19E4
Tomislavgrad 20G3
Tomsk 24J4
Toms River 48D2
Tonalá 50F5
Tondano 29E7
Tønder 11F9
Tonga country 39I4
Tongaat 37J5
Tongatapu Group is 39I4
Tongchuan 27J3
Tongduch'ŏn 31B5
Tonghae 31C5
Tonghua 30C3
Tongliao 27L2
Tongling 27K3
Tongyeong 31C6
Tonk 27G4
Tonle Sap l. 29C6
Tønsberg 11G7
Tooele 46E3
Toowoomba 42E1
Topeka 47H4
Topol'čany 13Q6
Torbalı 21L5
Torbat-e Heydarīyeh 26F3
Torbat-e Jām 26F3
Torbeyevo 23I5
Torgau 13N5
Tornäälven r. 10N4
Tornio 10N4
Toronto 48B1
Toropets 22F4
Tororo 34D3
Torquay 15D8
Torrance 49C4
Torrão 19B5

Torre del Greco 20F4
Torrelavega 19D2
Torrens, Lake imp. l. 41H6
Torrent 19F4
Torreón 46G6
Torres 55A5
Torres Novas 19B4
Torres Strait strait 38E2
Torres Vedras 19B4
Torrevieja 19F5
Torridge r. 15C8
Torridon, Loch b. 16D3
Tórshavn 10□¹
Tortona 20C2
Tortosa 19G3
Toruń 11J10
Tory Island 17D2
Tory Sound sea chan. 17D2
Torzhok 22G4
Tosa 31D6
Toscano, Arcipelago is 20C3
Toshkent 27F2
Tosno 22I4
Tostado 54D3
Tosya 23I8
Tot'ma 22I4
Totness 53K5
Totton 15F8
Tottori 31D6
Touba 32B3
Touba 32C4
Touboro 33E4
Tougan 32C3
Touggourt 32D1
Toul 18G2
Toulon 18G5
Toulouse 18E5
Touros 53K5
Tours 18E3
Tovuz 23J8
Towada 30F4
Townsville 41J3
Towson 48C3
Toyama 31E5
Toyohashi 31E6
Toyama 31E5
Toyonaka 31D6
Toyota 31E6
Toyooka 31D6
Tozeur 32D1
Tqibuli 23I8
Trabotivište 21J4
Trabzon 23I7
Tracy 49B1
Trá Li r. 32D2
Trail 46D2
Trakai 11N9
Trakt 22K3
Tralee 17C5
Tralee Bay 17B5
Tranås 11I7
Transantarctic Mountains 56B4
Transylvanian Alps mts 21J2
Transylvanian Basin plat. 21K1
Trapani 20E5
Traralgon 42C7
Traverse City 47J3
Třebíč 13O6
Trebinje 20H3
Trebišov 23D6
Trebnje 20F2
Treinta y Tres 54F4
Trelew 54C6
Trelleborg 11H9
Tremonton 46E3
Trenčín 13Q6
Trenque Lauquén 54D5
Trent r. 15G5
Trento 20D1
Trenton 47J3
Trenton 48D2
Treorchy 15D7
Tres Arroyos 54D5
Três Corações 55B3
Três Lagoas 55A3
Três Marias, Represa resr 55B2
Três Pontas 55B3
Três Rios 55C3
Treviglio 20C2
Treviso 20E2
Triangle 48C3
Trier 13K6
Trieste 20E2
Trieste, Gulf of 20E2
Trikala 21J5
Trincomalee 27H6
Trindade 46G4
Trindade 55B2
Trinidad 51L6
Trinidad 52F6
Trinidad 54E4
Trinidad and Tobago country 51L6
Tripoli 20E7
Tripoli 33E1
Tripoli 33E1
Tristan da Cunha i. 6
Trnava 13P6
Troisdorf 13K5
Trois-Rivières 45K5
Troitskaya 23J7
Trollhättan 11H7
Tromsø 10K2
Trondheim 10G5
Troon 16E5
Trosnan hill 17F2
Trout Lake 44F3
Trowbridge 15E7
Troy 48E1
Troyan 21K3
Troyes 18G2
Trujillo 19D4
Trujillo 51G5
Trujillo 52C5
Truro 15B8
Truro 47L5
Truth or Consequences 46F5

Tswelelang 37G4
Tsyelyakhany 11N10
Tsyurupyns'k 21O1
Tuamotu Islands 6
Tuapse 23I7
Tubarão 55A5
Tübingen 13L6
Tubmanburg 32B4
Tubruq 33F1
Tucano 53K6
Tucson 46E5
Tucumcari 46G4
Tucupita 52F2
Tucuruí 53I4
Tucuruí, Represa resr 53I4
Tudela 19F2
Tudun Wada 32D3
Tuguegarao 29E6
Tukums 11M8
Tukuyu 35D4
Tulancingo 50E4
Tulare 49C2
Tulcán 52C3
Tulcea 21M2
Tulihe 30A2
Tullamore 17E4
Tulle 18E4
Tullow 17F5
Tottori 31D6
Tulsa 47H4
Tulú 52C3
Tumaco 52C3
Tumahole 37H4
Tumba 11J7
Tumbarumba 42D5
Tumbes 52B4
Tumby Bay 41H6
Tumen 30C4
Tumu 32C3
Tumucumaque, Serra hills 53G3
Tumut 42D5
Tunbridge Wells, Royal 15H7
Tuncurry 42F4
Tunduru 35D5
Tungor 30F1
Tunis 20D6
Tunis, Golfe de g. 20D6
Tunisia country 32D1
Tunja 52D2
Tupã 55A3
Tupelo 47J5
Tupiza 52E8
Tupungato, Cerro mt. 54C4
Tura 25L3
Turan Lowland 26F2
Turbo 52C2
Turda 21J1
Turgay 26F2
Türgovishte 21L3
Turgutlu 21L5
Turin 20B2
Turkana, Lake salt l. 34D3
Turkestan 26F2
Turkey country 26C3
Turki 23I6
Türkmenabat 26F3
Türkmenbaşy 26E2
Turkmenistan country 26E2
Turks and Caicos Islands terr. 51J4
Turkwel watercourse 34D3
Turlock 49B2
Turmalina 55C2
Turneffe Islands atoll 50G5
Turnu Măgurele 21K3
Turpan 27H2
Turriff 16G3
Tuscaloosa 47J5
Tuscarora Mountains hills 48C2
Tuskegee 47J5
Tussey Mountains hills 48B2
Tutayev 22I4
Tuticorin 27G6
Tuttlingen 13L7
Tutubu 35D4
Tuvalu country 39H2
Tuwayq, Jabal mts 34E1
Tuwwal 34D1
Tuxpan 50E4
Tuxtla Gutiérrez 50F5
Tuy Hoa 29C6
Tuz, Lake salt l. 26C3
Tuzha 22J4
Tuz Khurmātū 33H1
Tuzla 20H2
Tver' 22G4
Tweed r. 16G5
Tweed Heads 42F2
Twentynine Palms 46F5
Twin Falls 46E3
Twizel 43C7
Tyler 47H5
Tymovskoye 30F2
Tynda 25N4
Tynemouth 14F3
Tyre 33G1
Tyrrell, Lake dry lake 38E5
Tyrrhenian Sea 20D4
Tyukalinsk 24I4
Tyumen' 24H4
Tywyn 15C6

U

Uauá 53K5
Ubá 55B2
Ubaí 55B2
Ubaitaba 55D1
Ubangi r. 34B4
Ube 31C6
Úbeda 19E4
Uberaba 55B2
Uberlândia 55A2
Ubon Ratchathani 46F5
Ubu 23J8
Ucar 23J8
Ucayali r. 52D4
Ucharal 27H2
Uchiura-wan b. 30F4
Uckfield 15H8
Udaipur 27G4
Uddevalla 11G7
Udimskiy 22J3
Udine 20E1
Udomlya 22G4
Udon Thani 29C6
Udupi 27G5
Uele r. 34C3
Uelzen 13M4
Ufa 24G4
Ugab watercourse 35B6
Uganda country 34D3
Uglegorsk 30F2
Uglich 22H4
Ugra 23G5